RIFF REB'S

MEN AT SEA

Translated by Joe Johnson
Translation Lettering by T. Perran Mitchell

DEAD RECKONING
Annapolis, Maryland

MEN AT SEA

CONTENTS

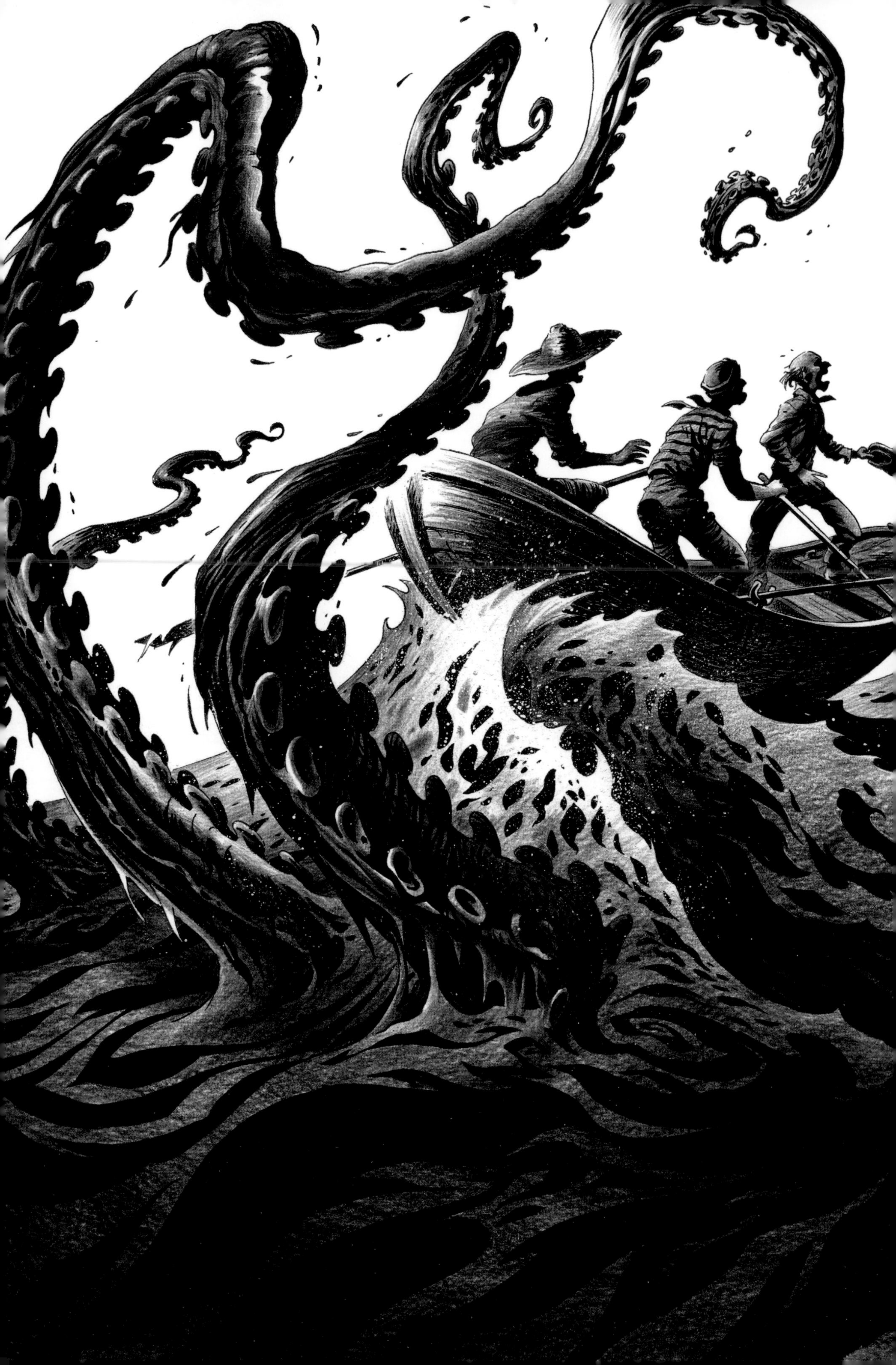

Sometimes it's attributed to Plato, sometimes to Aristotle, his disciple.
It is also the accepted citation for a work about the sea.
Dare I say, it's the most shiplike?

Nevertheless, to last for so many centuries, to possess such a part of eternity, a rare quality,
it must be the perfect dose between the categorical and the absurd.

It is, in any case, the most suitable one for the volume you have in your hand.

"There are three sorts of people, the living,
the dead, and those who are at sea."

Riff Reb's

This volume is dedicated to rockin' Christian, who chose to go from one condition to the other while bypassing that of a seafarer.

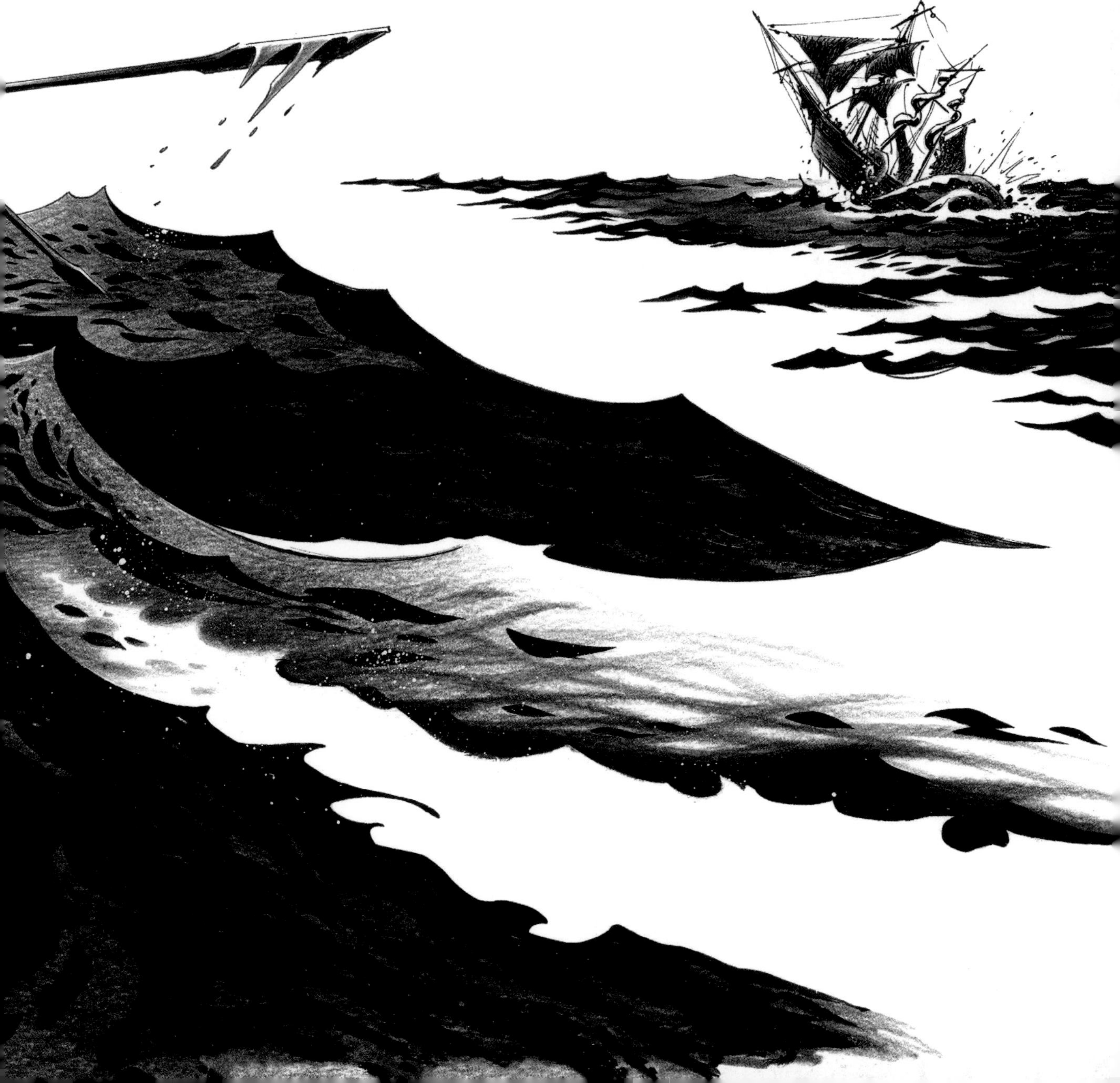

The Sea Horses

based on WILLIAM HOPE HODGSON

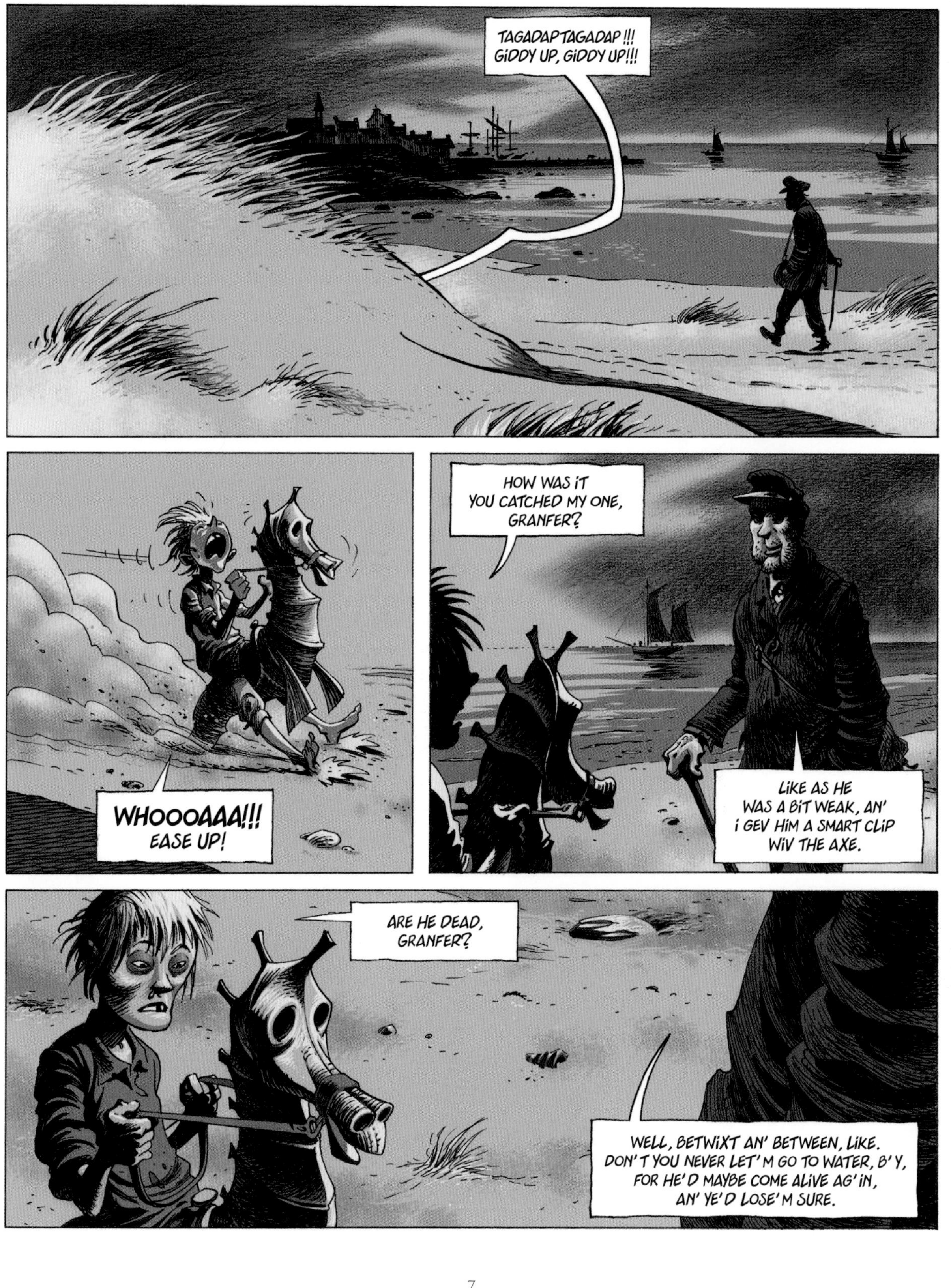
TAGADAPTAGADAP!!! GIDDY UP, GIDDY UP!!!
WHOOOAAA!!! EASE UP!
HOW WAS IT YOU CATCHED MY ONE, GRANFER?
LIKE AS HE WAS A BIT WEAK, AN' I GEV HIM A SMART CLIP WIV THE AXE.
ARE HE DEAD, GRANFER?
WELL, BETWIXT AN' BETWEEN, LIKE. DON'T YOU NEVER LET'M GO TO WATER, B'Y, FOR HE'D MAYBE COME ALIVE AG'IN, AN' YE'D LOSE'M SURE.

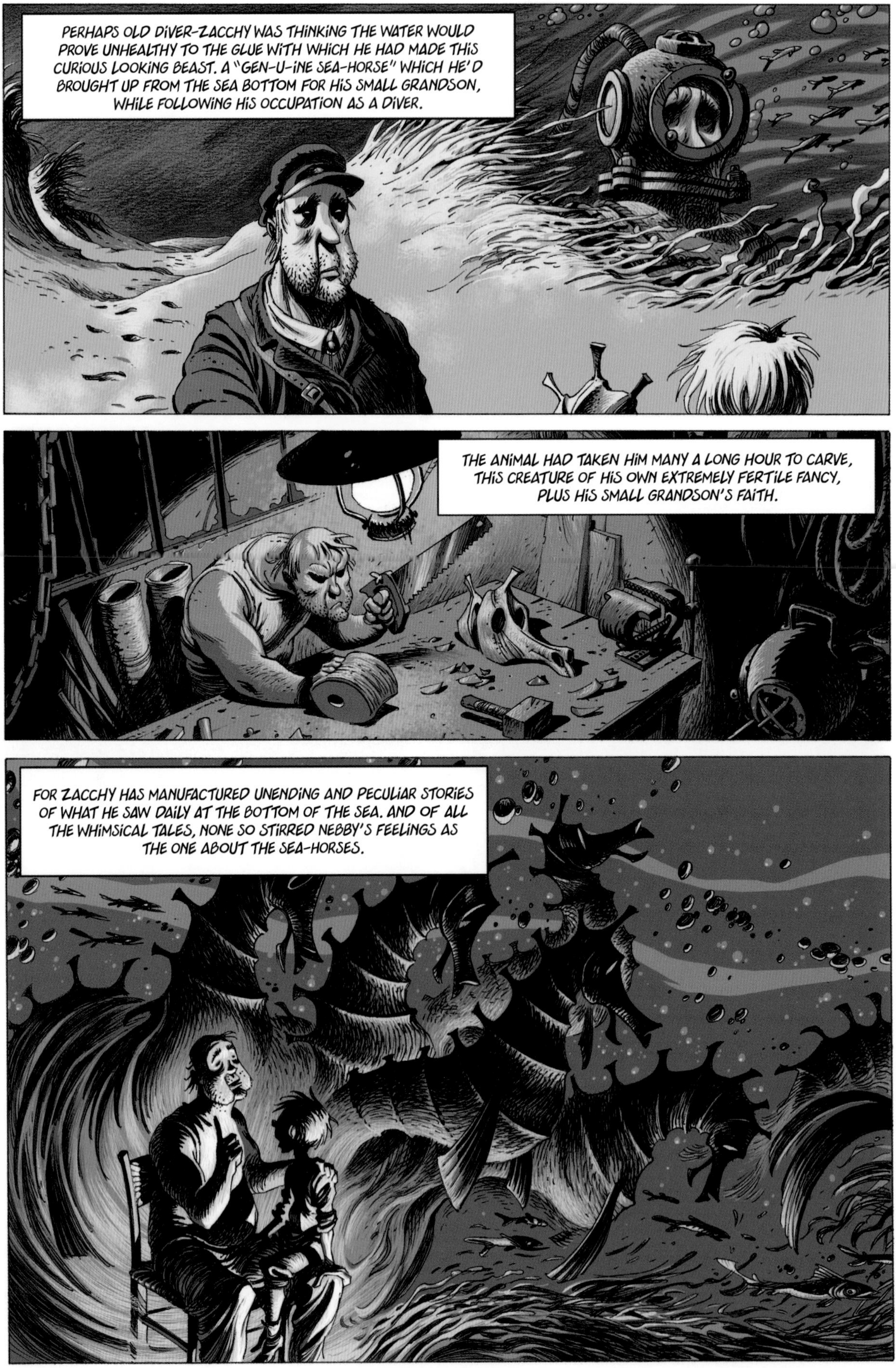
PERHAPS OLD DIVER-ZACCHY WAS THINKING THE WATER WOULD PROVE UNHEALTHY TO THE GLUE WITH WHICH HE HAD MADE THIS CURIOUS LOOKING BEAST. A "GEN-U-INE SEA-HORSE" WHICH HE'D BROUGHT UP FROM THE SEA BOTTOM FOR HIS SMALL GRANDSON, WHILE FOLLOWING HIS OCCUPATION AS A DIVER.
THE ANIMAL HAD TAKEN HIM MANY A LONG HOUR TO CARVE, THIS CREATURE OF HIS OWN EXTREMELY FERTILE FANCY, PLUS HIS SMALL GRANDSON'S FAITH.
FOR ZACCHY HAS MANUFACTURED UNENDING AND PECULIAR STORIES OF WHAT HE SAW DAILY AT THE BOTTOM OF THE SEA. AND OF ALL THE WHIMSICAL TALES, NONE SO STIRRED NEBBY'S FEELINGS AS THE ONE ABOUT THE SEA-HORSES.

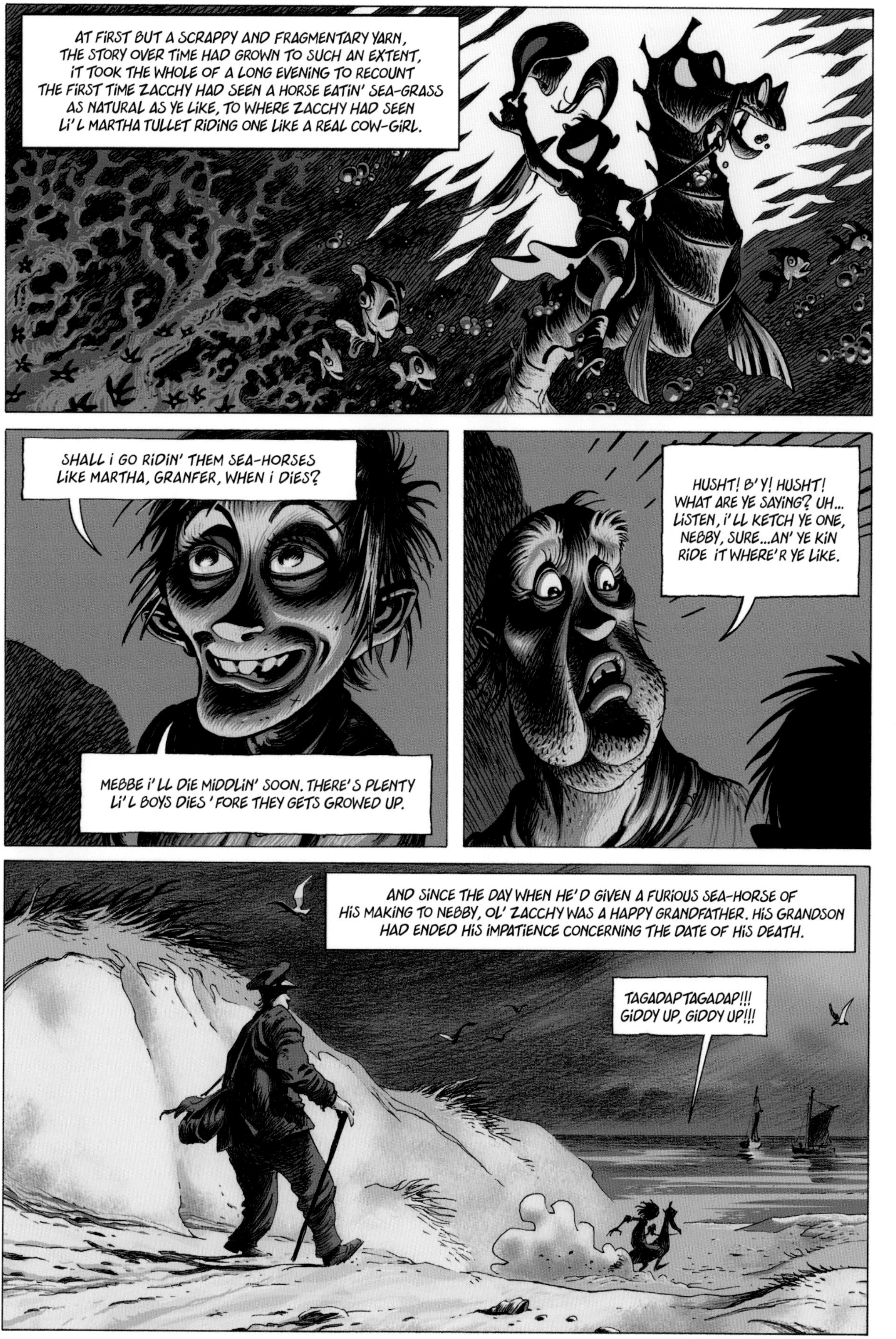
AT FIRST BUT A SCRAPPY AND FRAGMENTARY YARN, THE STORY OVER TIME HAD GROWN TO SUCH AN EXTENT, IT TOOK THE WHOLE OF A LONG EVENING TO RECOUNT THE FIRST TIME ZACCHY HAD SEEN A HORSE EATIN' SEA-GRASS AS NATURAL AS YE LIKE, TO WHERE ZACCHY HAD SEEN LI'L MARTHA TULLET RIDING ONE LIKE A REAL COW-GIRL.
SHALL I GO RIDIN' THEM SEA-HORSES LIKE MARTHA, GRANFER, WHEN I DIES?
MEBBE I'LL DIE MIDDLIN' SOON. THERE'S PLENTY LI'L BOYS DIES 'FORE THEY GETS GROWED UP.
HUSHT! B'Y! HUSHT! WHAT ARE YE SAYING? UH... LISTEN, I'LL KETCH YE ONE, NEBBY, SURE...AN' YE KIN RIDE IT WHERE'R YE LIKE.
AND SINCE THE DAY WHEN HE'D GIVEN A FURIOUS SEA-HORSE OF HIS MAKING TO NEBBY, OL' ZACCHY WAS A HAPPY GRANDFATHER. HIS GRANDSON HAD ENDED HIS IMPATIENCE CONCERNING THE DATE OF HIS DEATH.
TAGADAPTAGADAP!!! GIDDY UP, GIDDY UP!!!

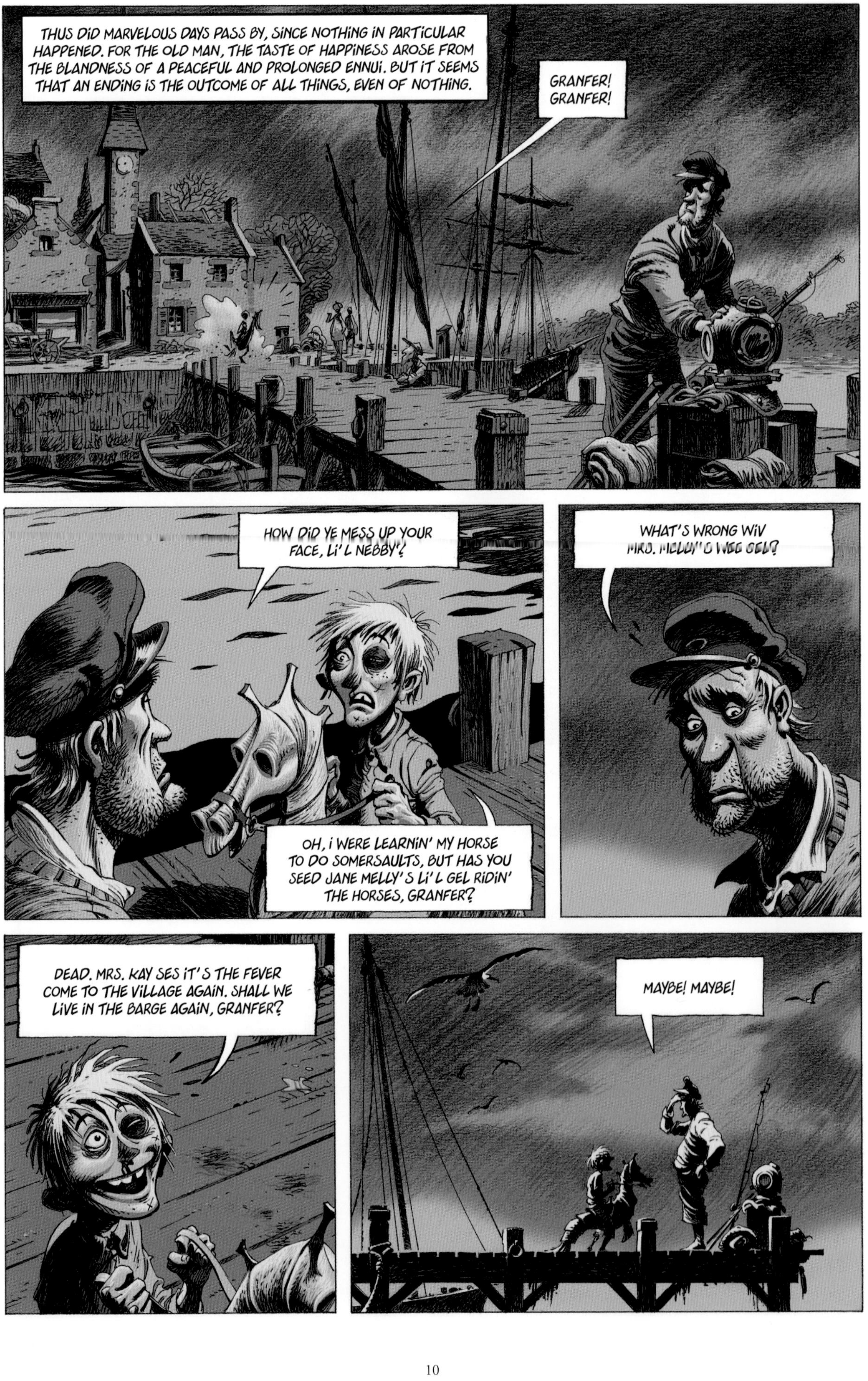

THUS DID MARVELOUS DAYS PASS BY, SINCE NOTHING IN PARTICULAR HAPPENED. FOR THE OLD MAN, THE TASTE OF HAPPINESS AROSE FROM THE BLANDNESS OF A PEACEFUL AND PROLONGED ENNUI. BUT IT SEEMS THAT AN ENDING IS THE OUTCOME OF ALL THINGS, EVEN OF NOTHING.
GRANFER! GRANFER!
HOW DID YE MESS UP YOUR FACE, LI'L NEBBY?
OH, I WERE LEARNIN' MY HORSE TO DO SOMERSAULTS, BUT HAS YOU SEED JANE MELLY'S LI'L GEL RIDIN' THE HORSES, GRANFER?
WHAT'S WRONG WIV MRS. MELLY'S WEE GEL?
DEAD. MRS. KAY SES IT'S THE FEVER COME TO THE VILLAGE AGAIN. SHALL WE LIVE IN THE BARGE AGAIN, GRANFER?
MAYBE! MAYBE!

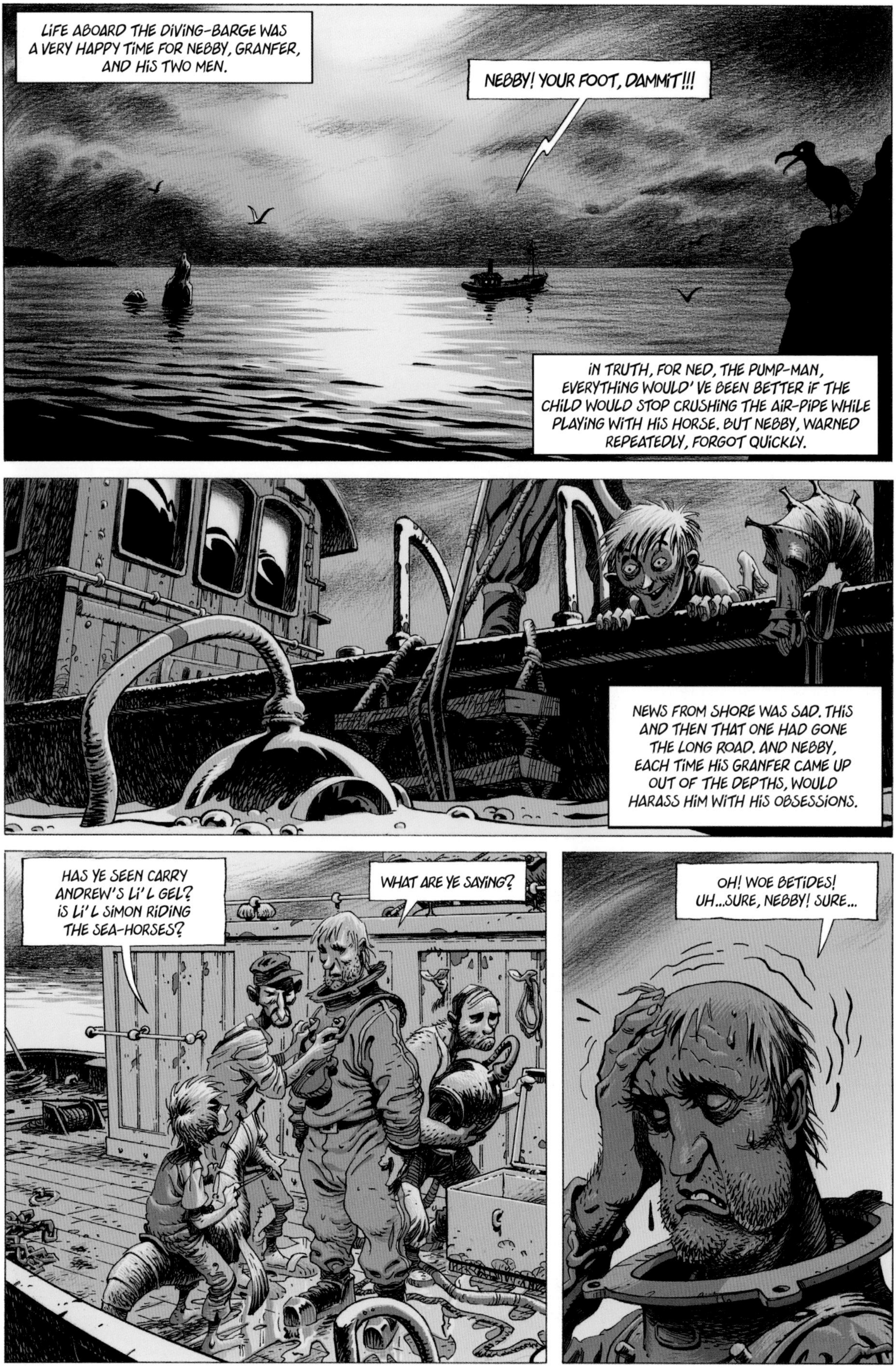
LIFE ABOARD THE DIVING-BARGE WAS A VERY HAPPY TIME FOR NEBBY, GRANFER, AND HIS TWO MEN.
NEBBY! YOUR FOOT, DAMMIT!!!
IN TRUTH, FOR NED, THE PUMP-MAN, EVERYTHING WOULD'VE BEEN BETTER IF THE CHILD WOULD STOP CRUSHING THE AIR-PIPE WHILE PLAYING WITH HIS HORSE. BUT NEBBY, WARNED REPEATEDLY, FORGOT QUICKLY.
NEWS FROM SHORE WAS SAD. THIS AND THEN THAT ONE HAD GONE THE LONG ROAD. AND NEBBY, EACH TIME HIS GRANFER CAME UP OUT OF THE DEPTHS, WOULD HARASS HIM WITH HIS OBSESSIONS.
HAS YE SEEN CARRY ANDREW'S LI'L GEL? IS LI'L SIMON RIDING THE SEA-HORSES?
WHAT ARE YE SAYING?
OH! WOE BETIDES! UH...SURE, NEBBY! SURE...

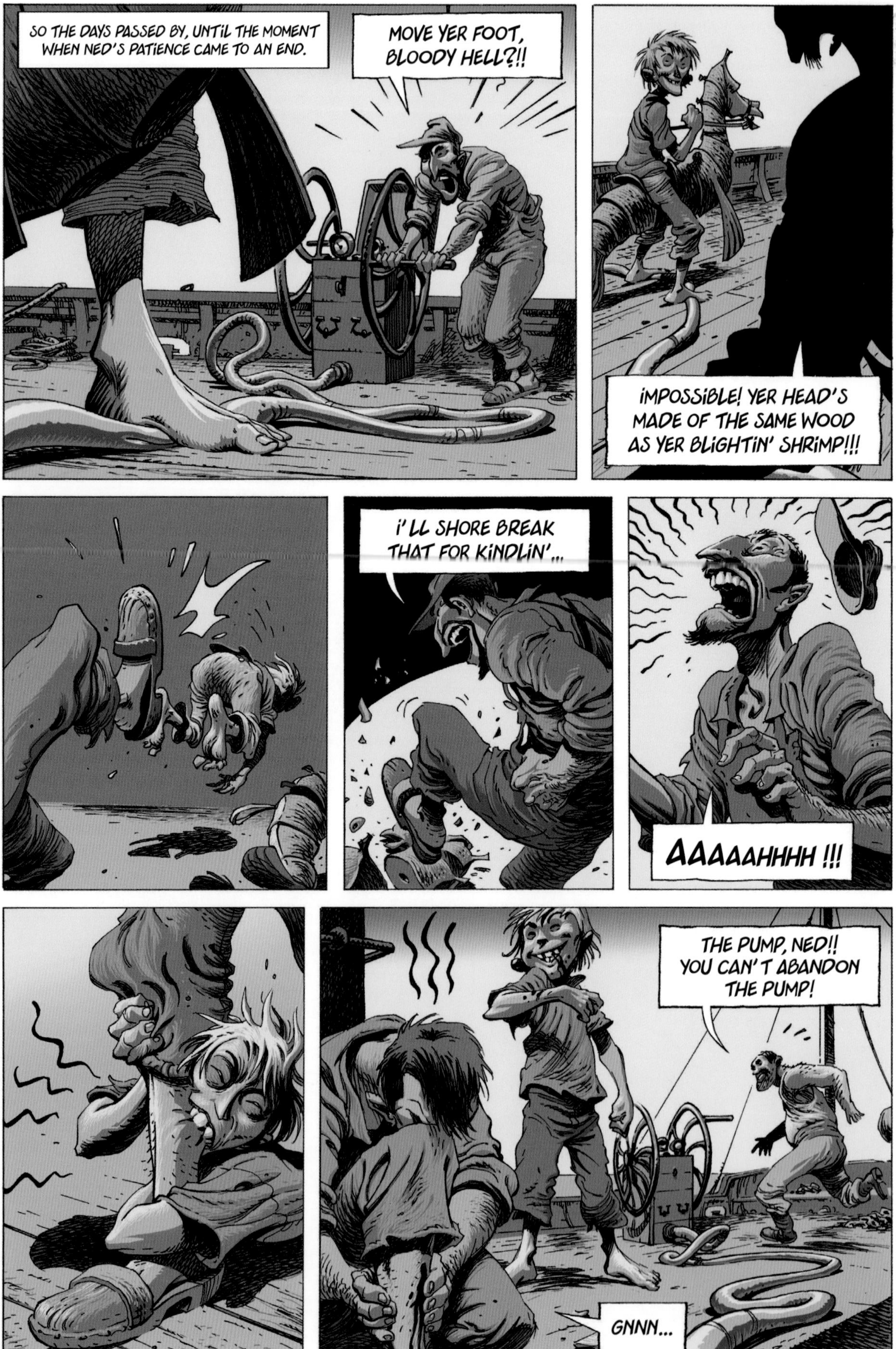
SO THE DAYS PASSED BY, UNTIL THE MOMENT WHEN NED'S PATIENCE CAME TO AN END.
MOVE YER FOOT, BLOODY HELL?!!
IMPOSSIBLE! YER HEAD'S MADE OF THE SAME WOOD AS YER BLIGHTIN' SHRIMP!!!
I'LL SHORE BREAK THAT FOR KINDLIN'...
AAAAAHHHH !!!
THE PUMP, NED!! YOU CAN'T ABANDON THE PUMP!
GNNN...

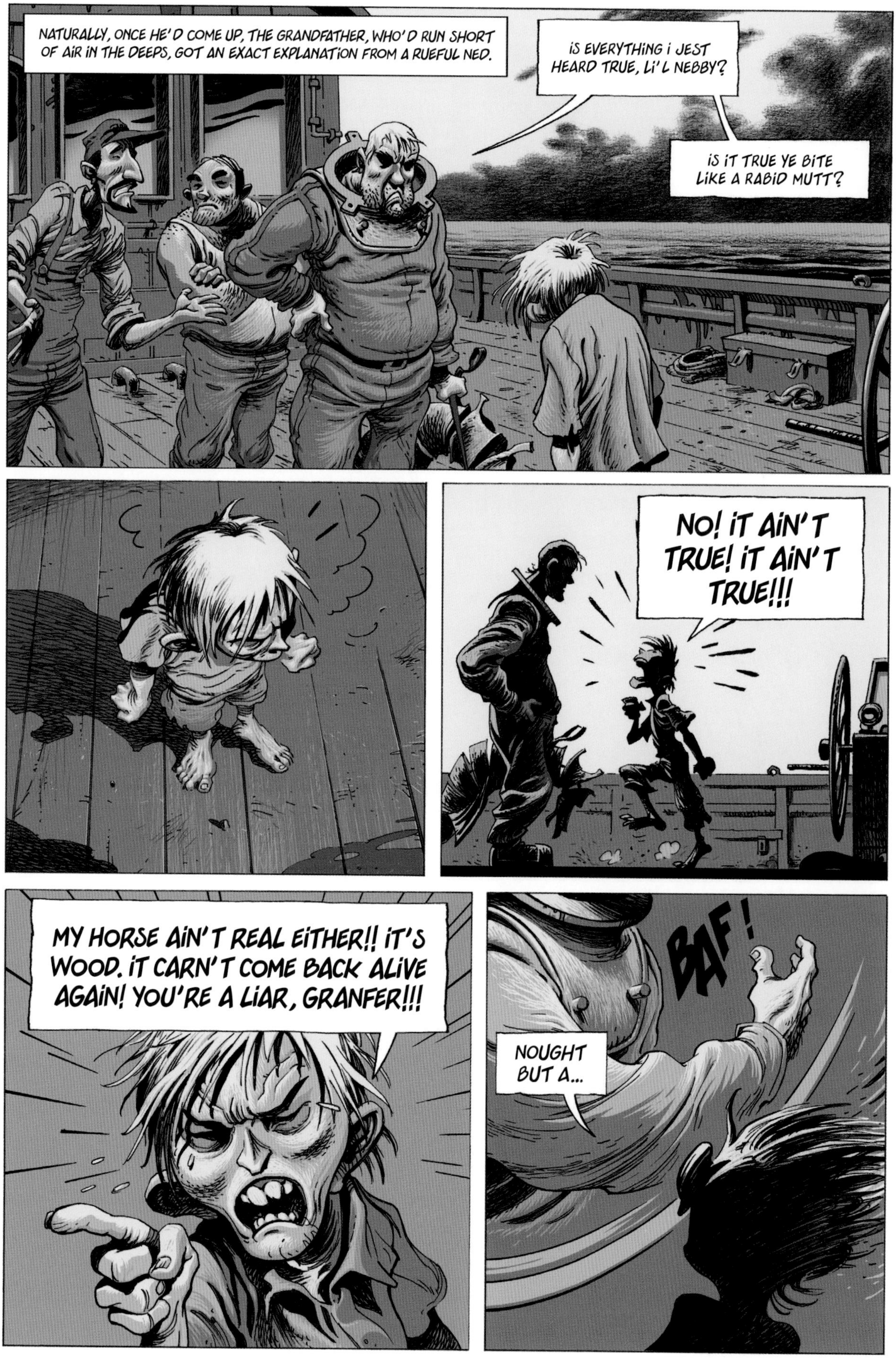
NATURALLY, ONCE HE'D COME UP, THE GRANDFATHER, WHO'D RUN SHORT OF AIR IN THE DEEPS, GOT AN EXACT EXPLANATION FROM A RUEFUL NED.
IS EVERYTHING I JEST HEARD TRUE, LI'L NEBBY?
IS IT TRUE YE BITE LIKE A RABID MUTT?
NO! IT AIN'T TRUE! IT AIN'T TRUE!!!
MY HORSE AIN'T REAL EITHER!! IT'S WOOD. IT CARN'T COME BACK ALIVE AGAIN! YOU'RE A LIAR, GRANFER!!!
NOUGHT BUT A...
BAF!

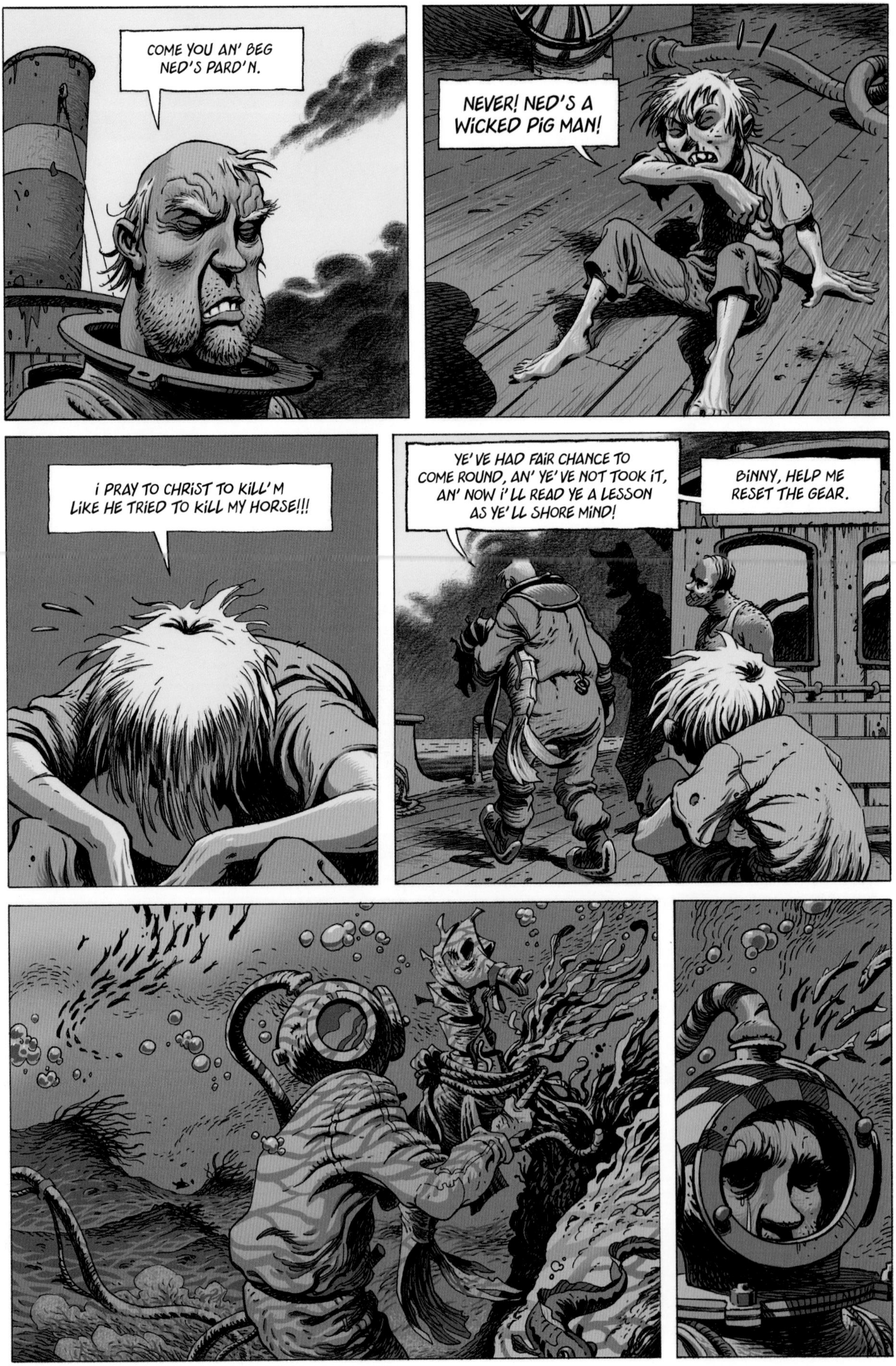

COME YOU AN' BEG NED'S PARD'N.
NEVER! NED'S A WICKED PIG MAN!
I PRAY TO CHRIST TO KILL'M LIKE HE TRIED TO KILL MY HORSE!!!
YE'VE HAD FAIR CHANCE TO COME ROUND, AN' YE'VE NOT TOOK IT, AN' NOW I'LL READ YE A LESSON AS YE'LL SHORE MIND!
BINNY, HELP ME RESET THE GEAR.

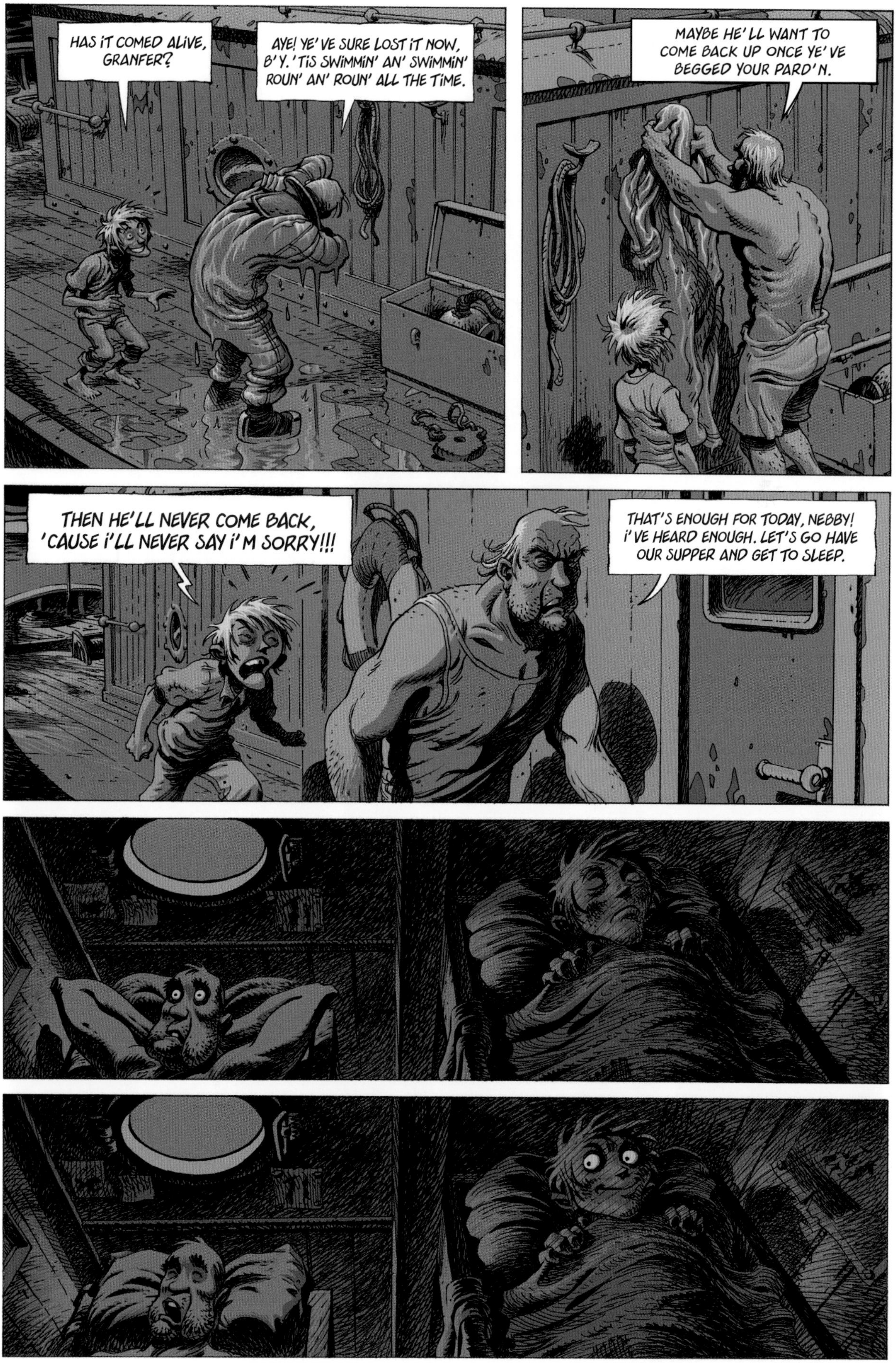
HAS iT COMED ALiVE, GRANFER?
AYE! YE'VE SURE LOST iT NOW, B'Y. 'TiS SWiMMiN' AN' SWiMMiN' ROUN' AN' ROUN' ALL THE TiME.
MAYBE HE'LL WANT TO COME BACK UP ONCE YE'VE BEGGED YOUR PARD'N.
THEN HE'LL NEVER COME BACK, 'CAUSE i'LL NEVER SAY i'M SORRY!!!
THAT'S ENOUGH FOR TODAY, NEBBY! i'VE HEARD ENOUGH. LET'S GO HAVE OUR SUPPER AND GET TO SLEEP.

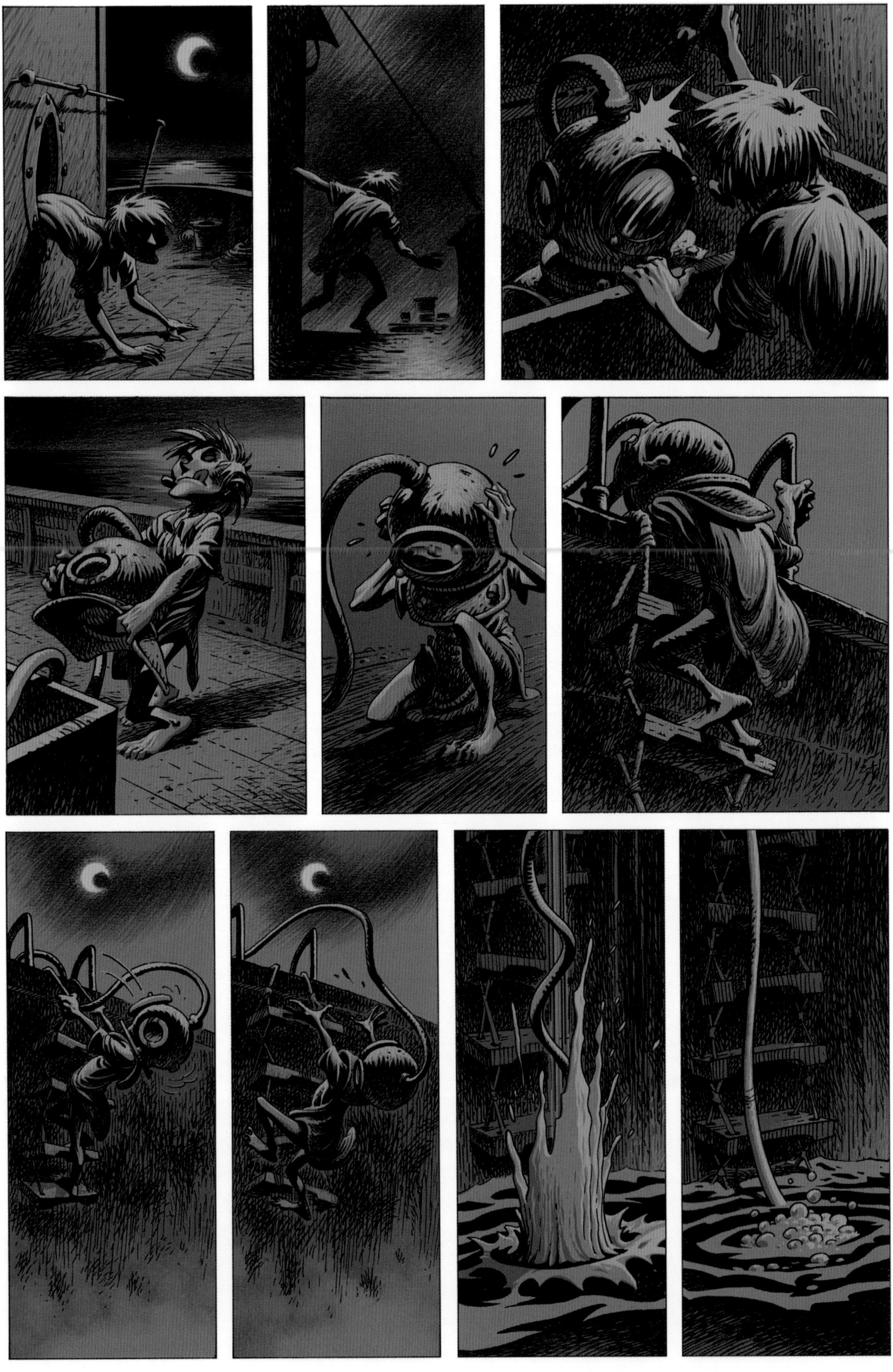

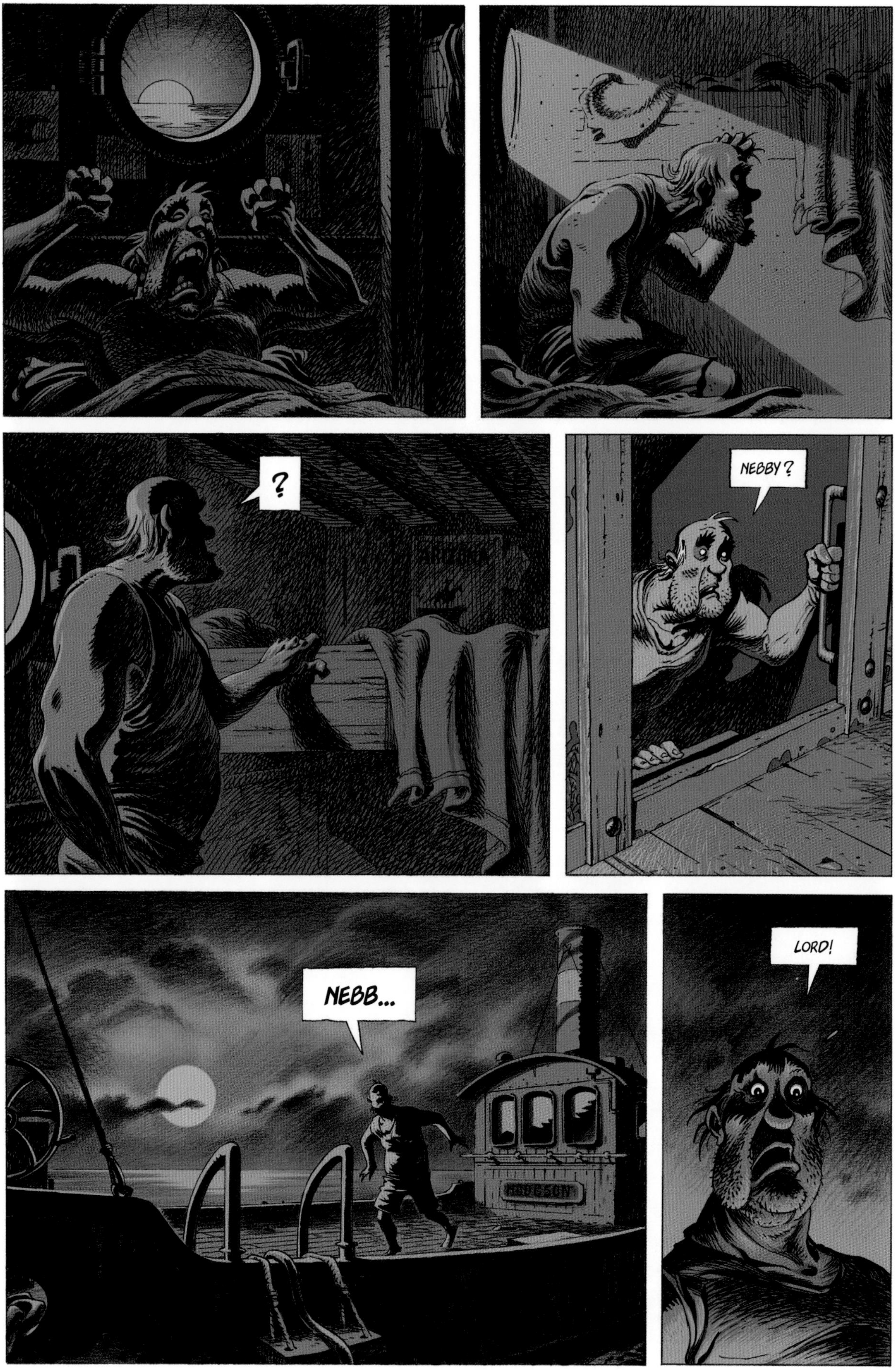
?
NEBBY?
NEBB...
LORD!

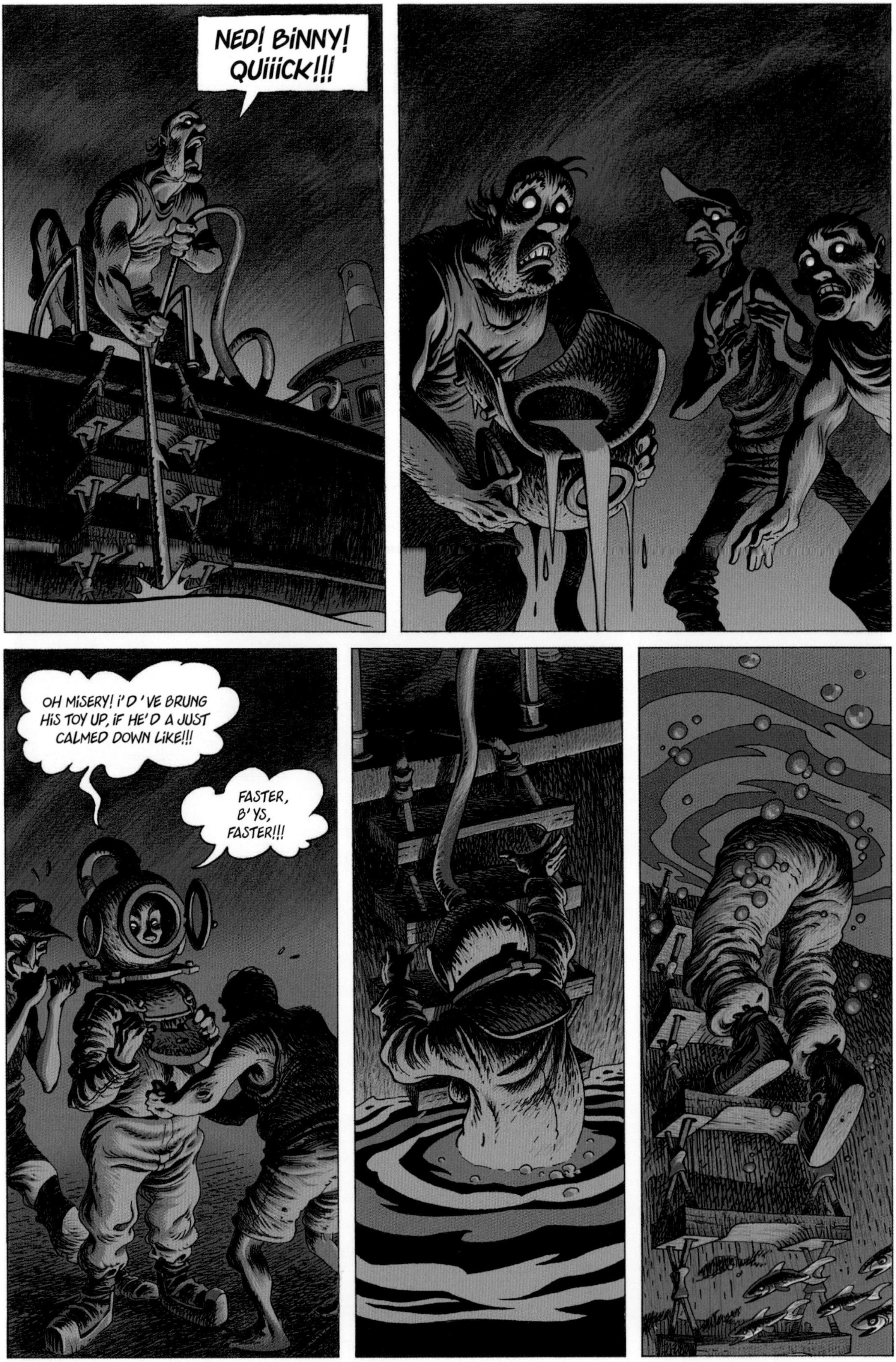
NED! BiNNY! QUiiiCK!!!
OH MiSERY! i'D 'VE BRUNG HiS TOY UP, iF HE'D A JUST CALMED DOWN LiKE!!!
FASTER, B'YS, FASTER!!!

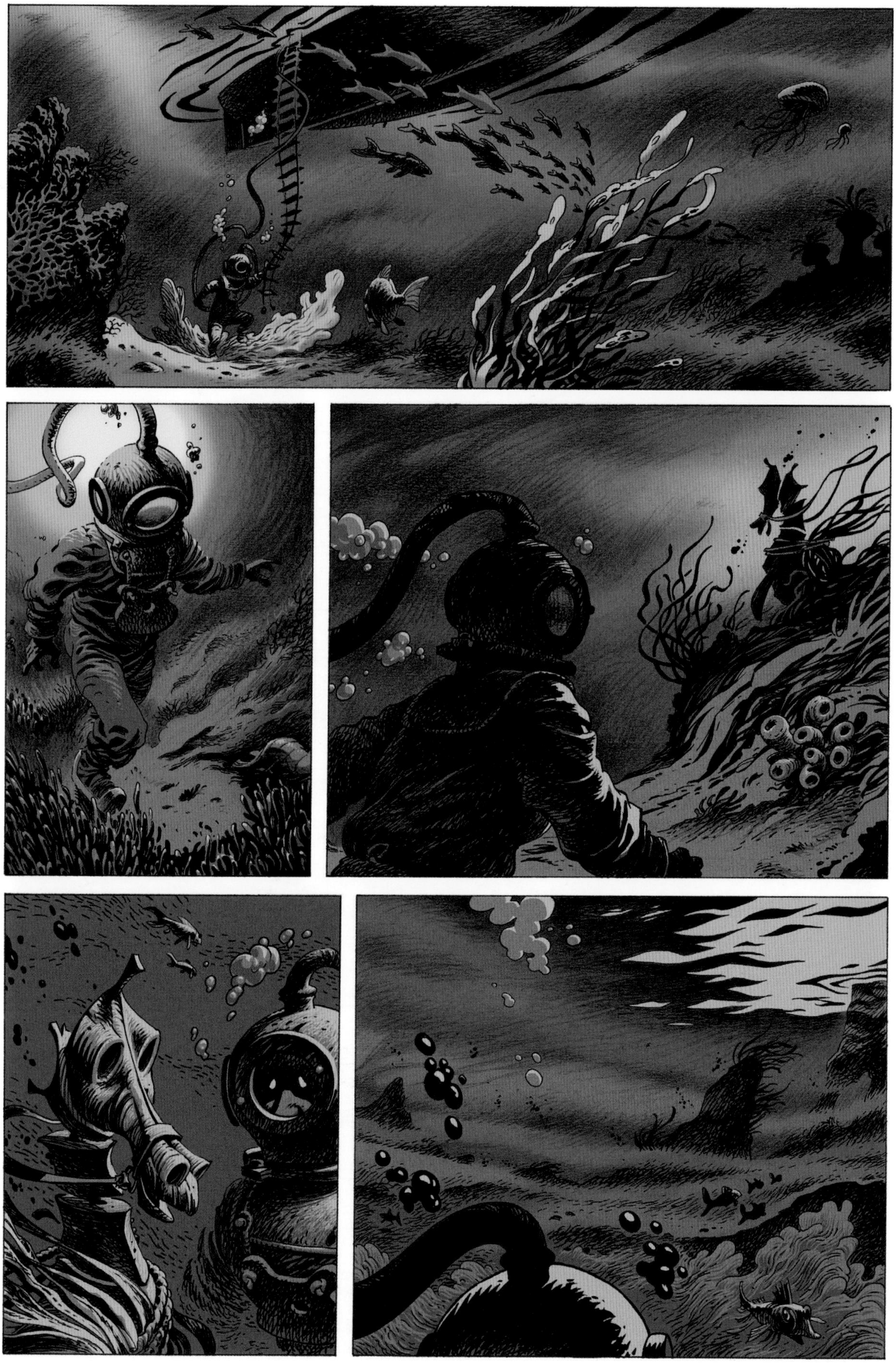

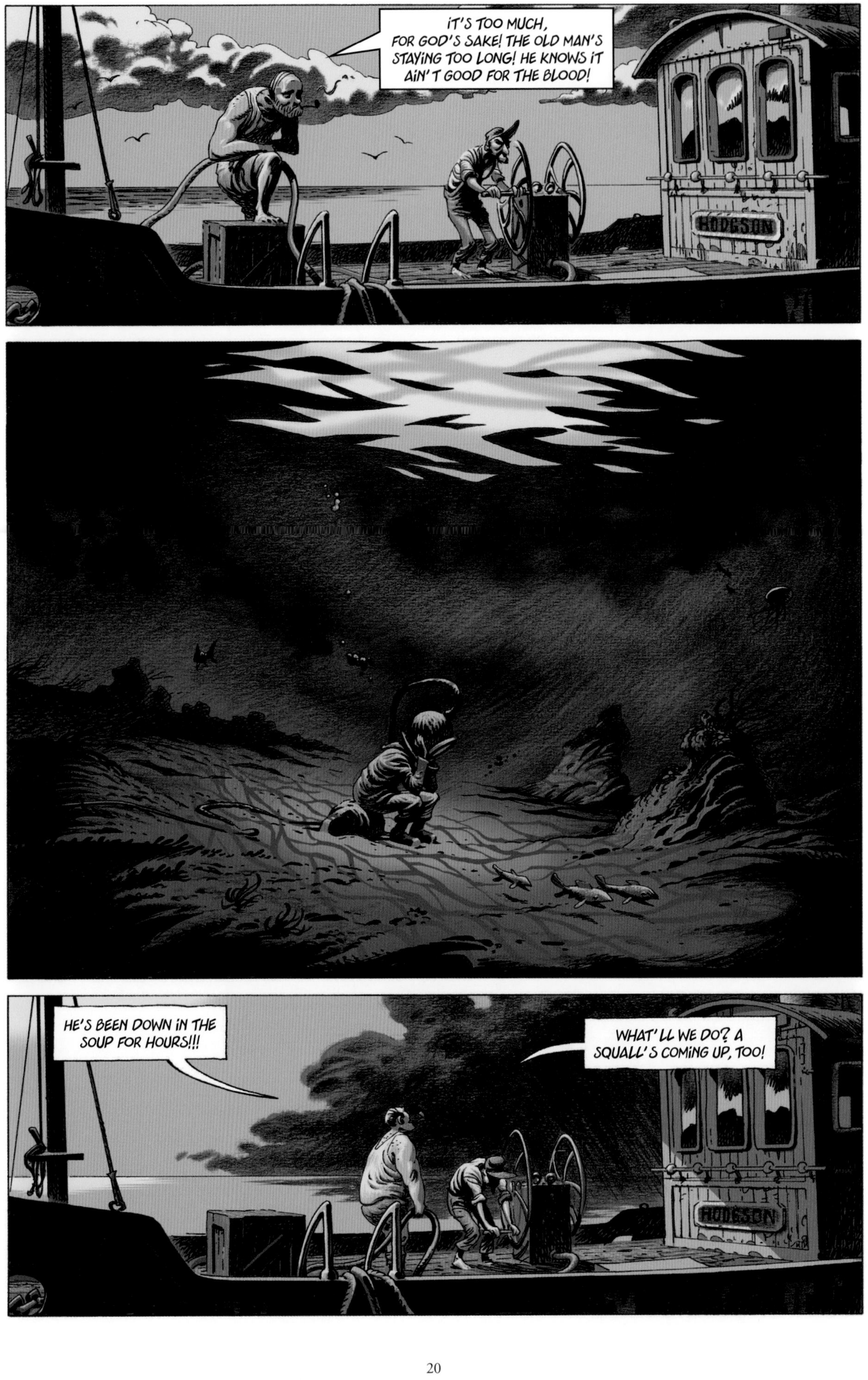
IT'S TOO MUCH, FOR GOD'S SAKE! THE OLD MAN'S STAYING TOO LONG! HE KNOWS IT AIN'T GOOD FOR THE BLOOD!
HODGSON
HE'S BEEN DOWN IN THE SOUP FOR HOURS!!!
WHAT'LL WE DO? A SQUALL'S COMING UP, TOO!
HODGSON

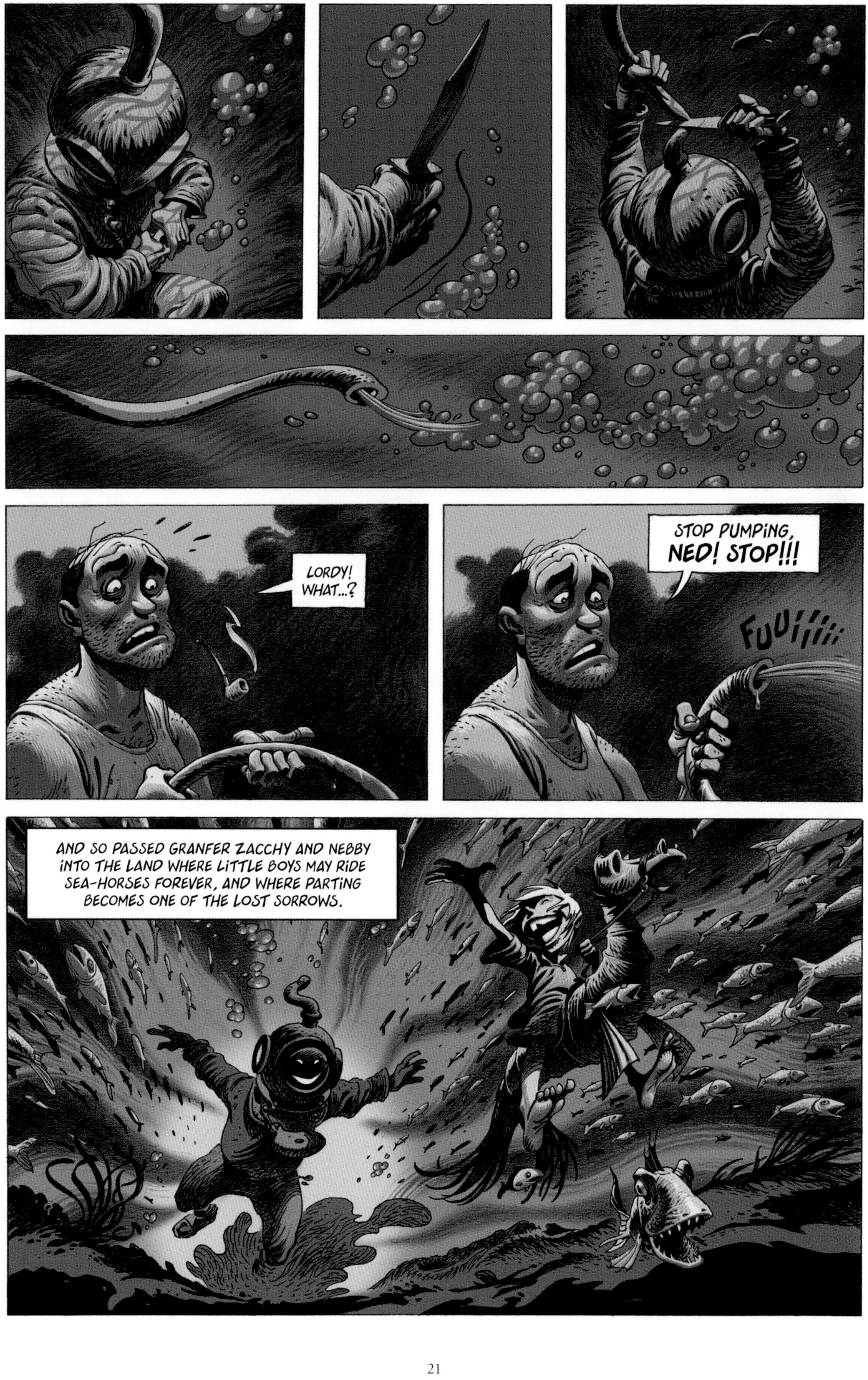
LORDY! WHAT...?
STOP PUMPING, NED! STOP!!!
FUUiiii
AND SO PASSED GRANFER ZACCHY AND NEBBY INTO THE LAND WHERE LITTLE BOYS MAY RIDE SEA-HORSES FOREVER, AND WHERE PARTING BECOMES ONE OF THE LOST SORROWS.

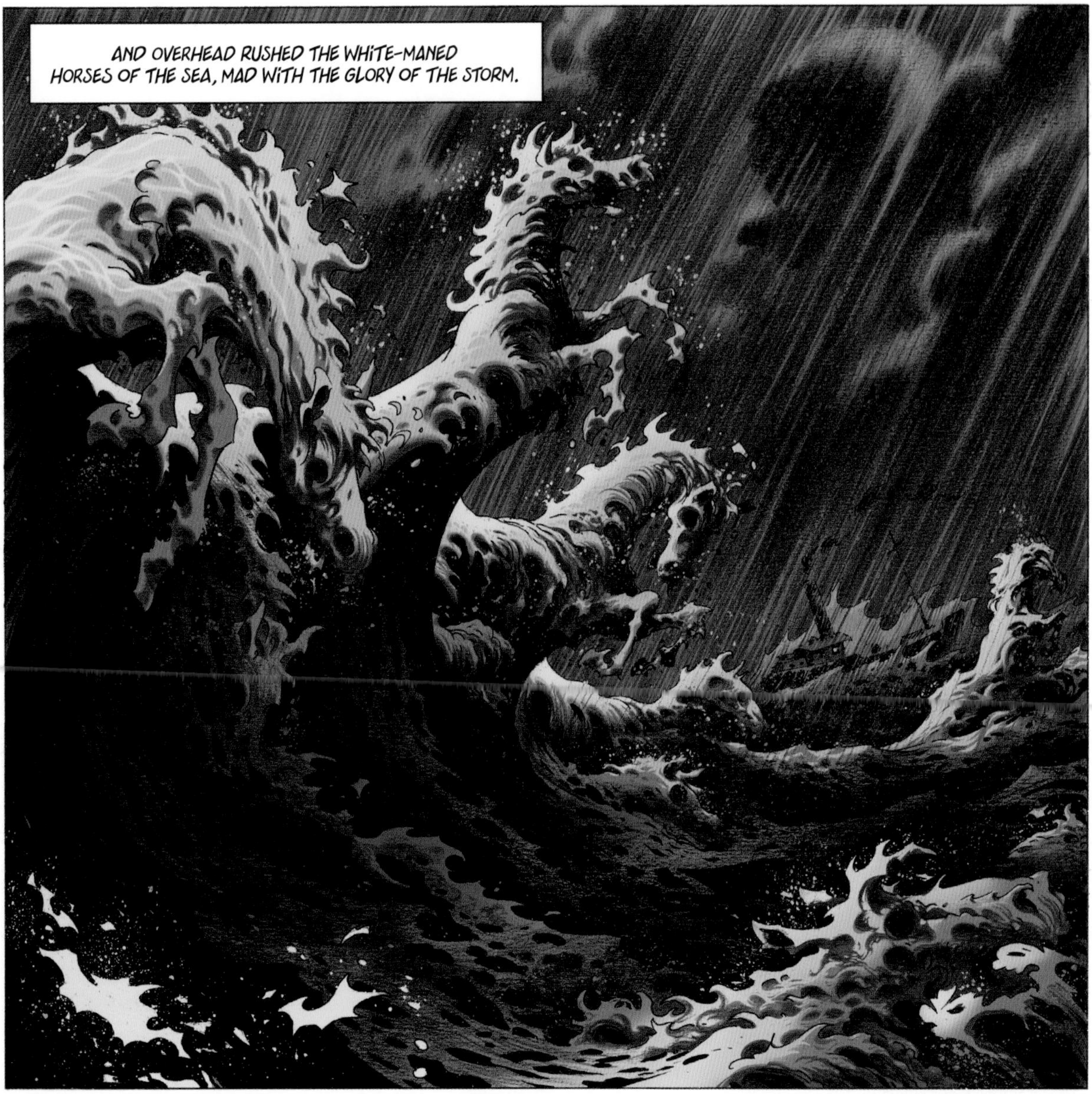
AND OVERHEAD RUSHED THE WHITE-MANED HORSES OF THE SEA, MAD WITH THE GLORY OF THE STORM.

The End

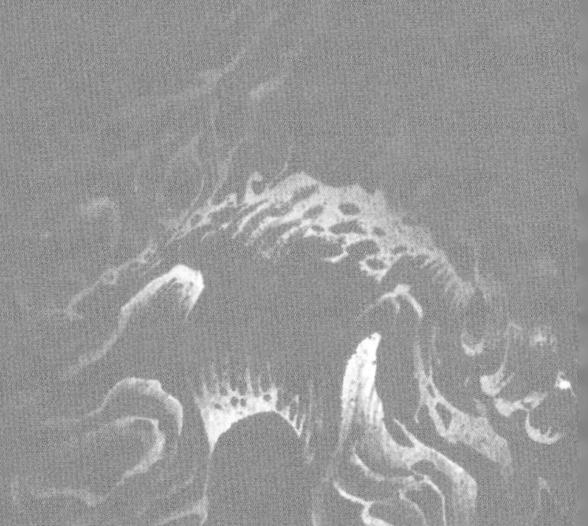

The Odyssey

based on HOMER

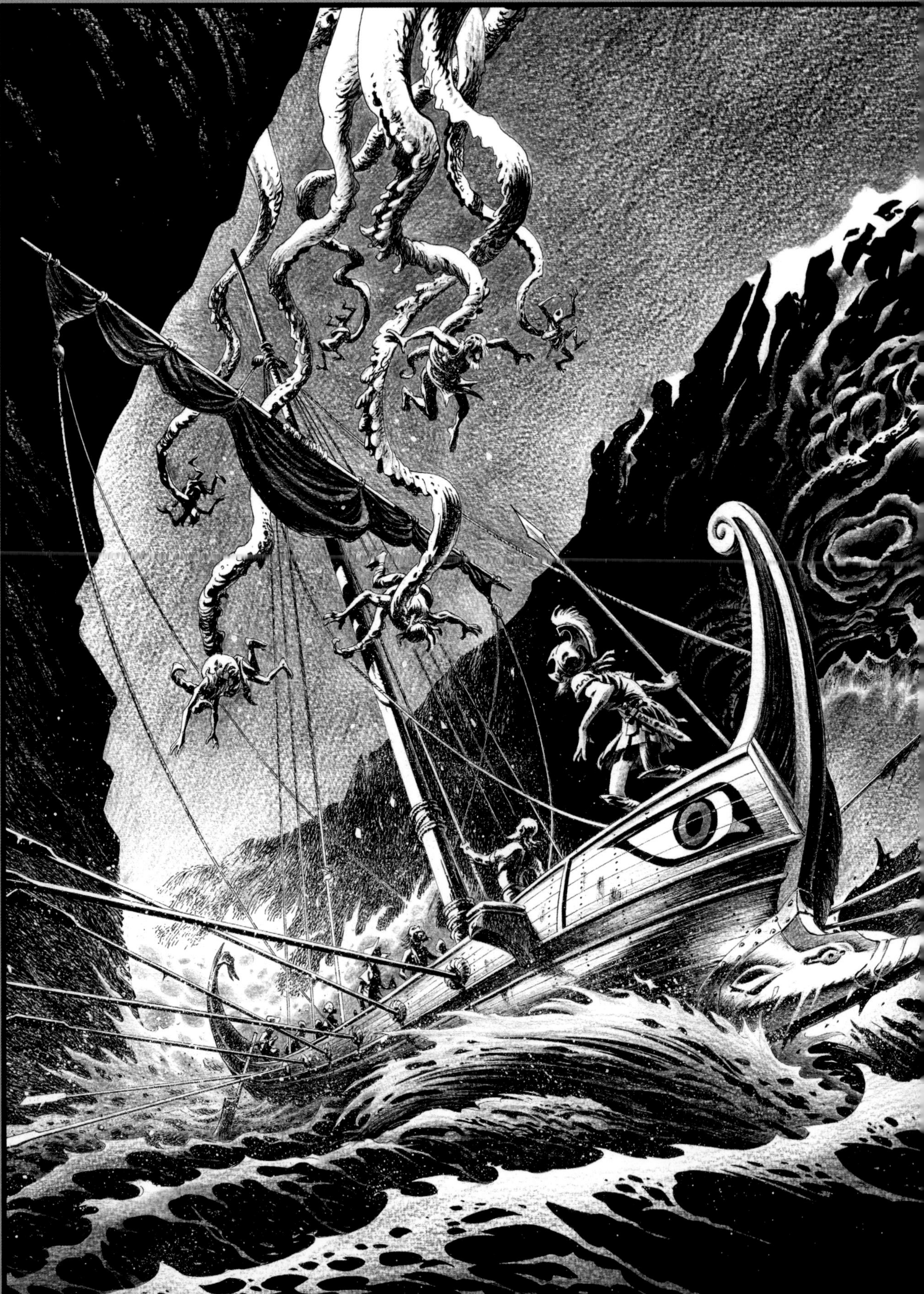

HOMER
The Odyssey

(Excerpt)

I'd forgotten that, in her sad counsel, Circe had enjoined me not to put on my shining armor; I put it on, grabbed two long spears, and went to the foredeck. I hoped to descry that Scylla of rock, ere she caused the ruin of my men… But I sought without seeing, and my eyes grew weary poring over the recesses of mist-covered rock…

We entered into the strait, sailing anxiously. On the one side, we had the divine Charybdis and, on the other, Scylla. When Charybdis belched, the entire sea boiled and seethed like a cauldron over a great flame: the spray surged up to the heights of the cliffs, covering them both. While Charybdis swallowed up the bitter sea anew, we could see her in her pit, in utter turmoil; the surrounding rock roared frightfully; at the very bottom appeared a seafloor of blue sand…Ah! The terror that possessed my men and made them blanch!

But while our eyes looked toward Charybdis, from which we feared our deaths, Scylla seized out of the hollow of our ship six of our comrades, the best and mightiest. Turning around to look at the ship and my men, I saw the others carried aloft, their feet and hands beating the air, screaming, crying out to me! Ulysses!

The Galley Slaves

based on PIERRE MAC ORLAN

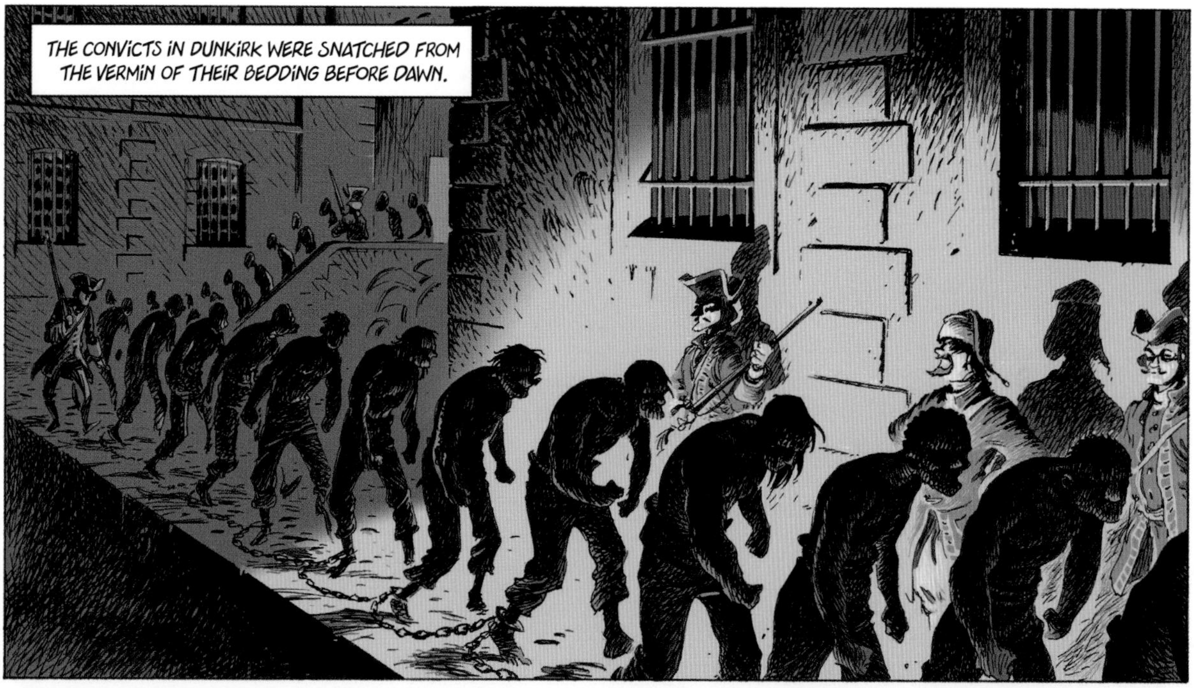
THE CONVICTS IN DUNKIRK WERE SNATCHED FROM THE VERMIN OF THEIR BEDDING BEFORE DAWN.

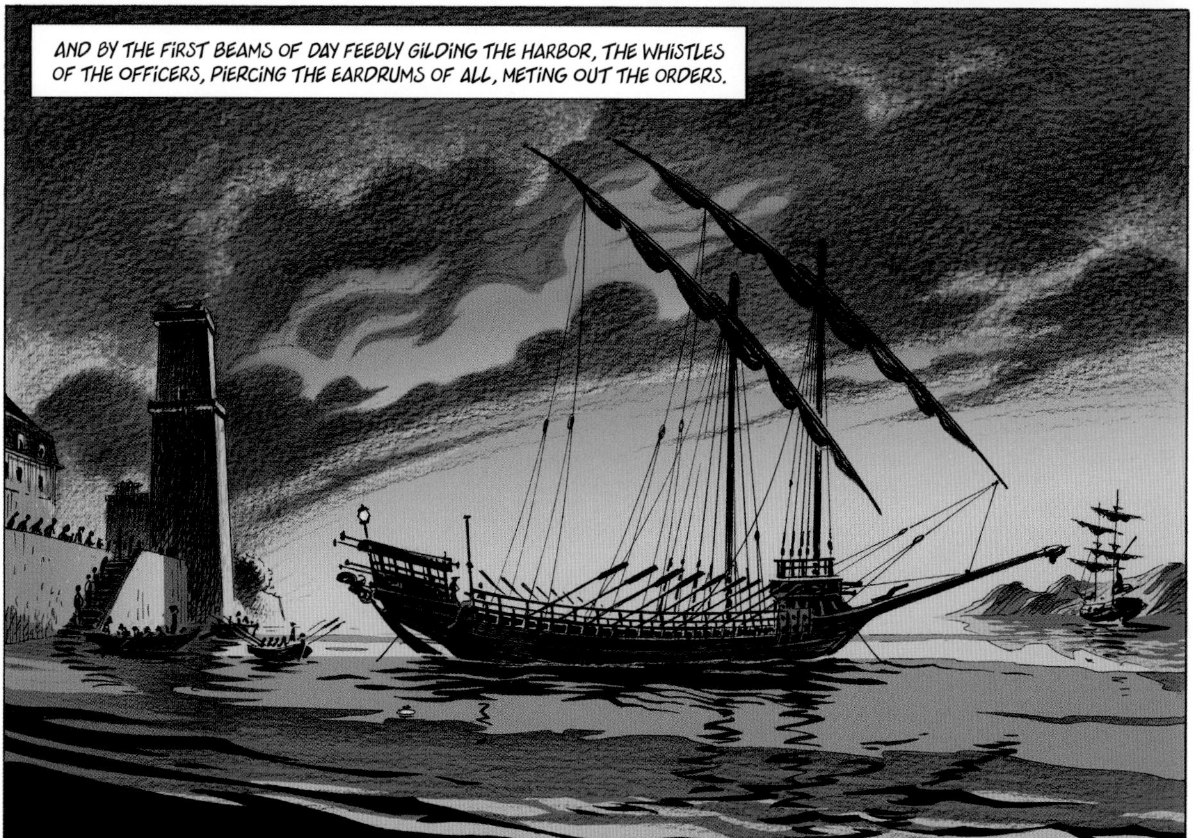
AND BY THE FIRST BEAMS OF DAY FEEBLY GILDING THE HARBOR, THE WHISTLES OF THE OFFICERS, PIERCING THE EARDRUMS OF ALL, METING OUT THE ORDERS.

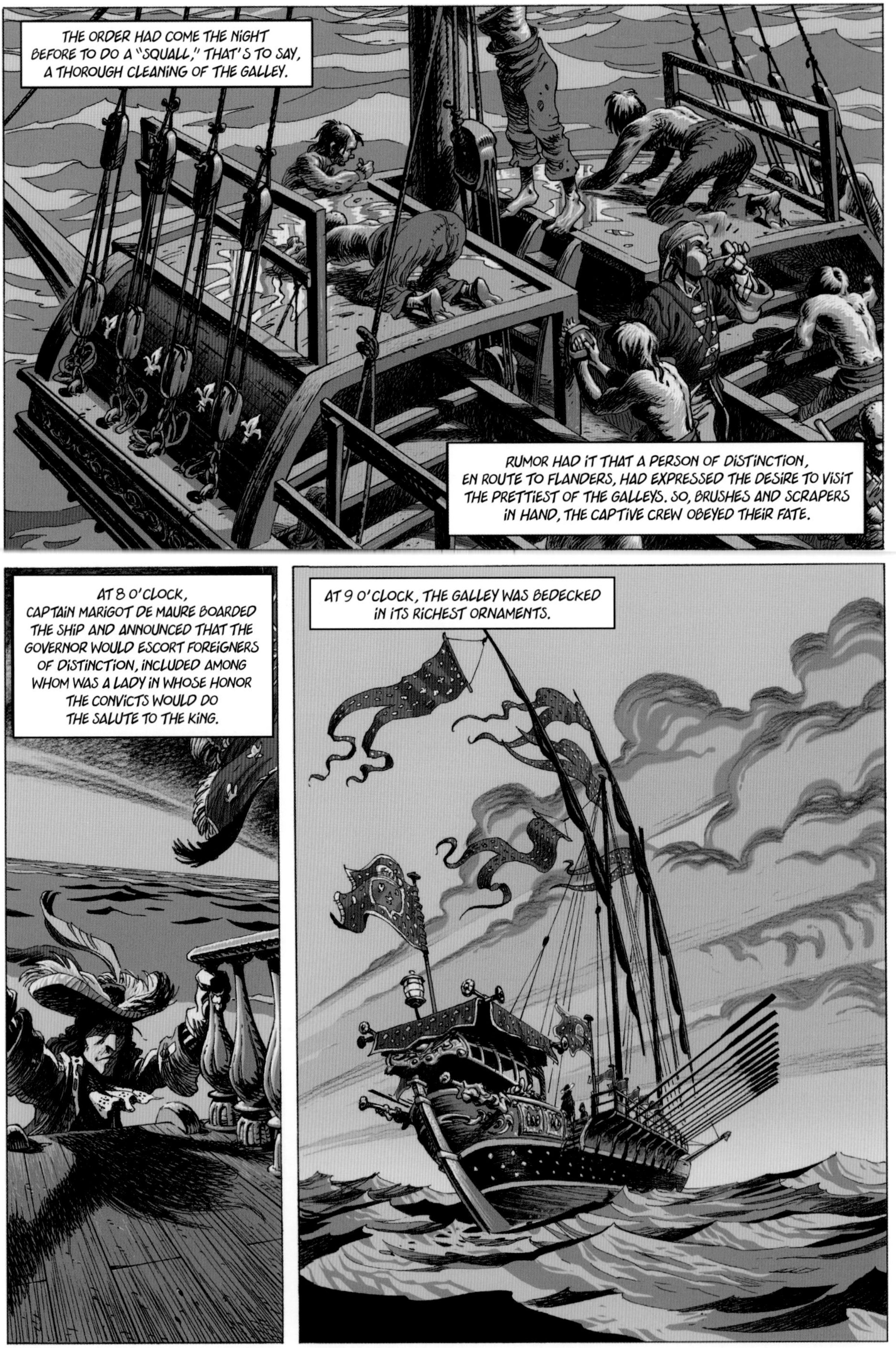
THE ORDER HAD COME THE NIGHT BEFORE TO DO A "SQUALL," THAT'S TO SAY, A THOROUGH CLEANING OF THE GALLEY.
RUMOR HAD IT THAT A PERSON OF DISTINCTION, EN ROUTE TO FLANDERS, HAD EXPRESSED THE DESIRE TO VISIT THE PRETTIEST OF THE GALLEYS. SO, BRUSHES AND SCRAPERS IN HAND, THE CAPTIVE CREW OBEYED THEIR FATE.
AT 8 O'CLOCK, CAPTAIN MARIGOT DE MAURE BOARDED THE SHIP AND ANNOUNCED THAT THE GOVERNOR WOULD ESCORT FOREIGNERS OF DISTINCTION, INCLUDED AMONG WHOM WAS A LADY IN WHOSE HONOR THE CONVICTS WOULD DO THE SALUTE TO THE KING.
AT 9 O'CLOCK, THE GALLEY WAS BEDECKED IN ITS RICHEST ORNAMENTS.

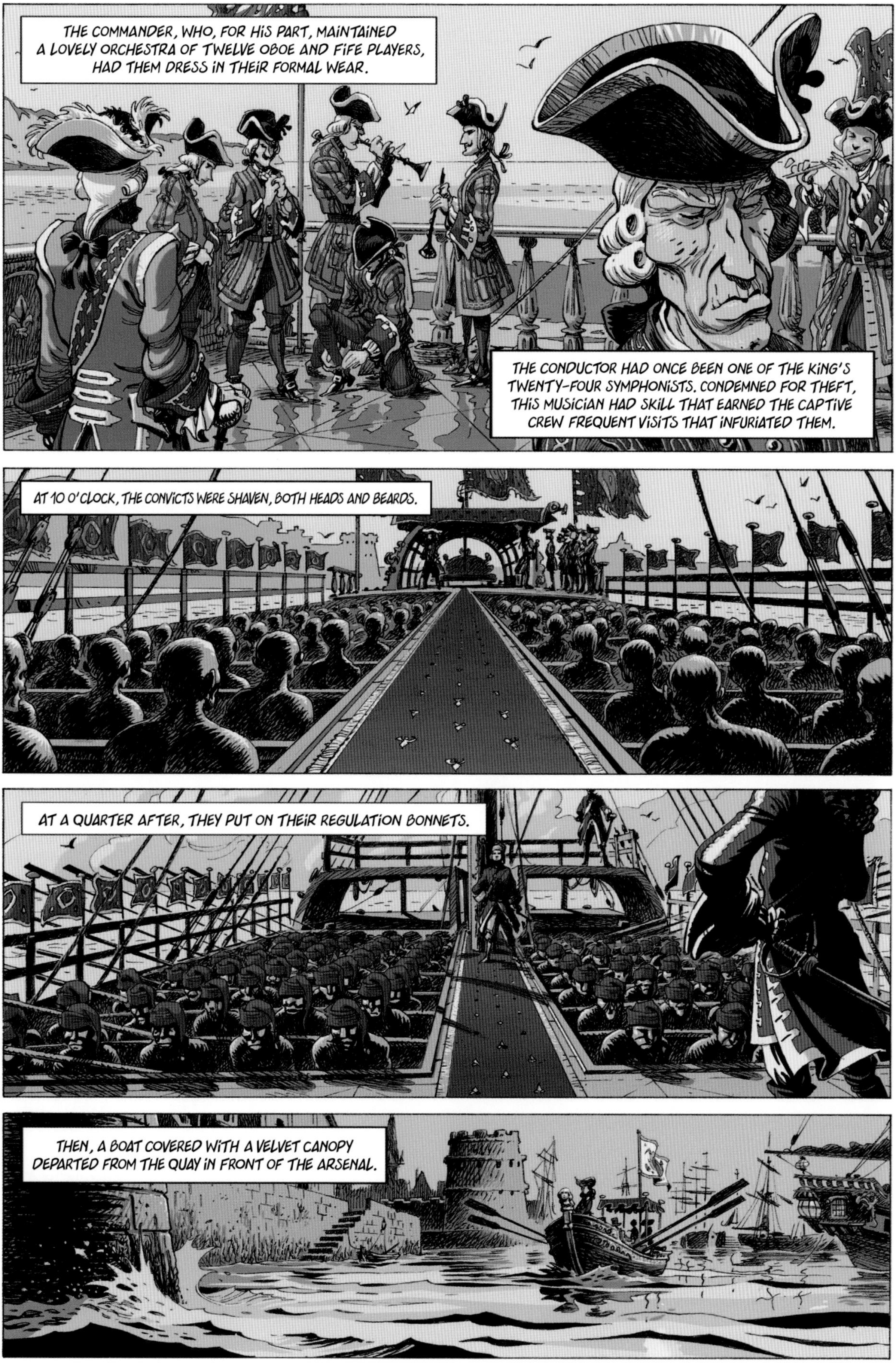
THE COMMANDER, WHO, FOR HIS PART, MAINTAINED A LOVELY ORCHESTRA OF TWELVE OBOE AND FIFE PLAYERS, HAD THEM DRESS IN THEIR FORMAL WEAR.
THE CONDUCTOR HAD ONCE BEEN ONE OF THE KING'S TWENTY-FOUR SYMPHONISTS. CONDEMNED FOR THEFT, THIS MUSICIAN HAD SKILL THAT EARNED THE CAPTIVE CREW FREQUENT VISITS THAT INFURIATED THEM.
AT 10 O'CLOCK, THE CONVICTS WERE SHAVEN, BOTH HEADS AND BEARDS.
AT A QUARTER AFTER, THEY PUT ON THEIR REGULATION BONNETS.
THEN, A BOAT COVERED WITH A VELVET CANOPY DEPARTED FROM THE QUAY IN FRONT OF THE ARSENAL.

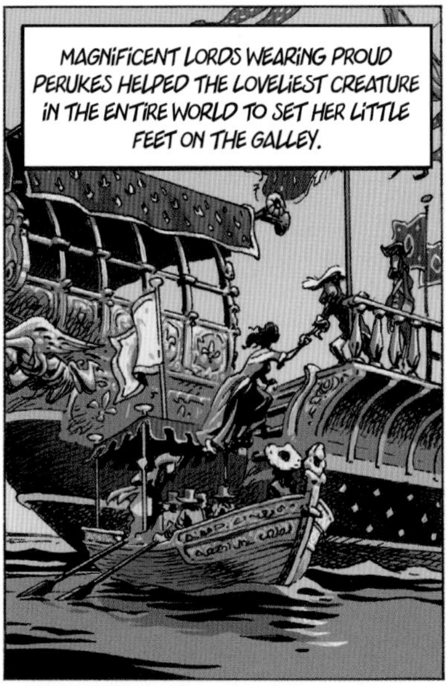
MAGNIFICENT LORDS WEARING PROUD PERUKES HELPED THE LOVELIEST CREATURE IN THE ENTIRE WORLD TO SET HER LITTLE FEET ON THE GALLEY.

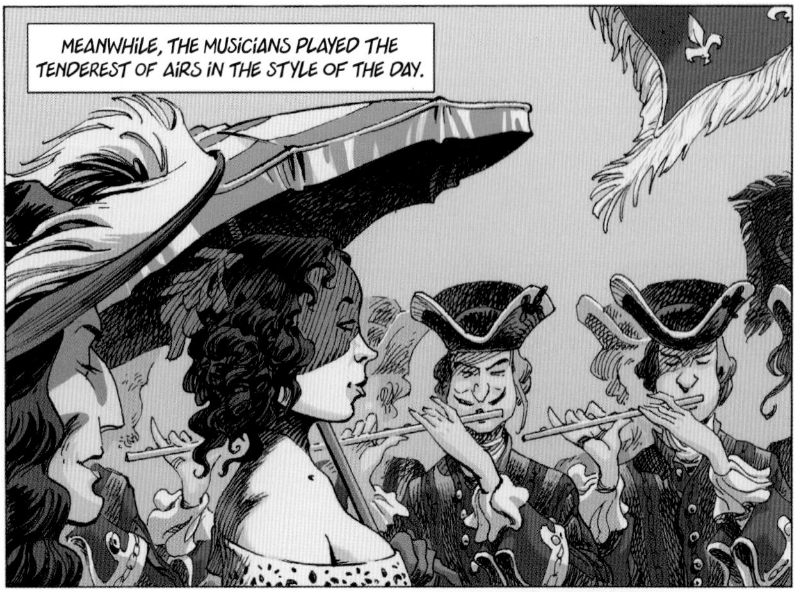
MEANWHILE, THE MUSICIANS PLAYED THE TENDEREST OF AIRS IN THE STYLE OF THE DAY.

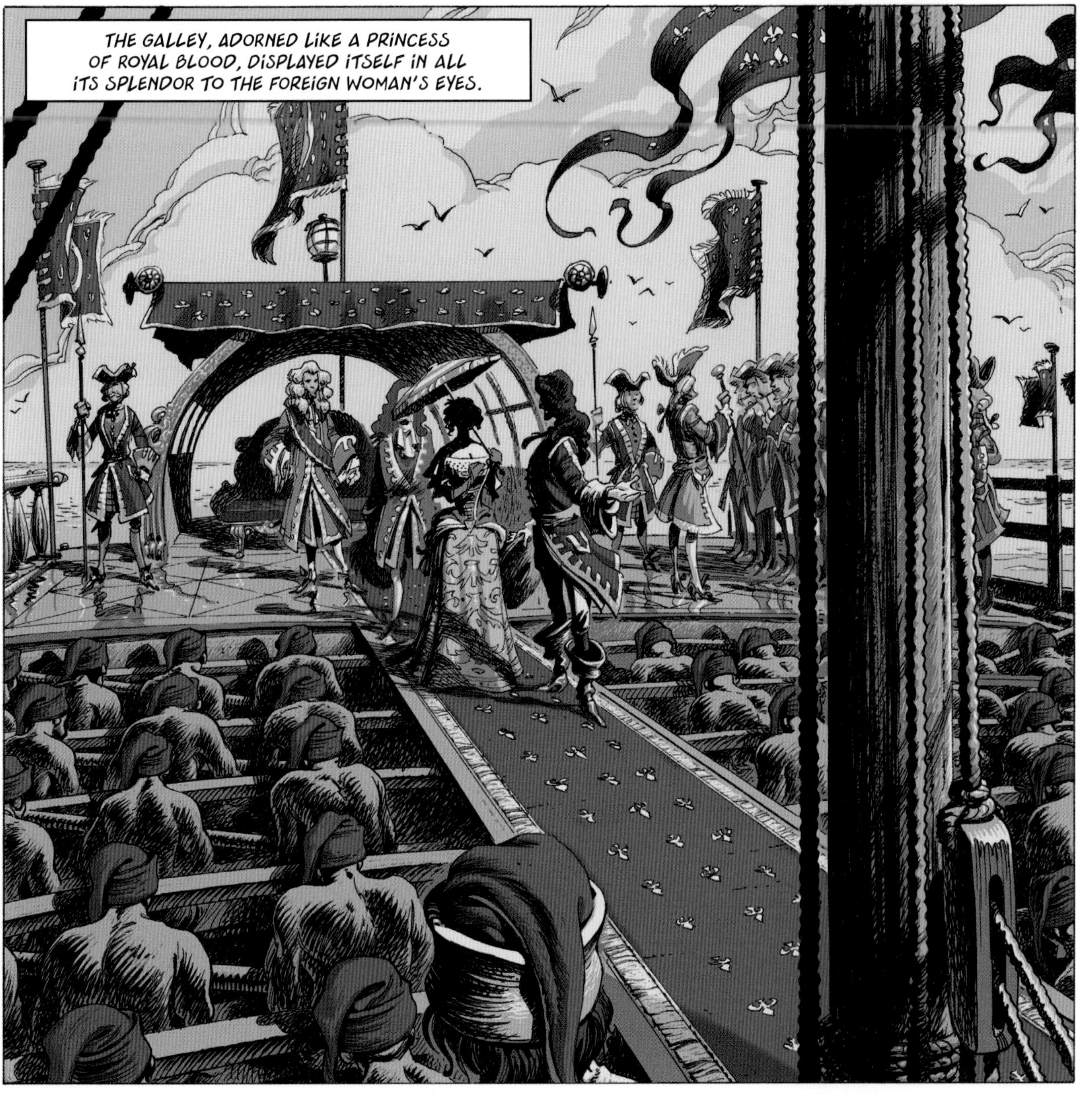
THE GALLEY, ADORNED LIKE A PRINCESS OF ROYAL BLOOD, DISPLAYED ITSELF IN ALL ITS SPLENDOR TO THE FOREIGN WOMAN'S EYES.

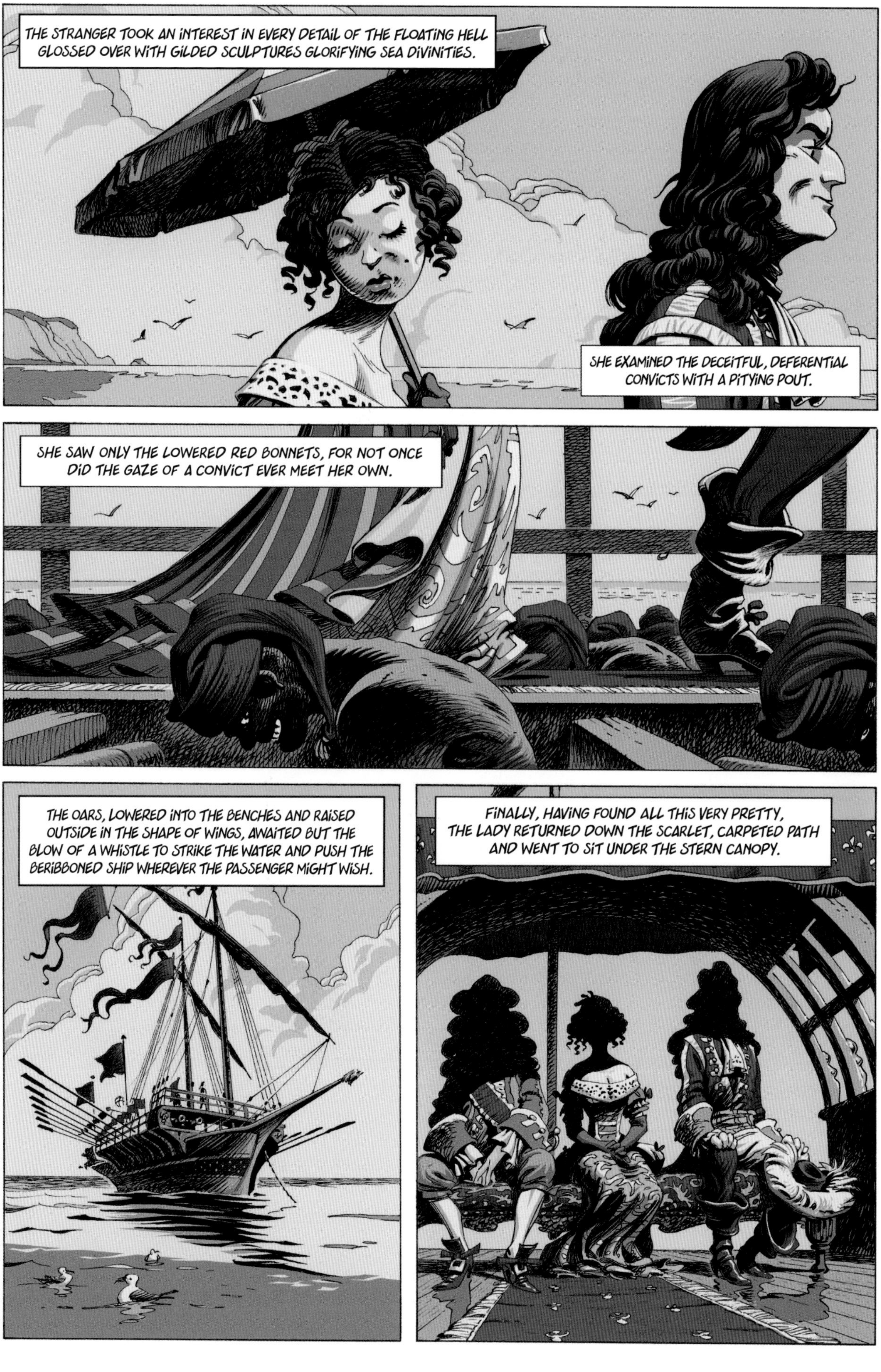
THE STRANGER TOOK AN INTEREST IN EVERY DETAIL OF THE FLOATING HELL GLOSSED OVER WITH GILDED SCULPTURES GLORIFYING SEA DIVINITIES.
SHE EXAMINED THE DECEITFUL, DEFERENTIAL CONVICTS WITH A PITYING POUT.
SHE SAW ONLY THE LOWERED RED BONNETS, FOR NOT ONCE DID THE GAZE OF A CONVICT EVER MEET HER OWN.
THE OARS, LOWERED INTO THE BENCHES AND RAISED OUTSIDE IN THE SHAPE OF WINGS, AWAITED BUT THE BLOW OF A WHISTLE TO STRIKE THE WATER AND PUSH THE BERIBBONED SHIP WHEREVER THE PASSENGER MIGHT WISH.
FINALLY, HAVING FOUND ALL THIS VERY PRETTY, THE LADY RETURNED DOWN THE SCARLET, CARPETED PATH AND WENT TO SIT UNDER THE STERN CANOPY.

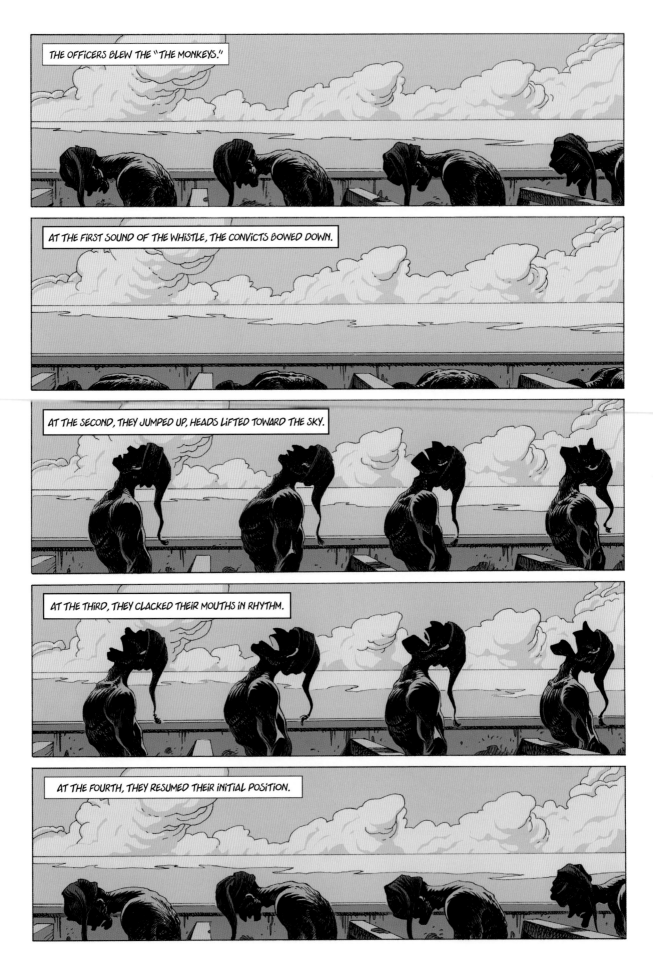

THE OFFICERS BLEW THE "THE MONKEYS."

AT THE FIRST SOUND OF THE WHISTLE, THE CONVICTS BOWED DOWN.

AT THE SECOND, THEY JUMPED UP, HEADS LIFTED TOWARD THE SKY.

AT THE THIRD, THEY CLACKED THEIR MOUTHS IN RHYTHM.

AT THE FOURTH, THEY RESUMED THEIR INITIAL POSITION.

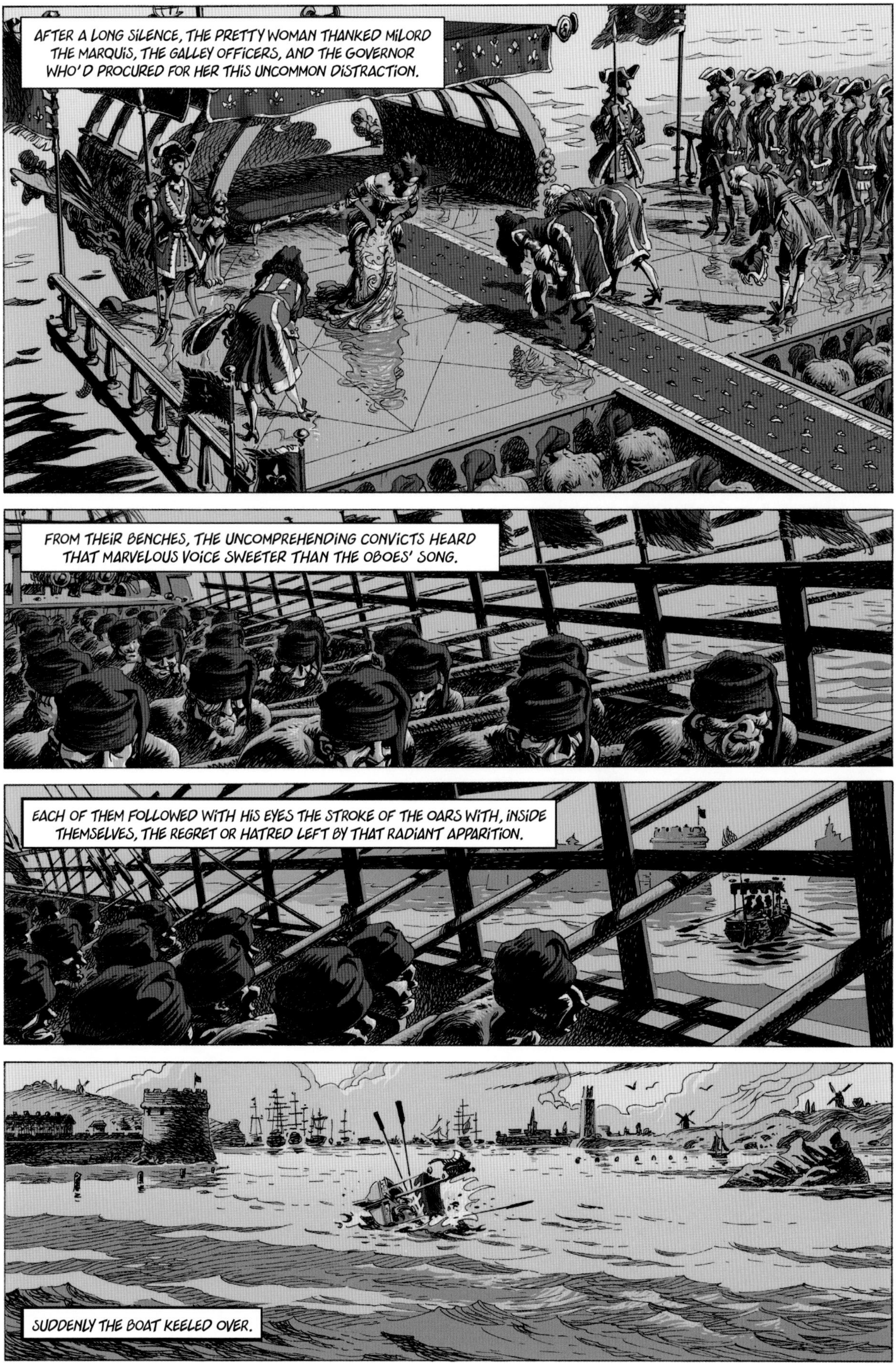
AFTER A LONG SILENCE, THE PRETTY WOMAN THANKED MILORD THE MARQUIS, THE GALLEY OFFICERS, AND THE GOVERNOR WHO'D PROCURED FOR HER THIS UNCOMMON DISTRACTION.
FROM THEIR BENCHES, THE UNCOMPREHENDING CONVICTS HEARD THAT MARVELOUS VOICE SWEETER THAN THE OBOES' SONG.
EACH OF THEM FOLLOWED WITH HIS EYES THE STROKE OF THE OARS WITH, INSIDE THEMSELVES, THE REGRET OR HATRED LEFT BY THAT RADIANT APPARITION.
SUDDENLY THE BOAT KEELED OVER.

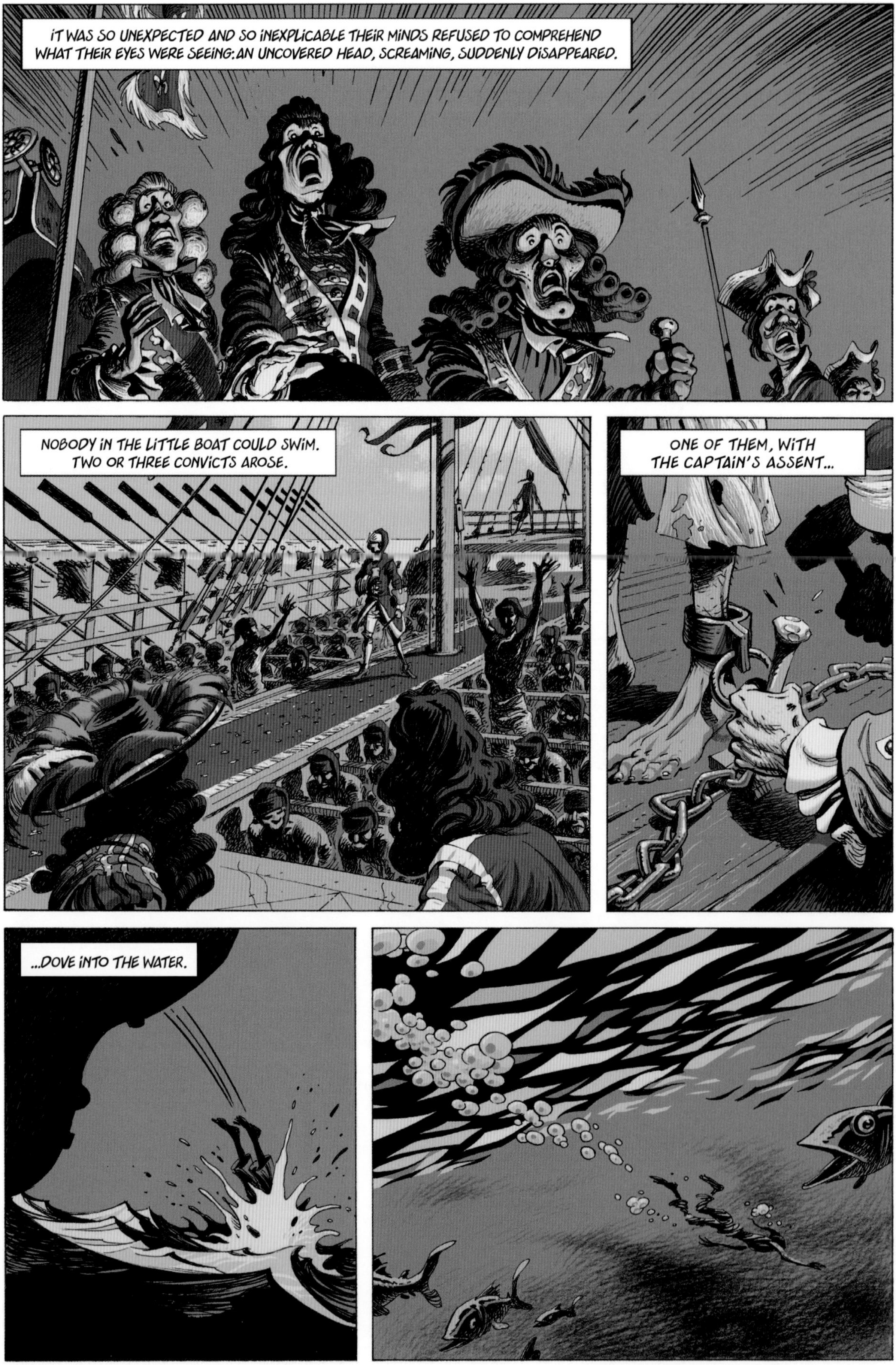
IT WAS SO UNEXPECTED AND SO INEXPLICABLE THEIR MINDS REFUSED TO COMPREHEND WHAT THEIR EYES WERE SEEING: AN UNCOVERED HEAD, SCREAMING, SUDDENLY DISAPPEARED.
NOBODY IN THE LITTLE BOAT COULD SWIM. TWO OR THREE CONVICTS AROSE.
ONE OF THEM, WITH THE CAPTAIN'S ASSENT...
...DOVE INTO THE WATER.

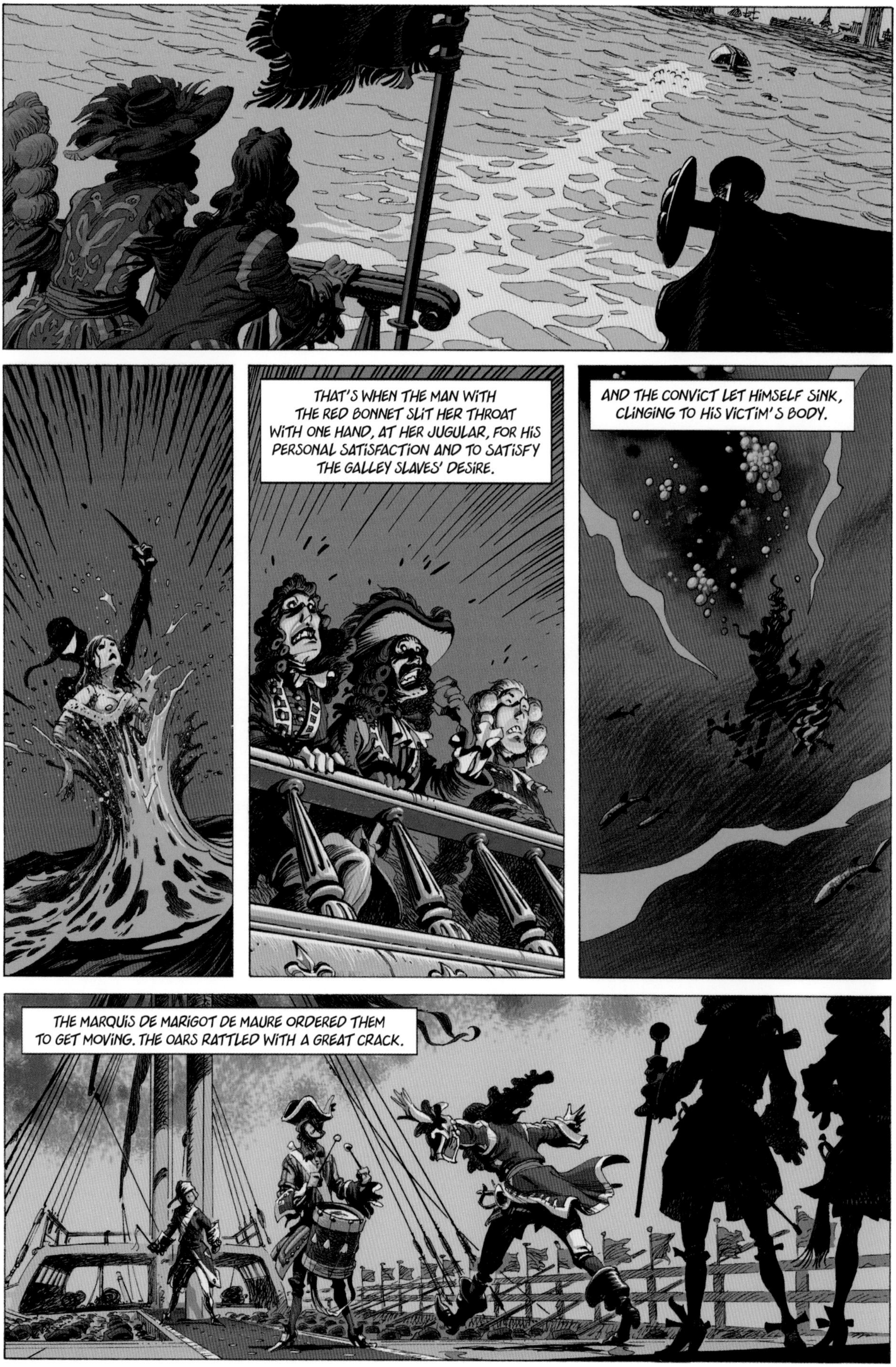
THAT'S WHEN THE MAN WITH THE RED BONNET SLIT HER THROAT WITH ONE HAND, AT HER JUGULAR, FOR HIS PERSONAL SATISFACTION AND TO SATISFY THE GALLEY SLAVES' DESIRE.
AND THE CONVICT LET HIMSELF SINK, CLINGING TO HIS VICTIM'S BODY.
THE MARQUIS DE MARIGOT DE MAURE ORDERED THEM TO GET MOVING. THE OARS RATTLED WITH A GREAT CRACK.

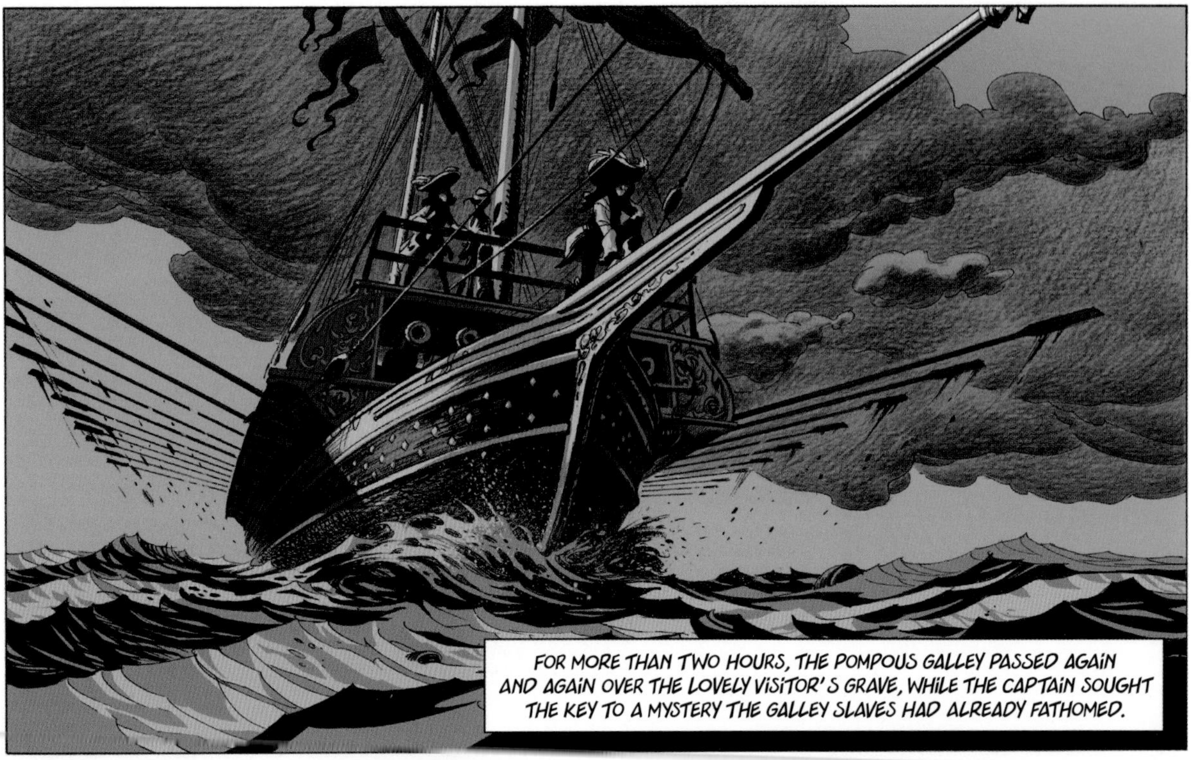
FOR MORE THAN TWO HOURS, THE POMPOUS GALLEY PASSED AGAIN AND AGAIN OVER THE LOVELY VISITOR'S GRAVE, WHILE THE CAPTAIN SOUGHT THE KEY TO A MYSTERY THE GALLEY SLAVES HAD ALREADY FATHOMED.

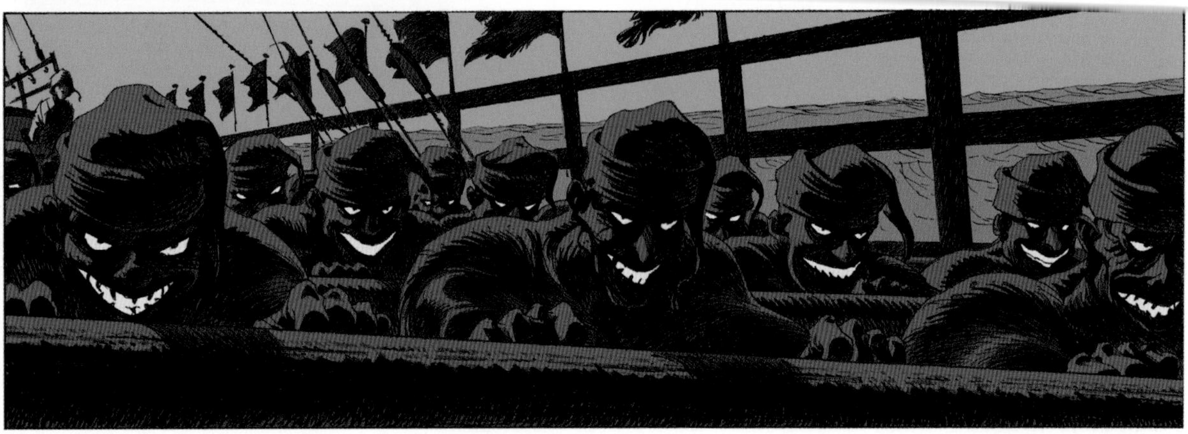

The End

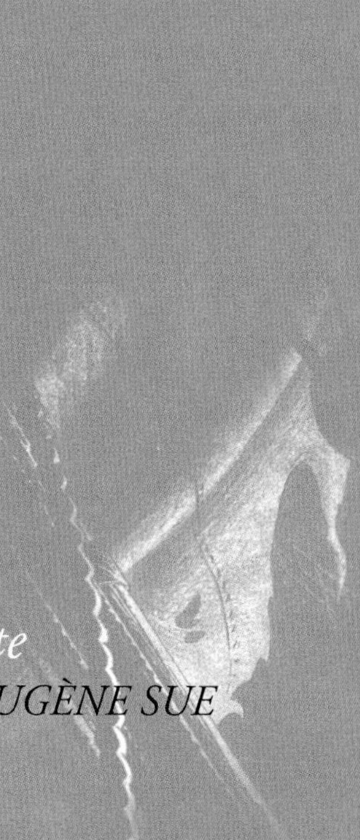

Kernok the Pirate

based on EUGÈNE SUE

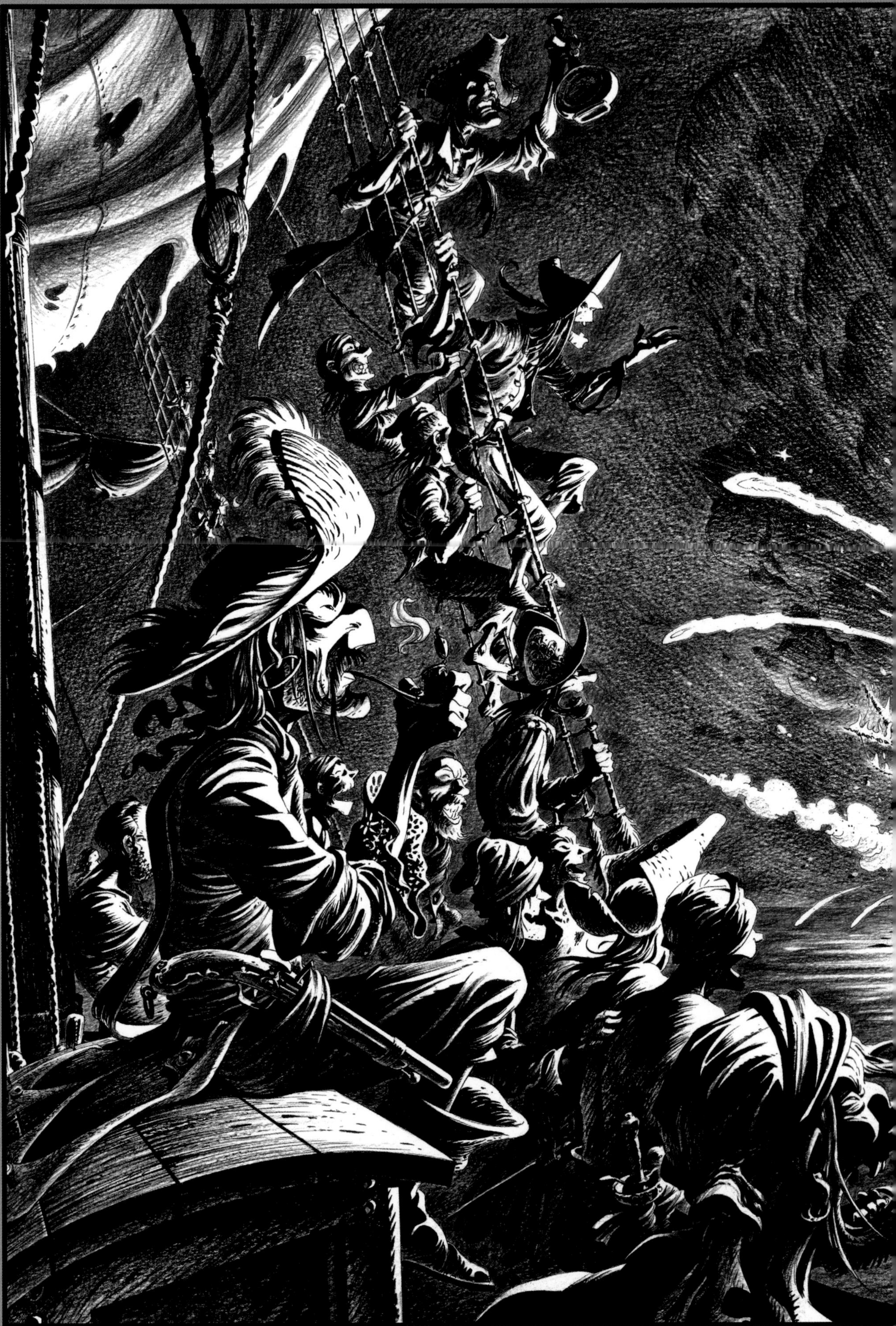

EUGÈNE SUE
Kernok the Pirate

(Excerpt)

Kernok had a surprise in store for his crew; he'd sent Master Zeli on board the Spanish ship, to remove the small bit of powder that might remain there, and to place flammable stuff in the hold and lower deck, then to bind as securely as possible the unfortunate Spaniards, who as yet suspected nothing.

The *San Pablo* was burning. The night was black, the air calm, the sea like a mirror. [...]

And a piercing cry… horrible… echoing into the distance, arose from the interior of the *San Pablo*, for its crew saw what fate awaited them.

"Now there's some music," said Kernok.
"They're singing hellishly off key," answered Zeli. […]

The cries of the Spaniards tied up amid that blazing inferno became so excruciating the pirates, almost despite themselves, howled savagely to drown out the harrowing voices of those wretched souls. [...]

Then murmured the pirate, while dozing off:
"They ought to be happy, for I've done it right: a ship of three hundred gross tons and three dozen Spaniards! That's respectable, but they'd better not get used to it. It's fine from time to time, though, for after all, you got to laugh a little."

The Far South

based on PIERRE MAC ORLAN

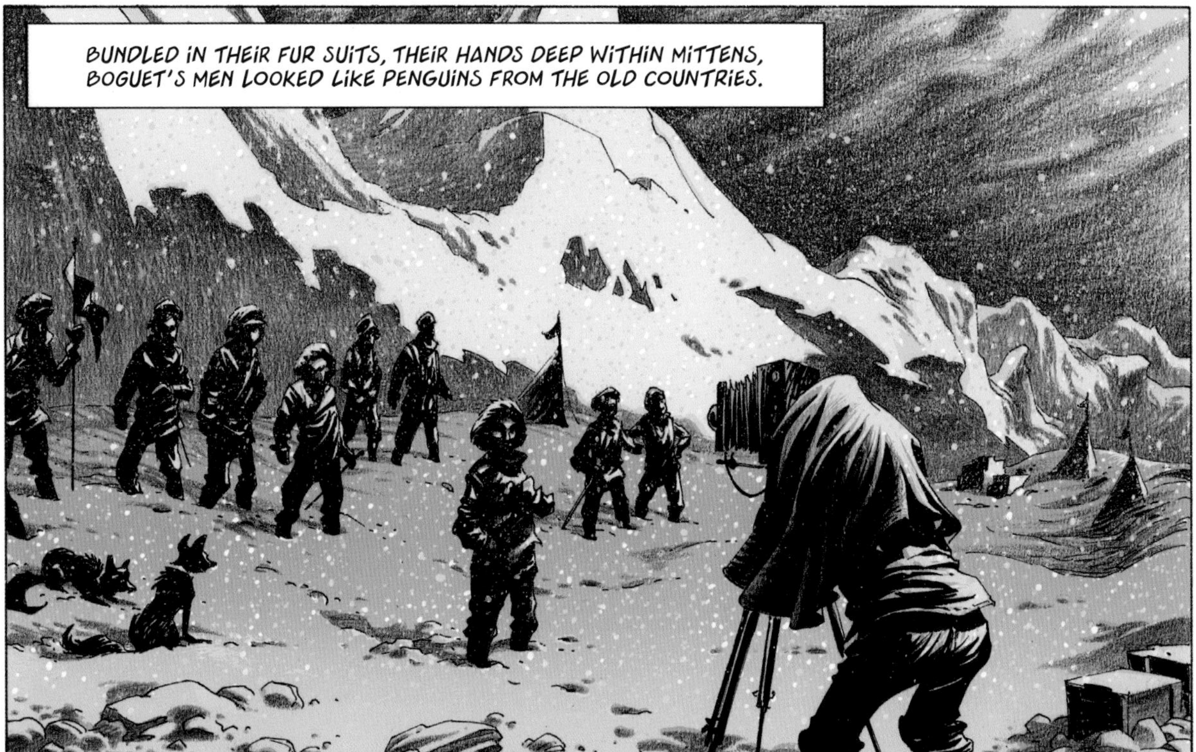
BUNDLED IN THEIR FUR SUITS, THEIR HANDS DEEP WITHIN MITTENS, BOGUET'S MEN LOOKED LIKE PENGUINS FROM THE OLD COUNTRIES.

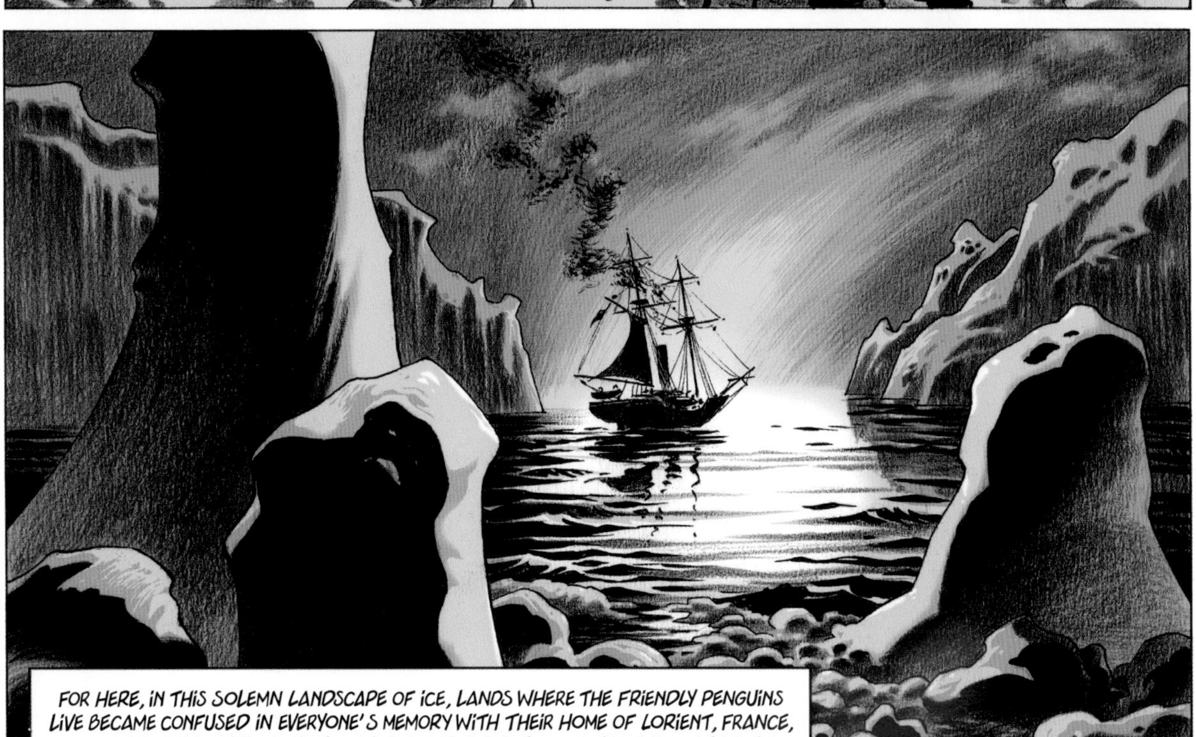
FOR HERE, IN THIS SOLEMN LANDSCAPE OF ICE, LANDS WHERE THE FRIENDLY PENGUINS LIVE BECAME CONFUSED IN EVERYONE'S MEMORY WITH THEIR HOME OF LORIENT, FRANCE, FROM WHICH THE EXPLORER'S YACHT HAD DEPARTED TO CONQUER THE SOUTH POLE.

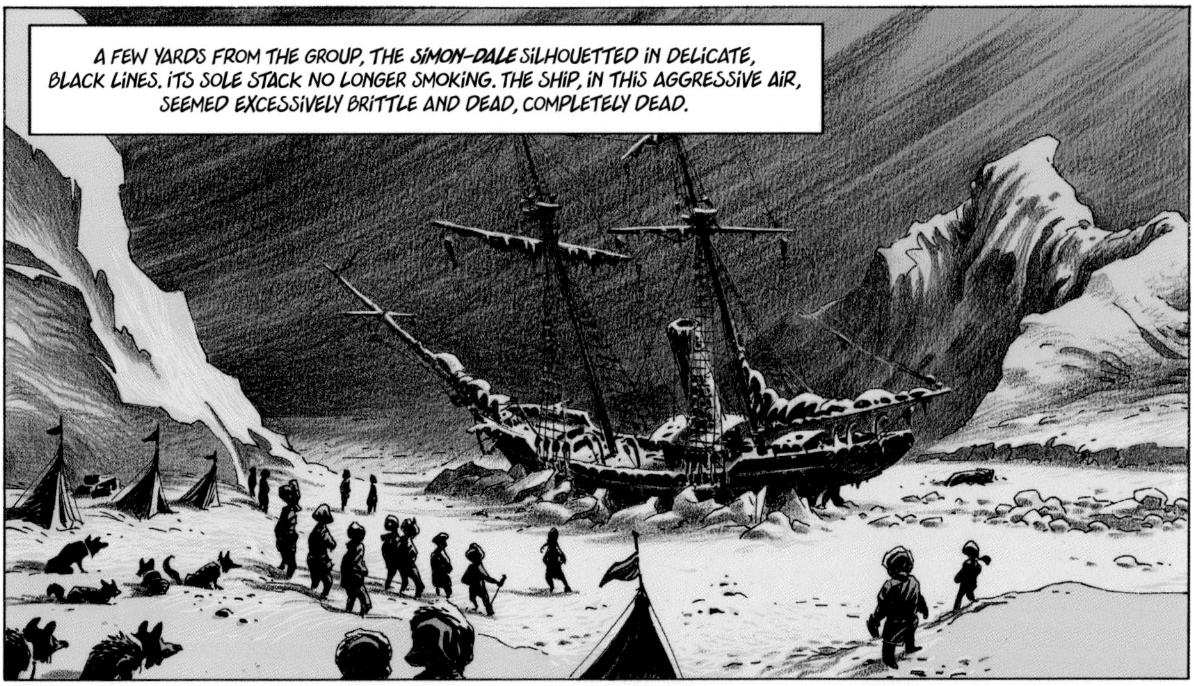
A FEW YARDS FROM THE GROUP, THE SIMON-DALE SILHOUETTED IN DELICATE, BLACK LINES. ITS SOLE STACK NO LONGER SMOKING. THE SHIP, IN THIS AGGRESSIVE AIR, SEEMED EXCESSIVELY BRITTLE AND DEAD, COMPLETELY DEAD.

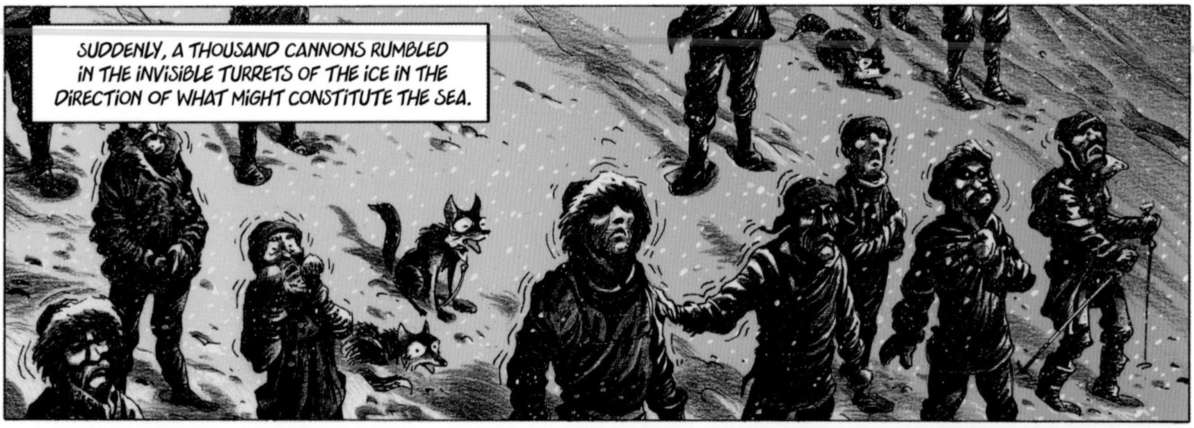
SUDDENLY, A THOUSAND CANNONS RUMBLED IN THE INVISIBLE TURRETS OF THE ICE IN THE DIRECTION OF WHAT MIGHT CONSTITUTE THE SEA.

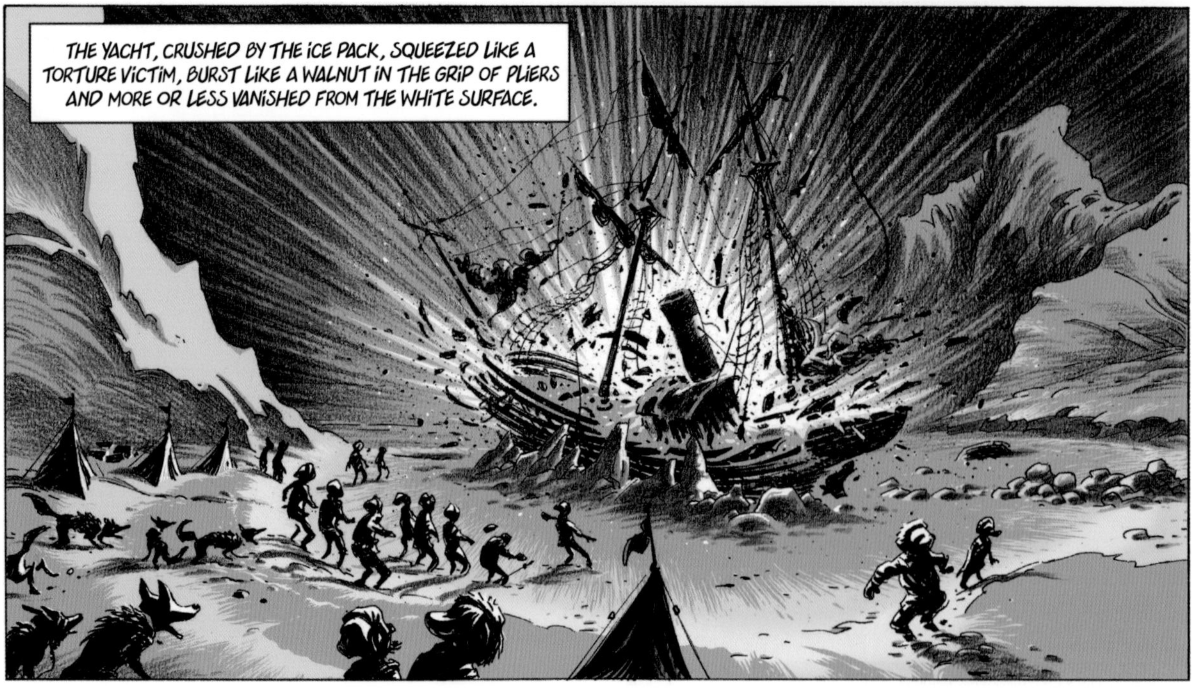
THE YACHT, CRUSHED BY THE ICE PACK, SQUEEZED LIKE A TORTURE VICTIM, BURST LIKE A WALNUT IN THE GRIP OF PLIERS AND MORE OR LESS VANISHED FROM THE WHITE SURFACE.

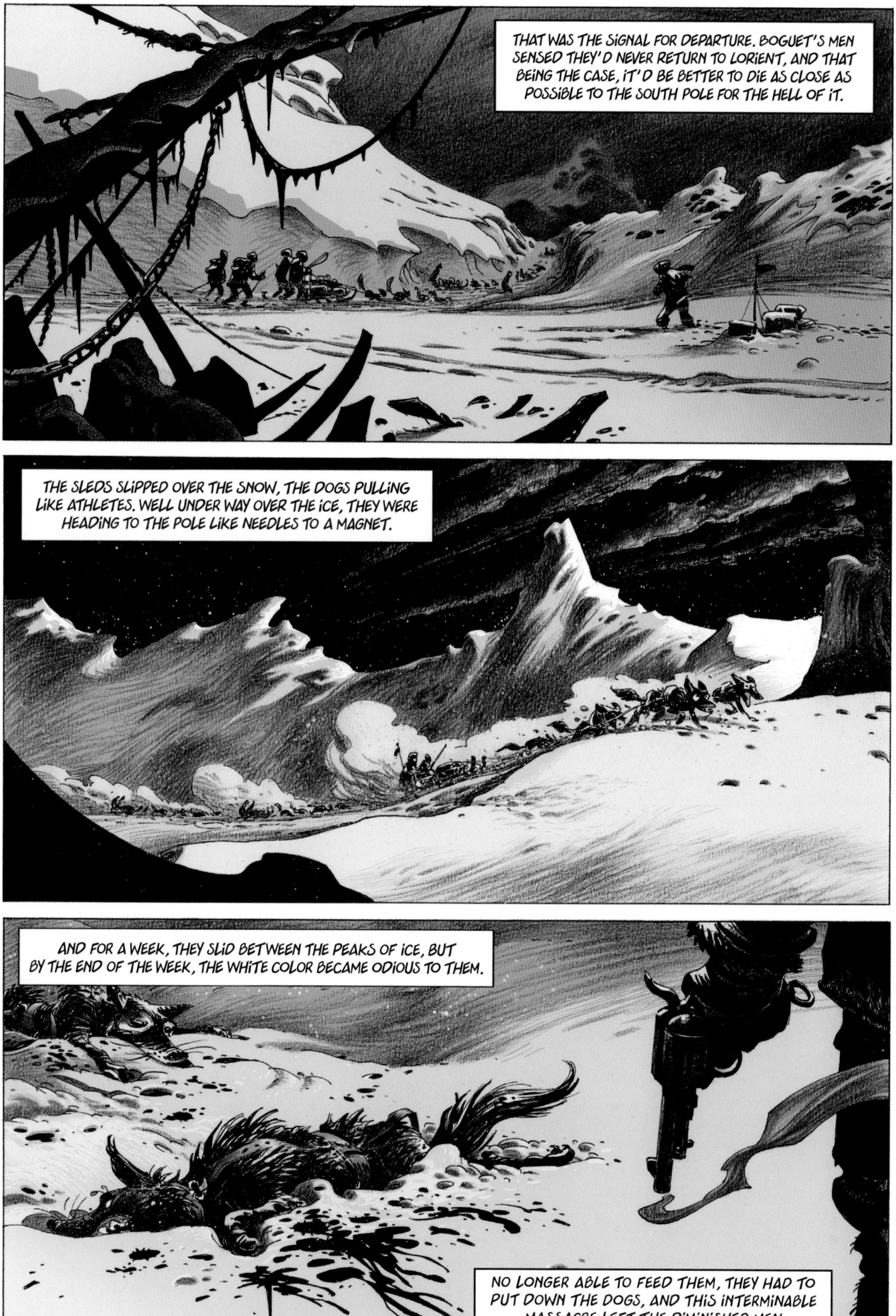
THAT WAS THE SIGNAL FOR DEPARTURE. BOGUET'S MEN SENSED THEY'D NEVER RETURN TO LORIENT, AND THAT BEING THE CASE, IT'D BE BETTER TO DIE AS CLOSE AS POSSIBLE TO THE SOUTH POLE FOR THE HELL OF IT.
THE SLEDS SLIPPED OVER THE SNOW, THE DOGS PULLING LIKE ATHLETES. WELL UNDER WAY OVER THE ICE, THEY WERE HEADING TO THE POLE LIKE NEEDLES TO A MAGNET.
AND FOR A WEEK, THEY SLID BETWEEN THE PEAKS OF ICE, BUT BY THE END OF THE WEEK, THE WHITE COLOR BECAME ODIOUS TO THEM.
NO LONGER ABLE TO FEED THEM, THEY HAD TO PUT DOWN THE DOGS, AND THIS INTERMINABLE MASSACRE LEFT THE DIMINISHED MEN DISGUSTED WITH THEMSELVES.

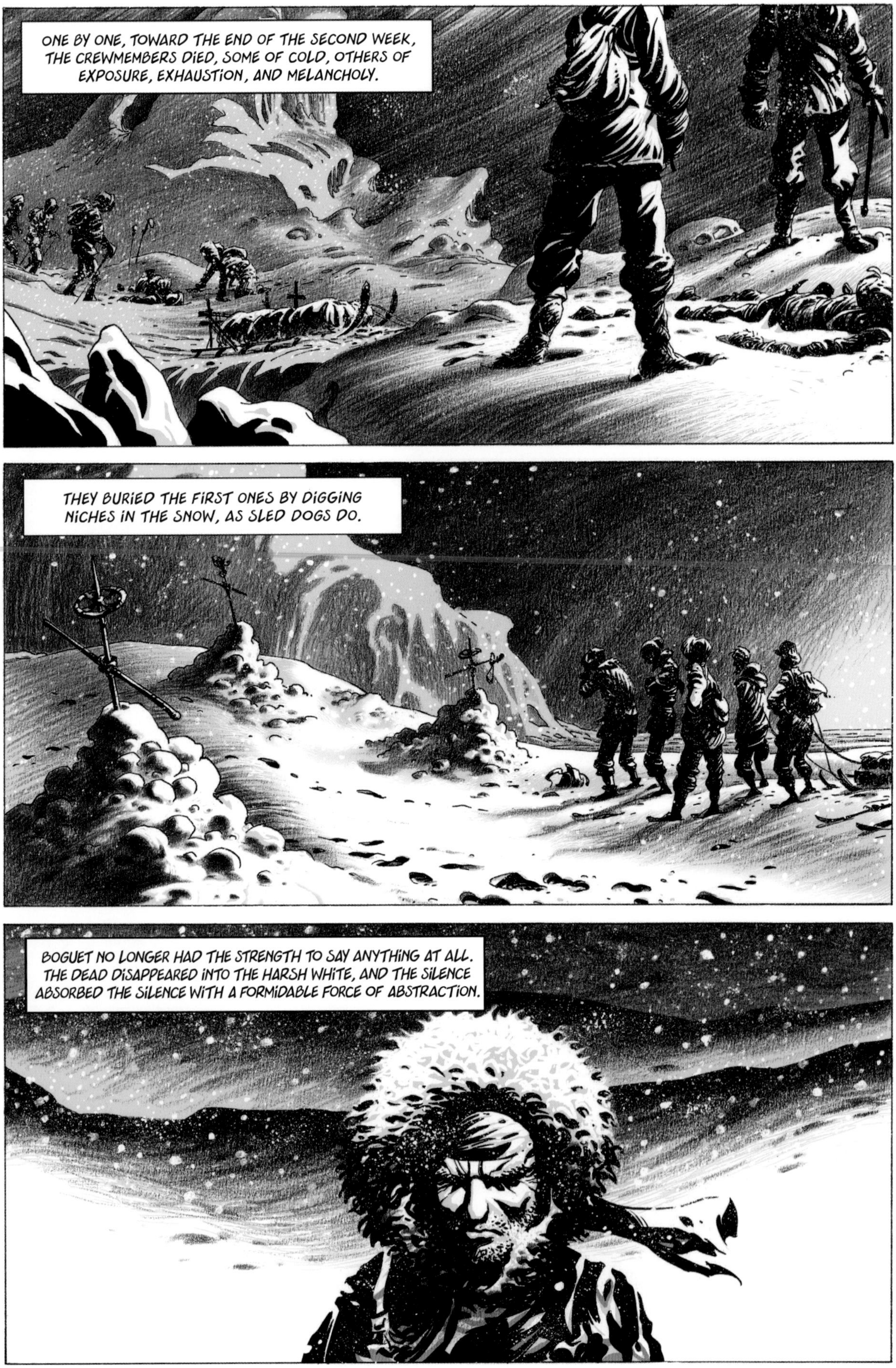
ONE BY ONE, TOWARD THE END OF THE SECOND WEEK, THE CREWMEMBERS DIED, SOME OF COLD, OTHERS OF EXPOSURE, EXHAUSTION, AND MELANCHOLY.
THEY BURIED THE FIRST ONES BY DIGGING NICHES IN THE SNOW, AS SLED DOGS DO.
BOGUET NO LONGER HAD THE STRENGTH TO SAY ANYTHING AT ALL. THE DEAD DISAPPEARED INTO THE HARSH WHITE, AND THE SILENCE ABSORBED THE SILENCE WITH A FORMIDABLE FORCE OF ABSTRACTION.

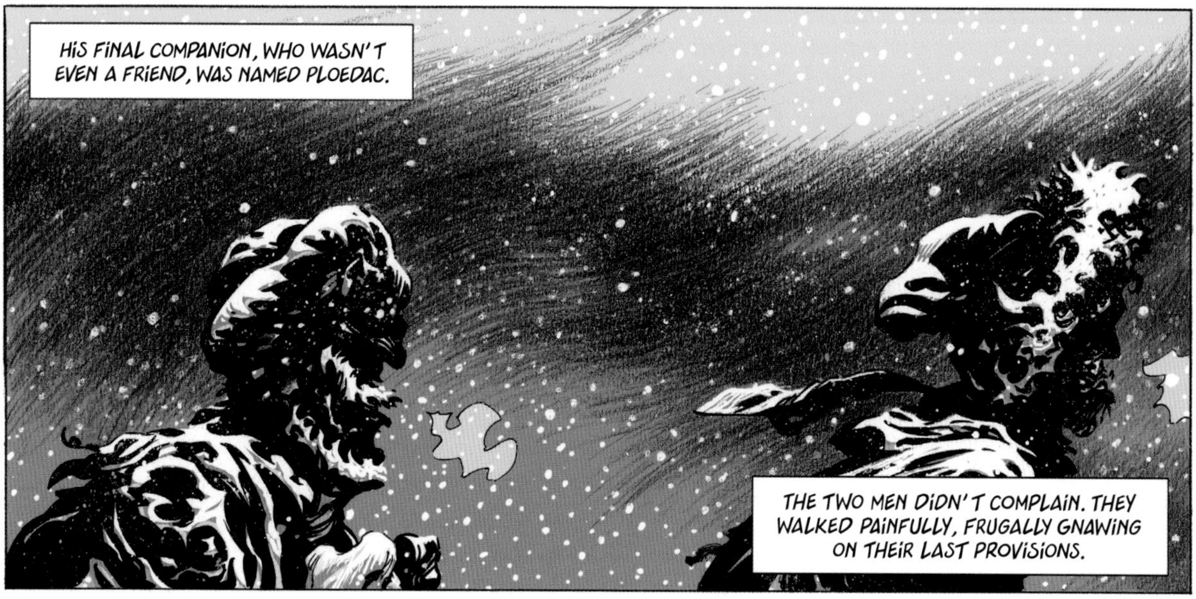
HIS FINAL COMPANION, WHO WASN'T EVEN A FRIEND, WAS NAMED PLOEDAC.
THE TWO MEN DIDN'T COMPLAIN. THEY WALKED PAINFULLY, FRUGALLY GNAWING ON THEIR LAST PROVISIONS.

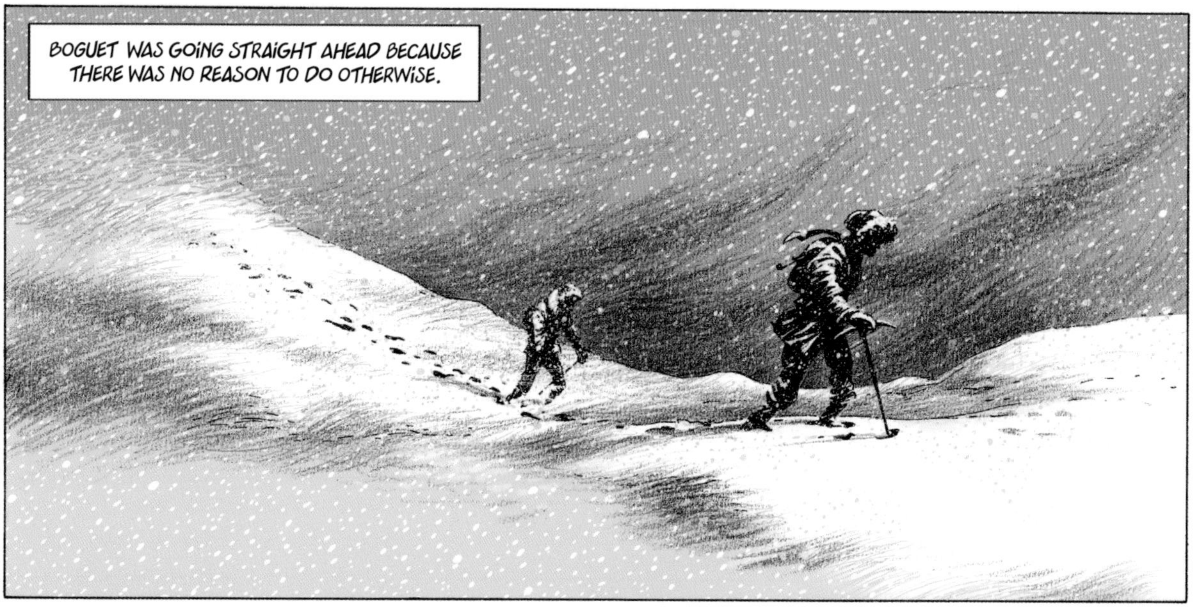
BOGUET WAS GOING STRAIGHT AHEAD BECAUSE THERE WAS NO REASON TO DO OTHERWISE.

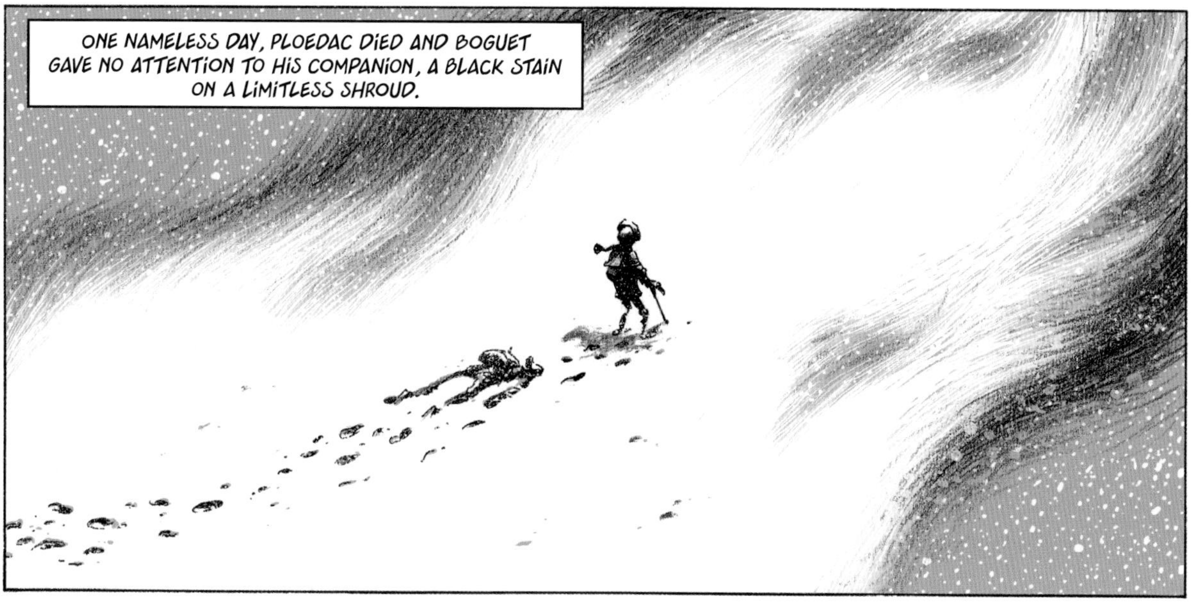
ONE NAMELESS DAY, PLOEDAC DIED AND BOGUET GAVE NO ATTENTION TO HIS COMPANION, A BLACK STAIN ON A LIMITLESS SHROUD.

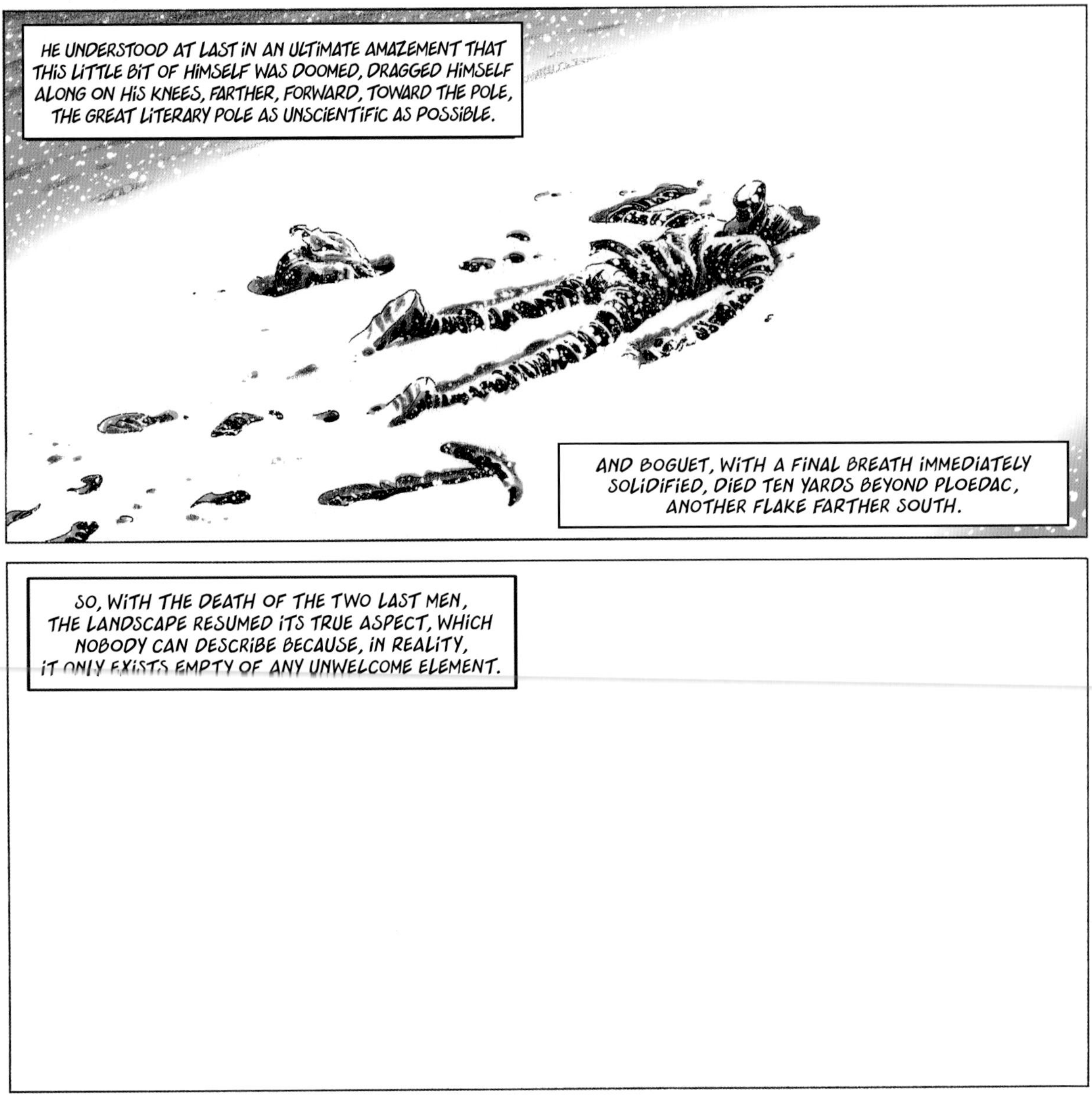
HE UNDERSTOOD AT LAST IN AN ULTIMATE AMAZEMENT THAT THIS LITTLE BIT OF HIMSELF WAS DOOMED, DRAGGED HIMSELF ALONG ON HIS KNEES, FARTHER, FORWARD, TOWARD THE POLE, THE GREAT LITERARY POLE AS UNSCIENTIFIC AS POSSIBLE.
AND BOGUET, WITH A FINAL BREATH IMMEDIATELY SOLIDIFIED, DIED TEN YARDS BEYOND PLOEDAC, ANOTHER FLAKE FARTHER SOUTH.
SO, WITH THE DEATH OF THE TWO LAST MEN, THE LANDSCAPE RESUMED ITS TRUE ASPECT, WHICH NOBODY CAN DESCRIBE BECAUSE, IN REALITY, IT ONLY EXISTS EMPTY OF ANY UNWELCOME ELEMENT.

The End

Malgorn the Whaler
based on ÉMILE CONDROYER

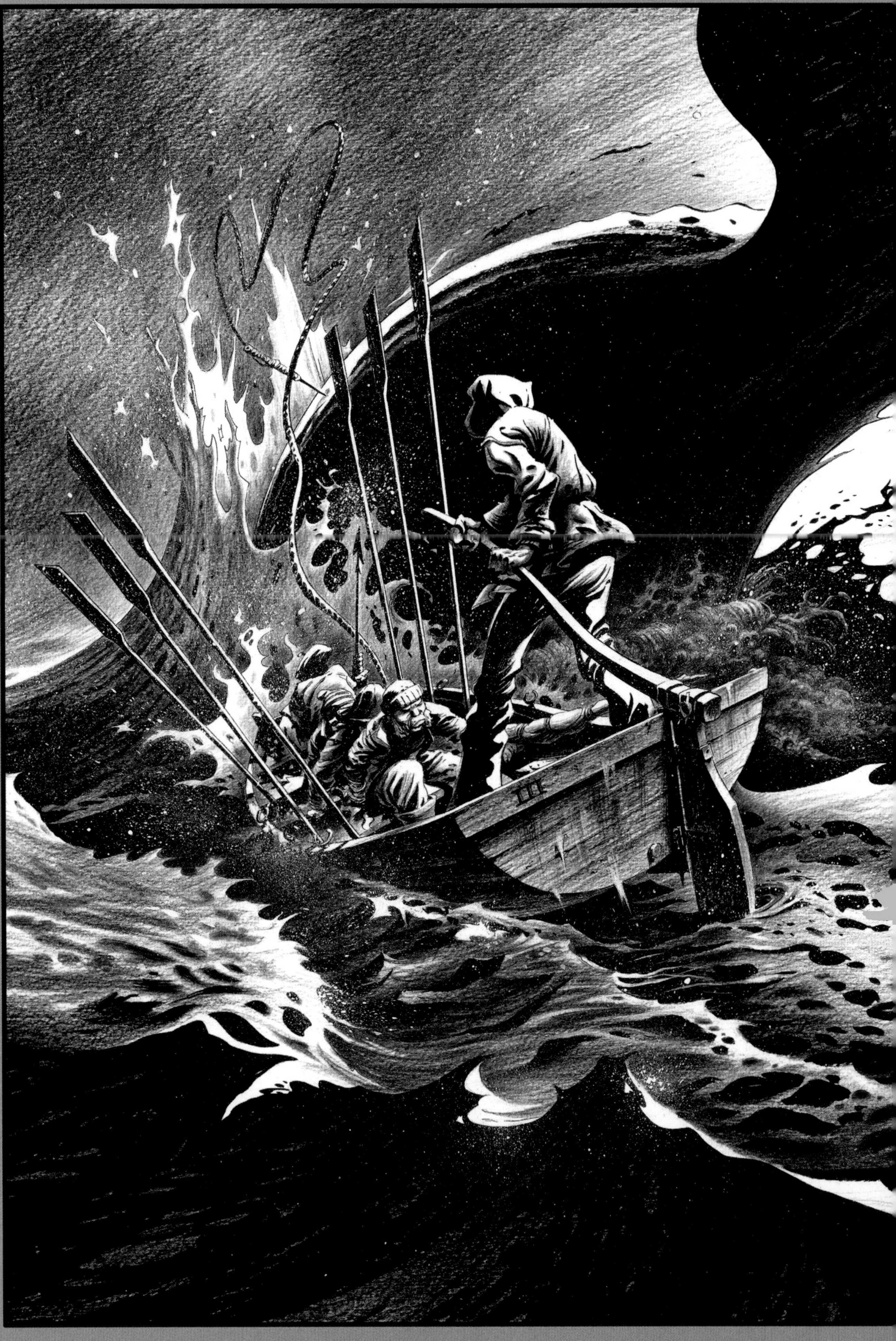

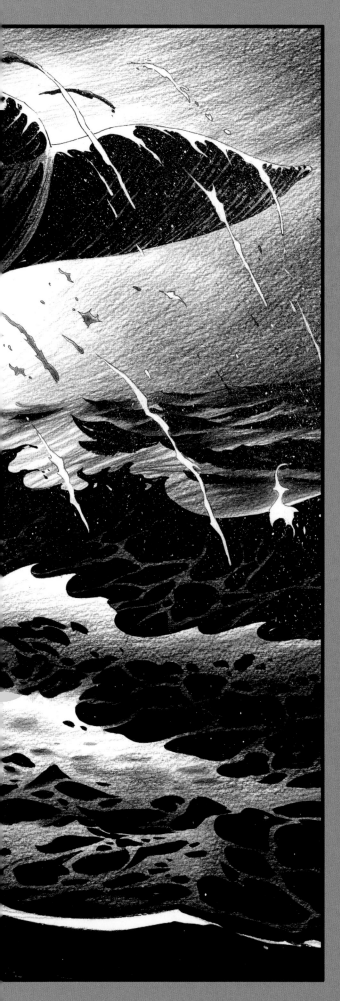

ÉMILE CONDROYER
Malgorn the Whaler

(Excerpt)

Malgorn, like the other rowers, was clutching at his bench. The line was vibrating on an intolerable note… The light hull reverberated from the crash of torrent against the stem rising bit by bit, rising too much even, for the wallowing stern was foundering in the fleeing eddies amid the waves with their lashing spray. Yawing swerved the boat against foaming, rolling waves. The boat fell back onto the water so hard Malgorn felt the shock in his bones like a falling rock. No one dared to move. The boat's slender planking of cedar groaned, ready to come apart at the slightest movement, in an unstable balance seemingly upon its single, straight keel. It was begetting the tempest, and the tempest accompanied its frenetic course with its gallop. Malgorn could make out the steering oar bending under the resistance of the water and Moisan, bent over like him like he'd been punched in the stomach by some Basque fellow. […]

Finally, breaking rules, he dared to turn his head a bit forward, toward the beast that was the cause for this infernal race, whose labored breathing sped up as it wearied. Beyond the silvered particles, he glimpsed its enormous, black, battered form, which, at times, surged out of a snowy havoc like a gloomy land of apocalypse and, at others, sank, rolling among its exhalations of fog. […]

Predisposed, he now underwent that of an astounding reality, a voluptuousness no longer funereal but light, with the awareness that there was nothing of importance other than this minute in which he was harnessing to his life the most legendary creature in the universe.

The Three Customs Officers

based on MARCEL SCHWOB

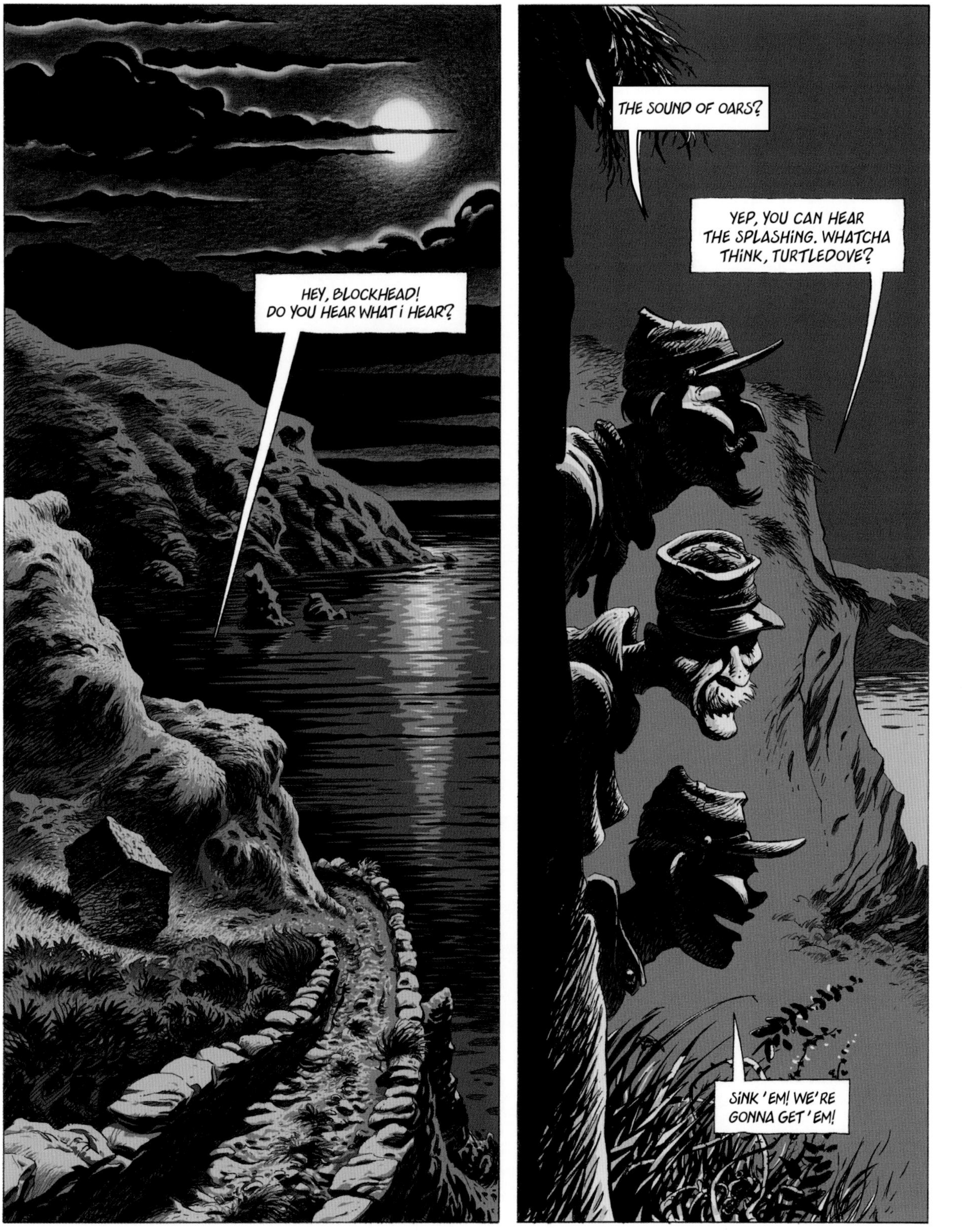

HEY, BLOCKHEAD! DO YOU HEAR WHAT I HEAR?
THE SOUND OF OARS?
YEP, YOU CAN HEAR THE SPLASHING. WHATCHA THINK, TURTLEDOVE?
SINK 'EM! WE'RE GONNA GET 'EM!

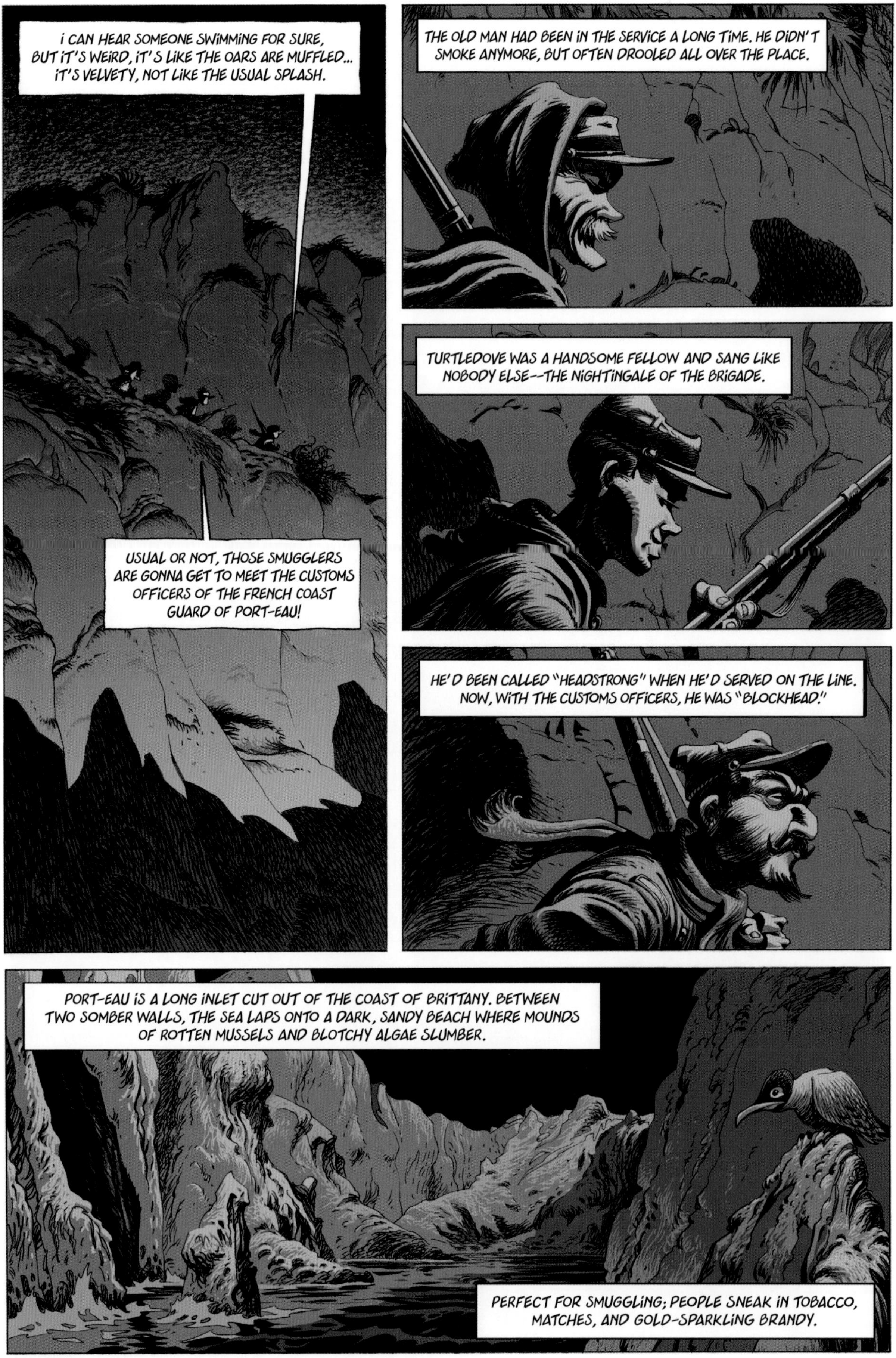
I CAN HEAR SOMEONE SWIMMING FOR SURE, BUT IT'S WEIRD, IT'S LIKE THE OARS ARE MUFFLED... IT'S VELVETY, NOT LIKE THE USUAL SPLASH.
USUAL OR NOT, THOSE SMUGGLERS ARE GONNA GET TO MEET THE CUSTOMS OFFICERS OF THE FRENCH COAST GUARD OF PORT-EAU!
THE OLD MAN HAD BEEN IN THE SERVICE A LONG TIME. HE DIDN'T SMOKE ANYMORE, BUT OFTEN DROOLED ALL OVER THE PLACE.
TURTLEDOVE WAS A HANDSOME FELLOW AND SANG LIKE NOBODY ELSE--THE NIGHTINGALE OF THE BRIGADE.
HE'D BEEN CALLED "HEADSTRONG" WHEN HE'D SERVED ON THE LINE. NOW, WITH THE CUSTOMS OFFICERS, HE WAS "BLOCKHEAD."
PORT-EAU IS A LONG INLET CUT OUT OF THE COAST OF BRITTANY. BETWEEN TWO SOMBER WALLS, THE SEA LAPS ONTO A DARK, SANDY BEACH WHERE MOUNDS OF ROTTEN MUSSELS AND BLOTCHY ALGAE SLUMBER.
PERFECT FOR SMUGGLING; PEOPLE SNEAK IN TOBACCO, MATCHES, AND GOLD-SPARKLING BRANDY.

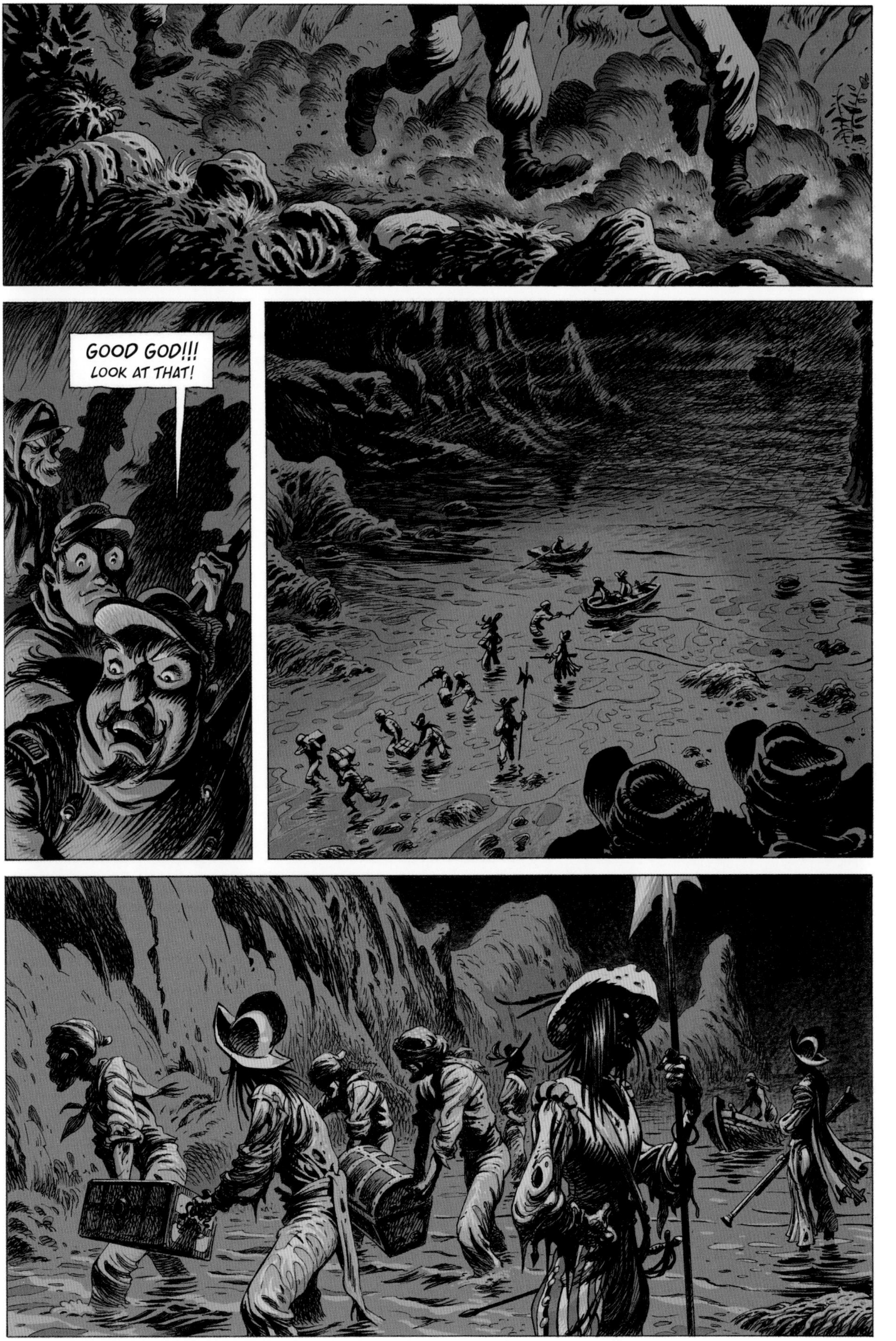
GOOD GOD!!!
LOOK AT THAT!

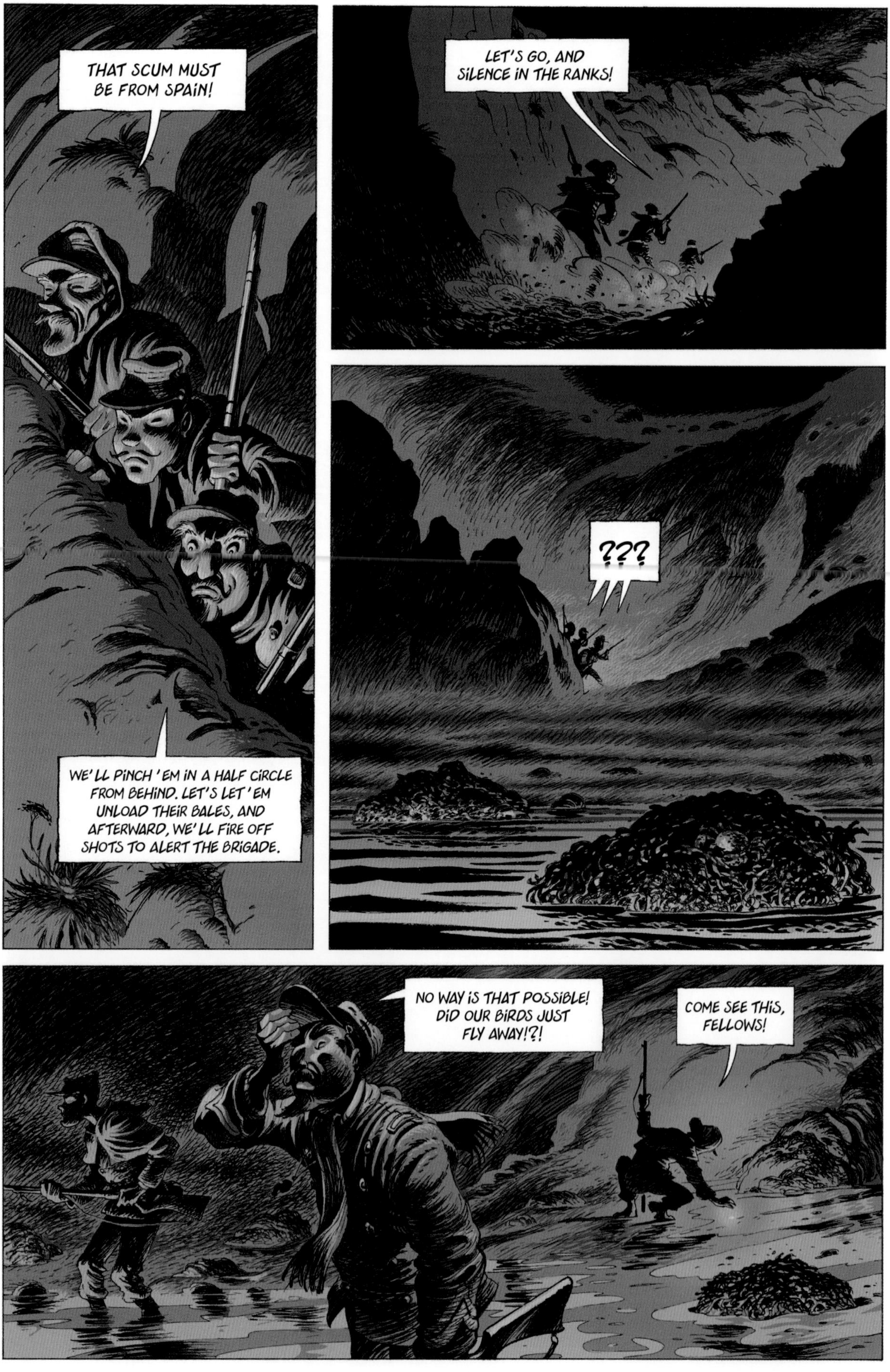
THAT SCUM MUST BE FROM SPAIN!
WE'LL PINCH 'EM IN A HALF CIRCLE FROM BEHIND. LET'S LET 'EM UNLOAD THEIR BALES, AND AFTERWARD, WE'LL FIRE OFF SHOTS TO ALERT THE BRIGADE.
LET'S GO, AND SILENCE IN THE RANKS!
???
NO WAY IS THAT POSSIBLE! DID OUR BIRDS JUST FLY AWAY!?!
COME SEE THIS, FELLOWS!

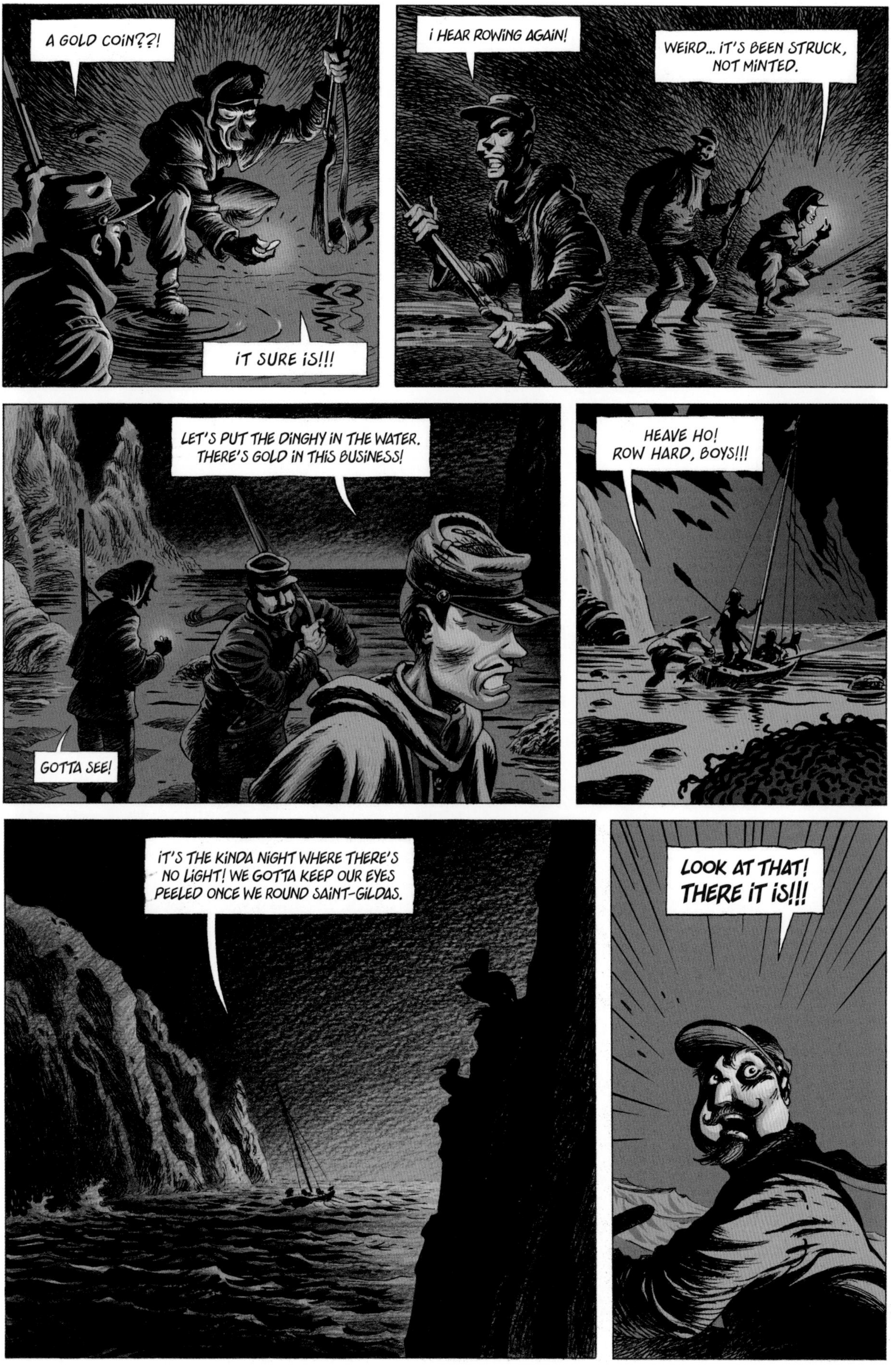
A GOLD COIN??!
IT SURE IS!!!
I HEAR ROWING AGAIN!
WEIRD... IT'S BEEN STRUCK, NOT MINTED.
LET'S PUT THE DINGHY IN THE WATER. THERE'S GOLD IN THIS BUSINESS!
GOTTA SEE!
HEAVE HO! ROW HARD, BOYS!!!
IT'S THE KINDA NIGHT WHERE THERE'S NO LIGHT! WE GOTTA KEEP OUR EYES PEELED ONCE WE ROUND SAINT-GILDAS.
LOOK AT THAT! THERE IT IS!!!

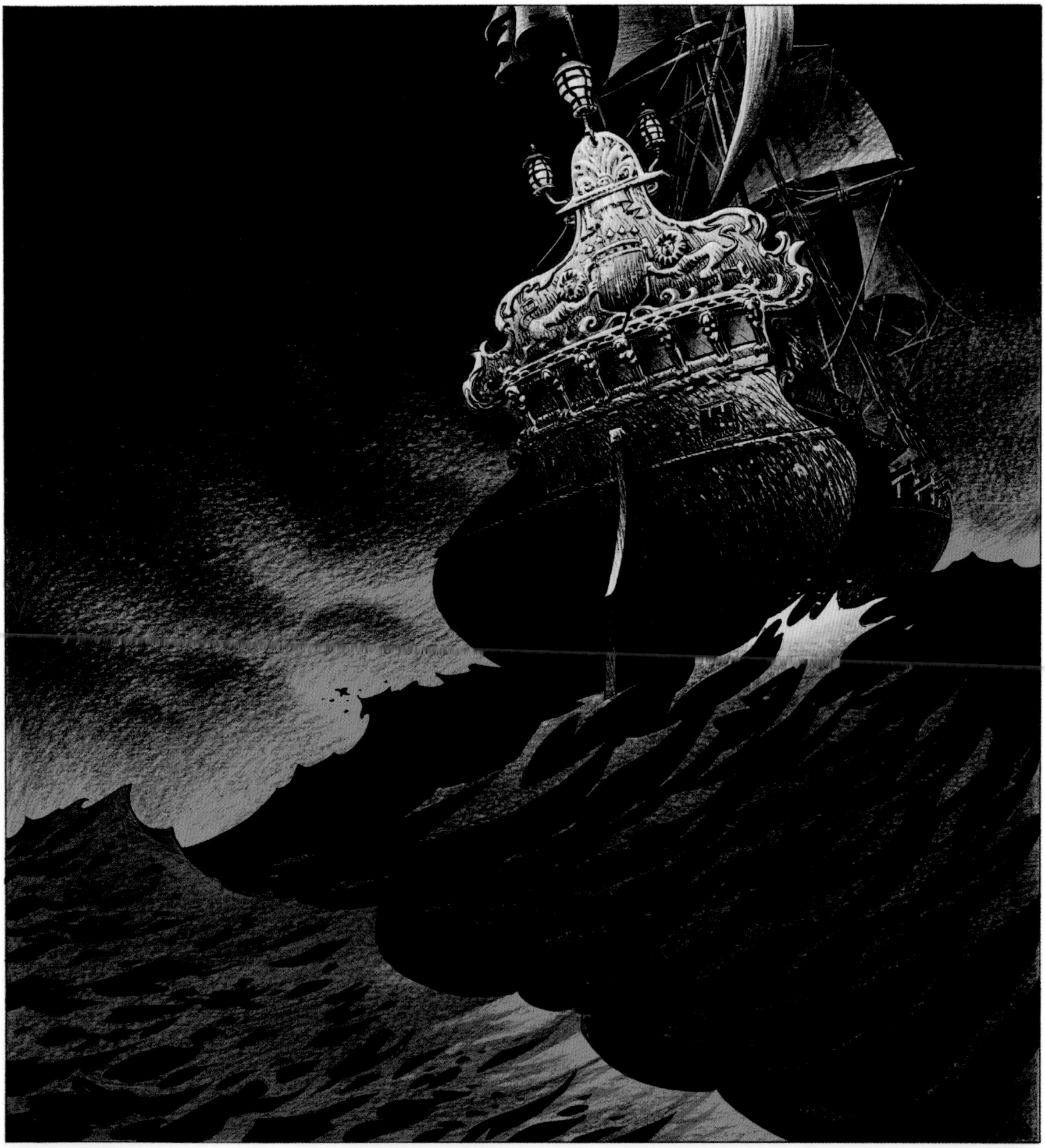

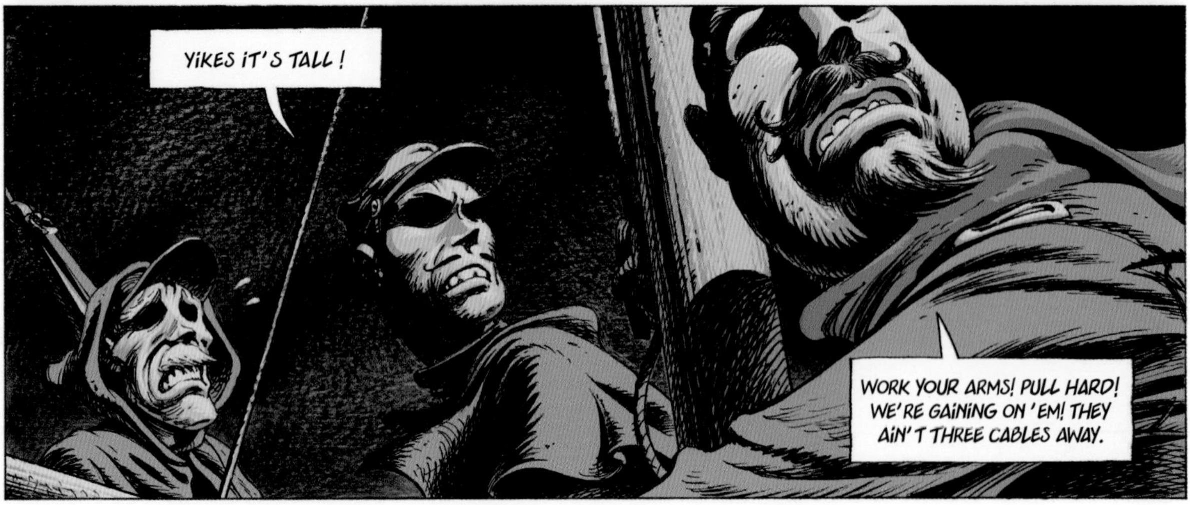
YIKES IT'S TALL!
WORK YOUR ARMS! PULL HARD! WE'RE GAINING ON 'EM! THEY AIN'T THREE CABLES AWAY.

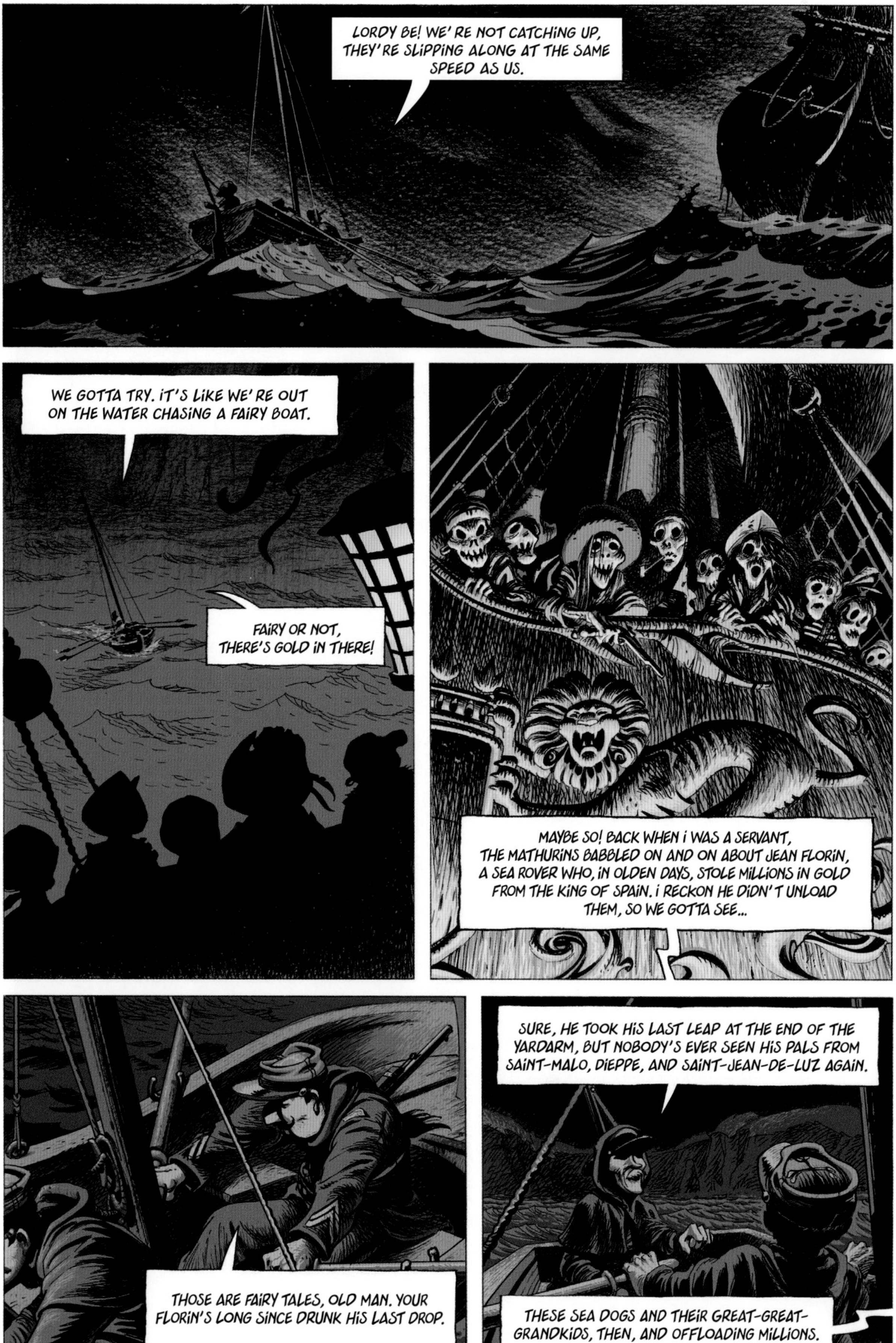
LORDY BE! WE'RE NOT CATCHING UP, THEY'RE SLIPPING ALONG AT THE SAME SPEED AS US.
WE GOTTA TRY. IT'S LIKE WE'RE OUT ON THE WATER CHASING A FAIRY BOAT.
FAIRY OR NOT, THERE'S GOLD IN THERE!
MAYBE SO! BACK WHEN I WAS A SERVANT, THE MATHURINS BABBLED ON AND ON ABOUT JEAN FLORIN, A SEA ROVER WHO, IN OLDEN DAYS, STOLE MILLIONS IN GOLD FROM THE KING OF SPAIN. I RECKON HE DIDN'T UNLOAD THEM, SO WE GOTTA SEE...
THOSE ARE FAIRY TALES, OLD MAN. YOUR FLORIN'S LONG SINCE DRUNK HIS LAST DROP.
SURE, HE TOOK HIS LAST LEAP AT THE END OF THE YARDARM, BUT NOBODY'S EVER SEEN HIS PALS FROM SAINT-MALO, DIEPPE, AND SAINT-JEAN-DE-LUZ AGAIN.
THESE SEA DOGS AND THEIR GREAT-GREAT-GRANDKIDS, THEN, AND OFFLOADING MILLIONS.

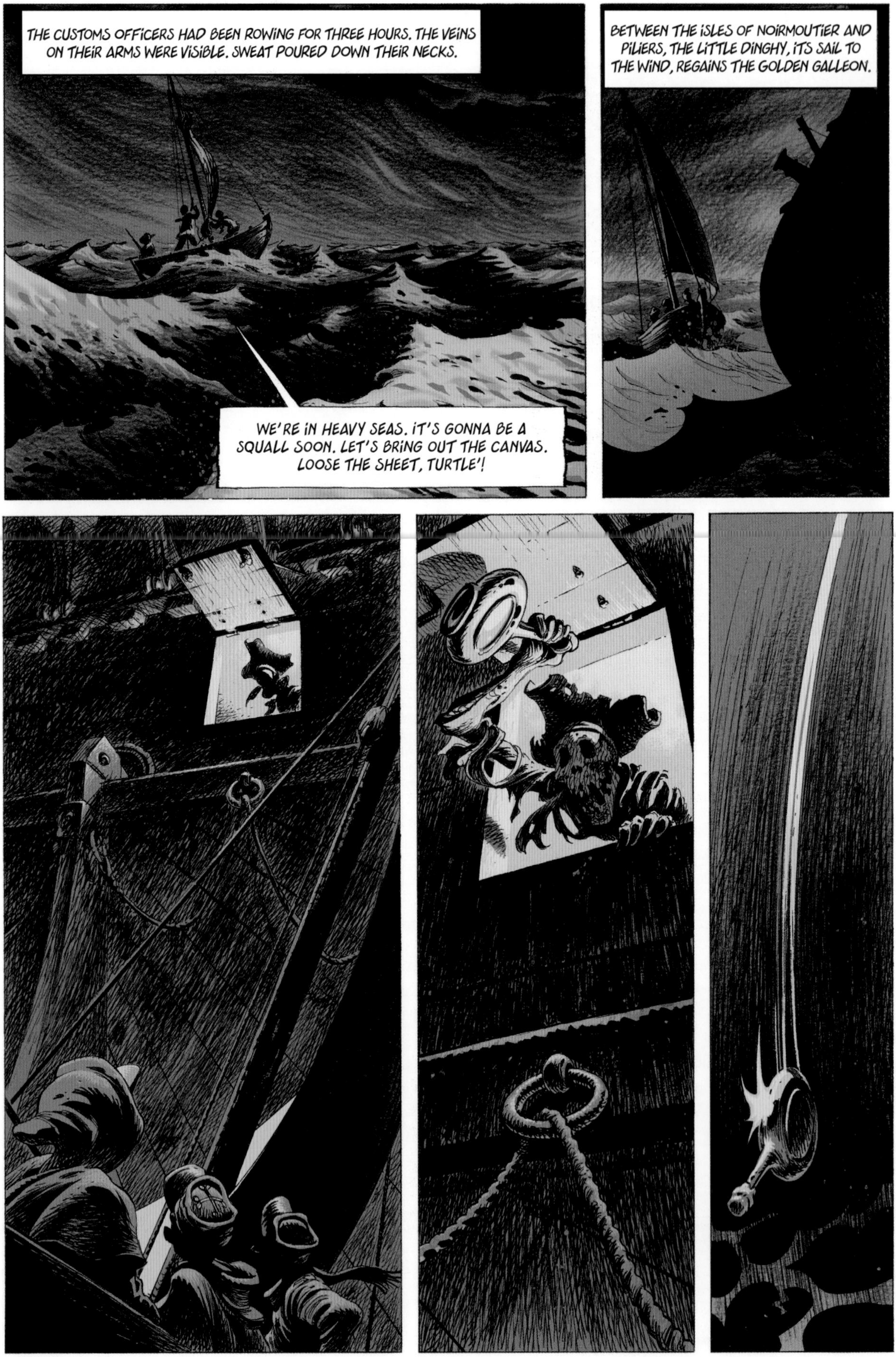
THE CUSTOMS OFFICERS HAD BEEN ROWING FOR THREE HOURS. THE VEINS ON THEIR ARMS WERE VISIBLE. SWEAT POURED DOWN THEIR NECKS.
WE'RE IN HEAVY SEAS. IT'S GONNA BE A SQUALL SOON. LET'S BRING OUT THE CANVAS. LOOSE THE SHEET, TURTLE'!
BETWEEN THE ISLES OF NOIRMOUTIER AND PILIERS, THE LITTLE DINGHY, ITS SAIL TO THE WIND, REGAINS THE GOLDEN GALLEON.

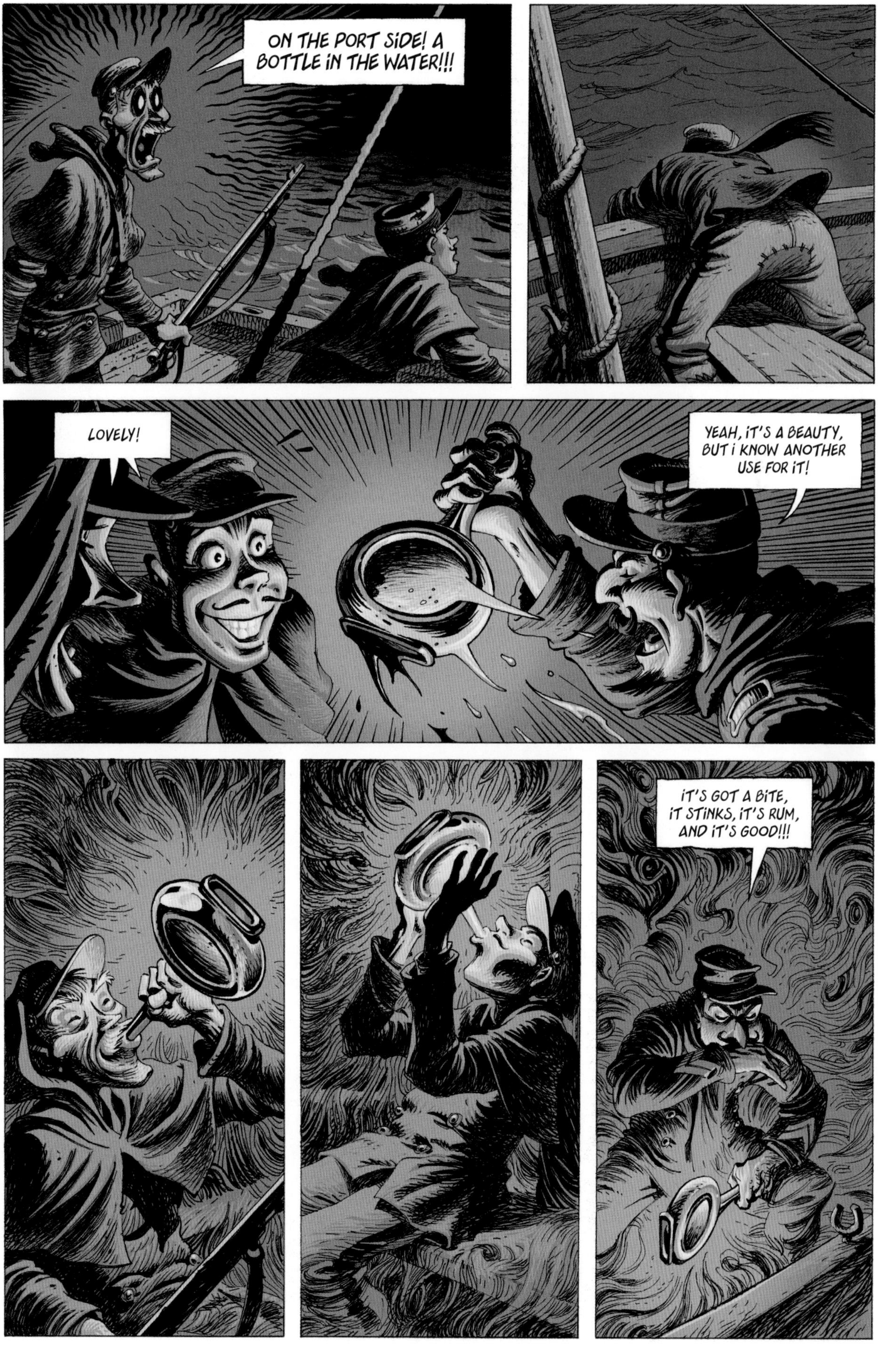
ON THE PORT SIDE! A BOTTLE IN THE WATER!!!
LOVELY!
YEAH, IT'S A BEAUTY, BUT I KNOW ANOTHER USE FOR IT!
IT'S GOT A BITE, IT STINKS, IT'S RUM, AND IT'S GOOD!!!

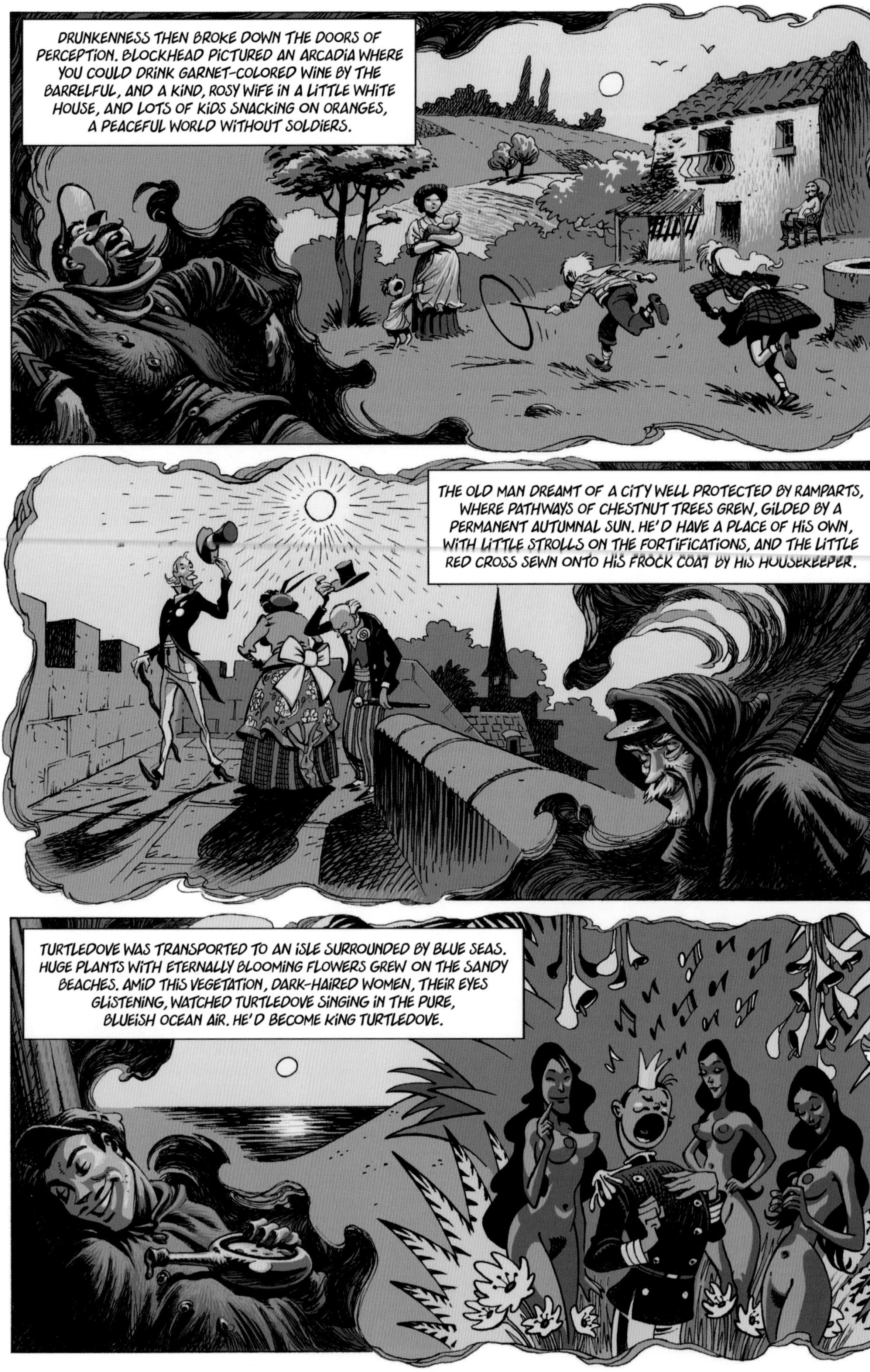
DRUNKENNESS THEN BROKE DOWN THE DOORS OF PERCEPTION. BLOCKHEAD PICTURED AN ARCADIA WHERE YOU COULD DRINK GARNET-COLORED WINE BY THE BARRELFUL, AND A KIND, ROSY WIFE IN A LITTLE WHITE HOUSE, AND LOTS OF KIDS SNACKING ON ORANGES, A PEACEFUL WORLD WITHOUT SOLDIERS.
THE OLD MAN DREAMT OF A CITY WELL PROTECTED BY RAMPARTS, WHERE PATHWAYS OF CHESTNUT TREES GREW, GILDED BY A PERMANENT AUTUMNAL SUN. HE'D HAVE A PLACE OF HIS OWN, WITH LITTLE STROLLS ON THE FORTIFICATIONS, AND THE LITTLE RED CROSS SEWN ONTO HIS FROCK COAT BY HIS HOUSEKEEPER.
TURTLEDOVE WAS TRANSPORTED TO AN ISLE SURROUNDED BY BLUE SEAS. HUGE PLANTS WITH ETERNALLY BLOOMING FLOWERS GREW ON THE SANDY BEACHES. AMID THIS VEGETATION, DARK-HAIRED WOMEN, THEIR EYES GLISTENING, WATCHED TURTLEDOVE SINGING IN THE PURE, BLUEISH OCEAN AIR. HE'D BECOME KING TURTLEDOVE.

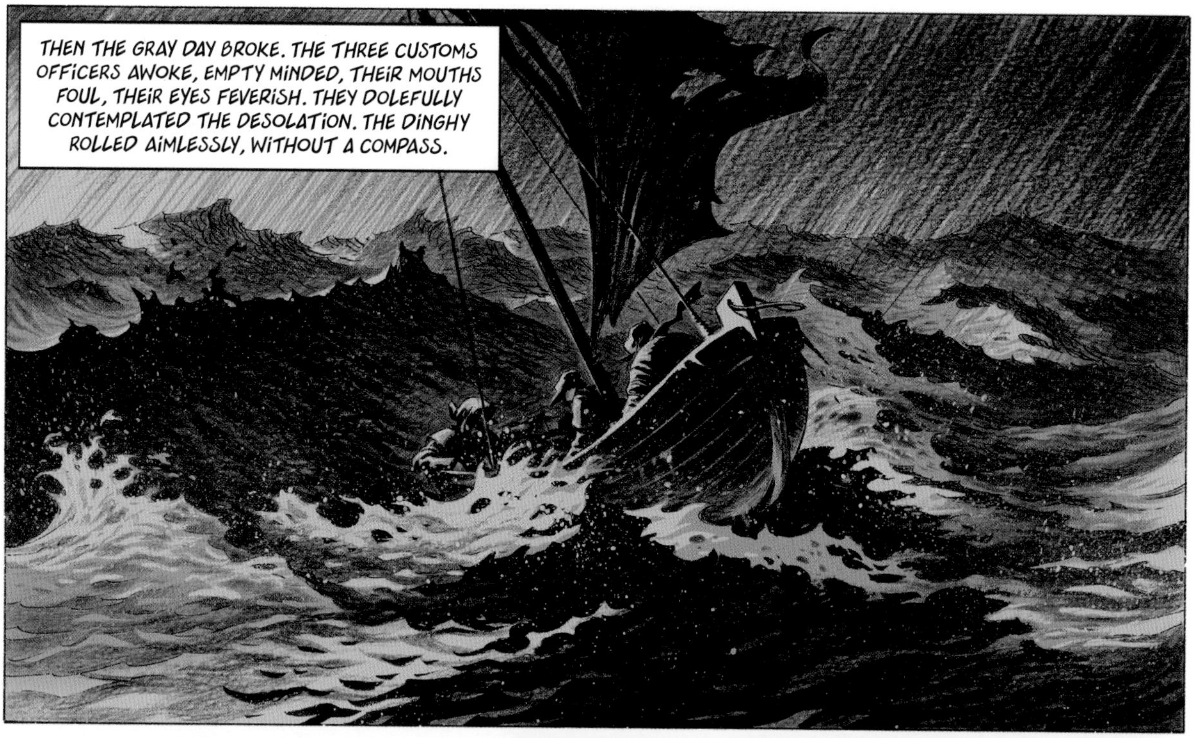
THEN THE GRAY DAY BROKE. THE THREE CUSTOMS OFFICERS AWOKE, EMPTY MINDED, THEIR MOUTHS FOUL, THEIR EYES FEVERISH. THEY DOLEFULLY CONTEMPLATED THE DESOLATION. THE DINGHY ROLLED AIMLESSLY, WITHOUT A COMPASS.

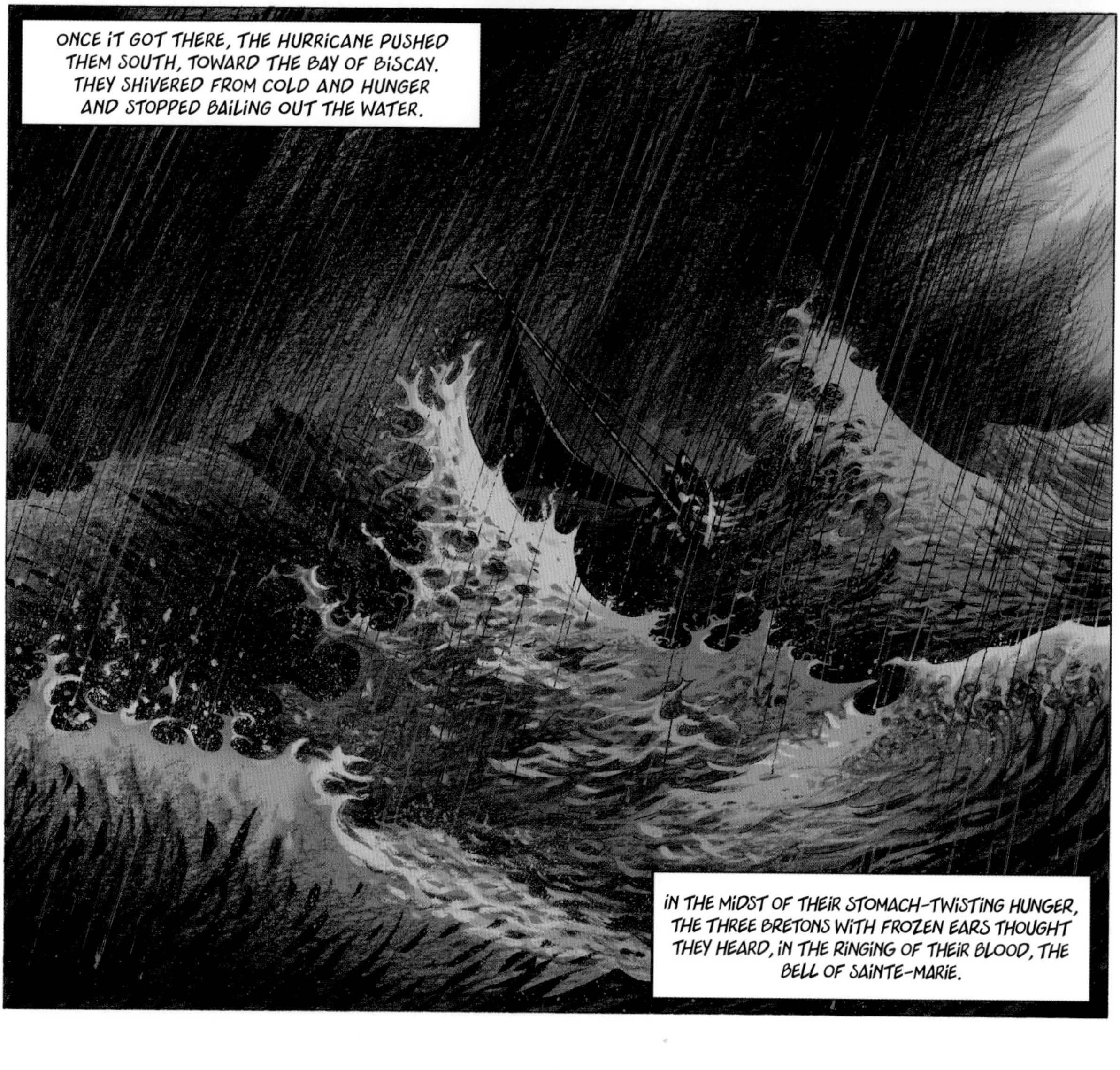
ONCE IT GOT THERE, THE HURRICANE PUSHED THEM SOUTH, TOWARD THE BAY OF BISCAY. THEY SHIVERED FROM COLD AND HUNGER AND STOPPED BAILING OUT THE WATER.
IN THE MIDST OF THEIR STOMACH-TWISTING HUNGER, THE THREE BRETONS WITH FROZEN EARS THOUGHT THEY HEARD, IN THE RINGING OF THEIR BLOOD, THE BELL OF SAINTE-MARIE.

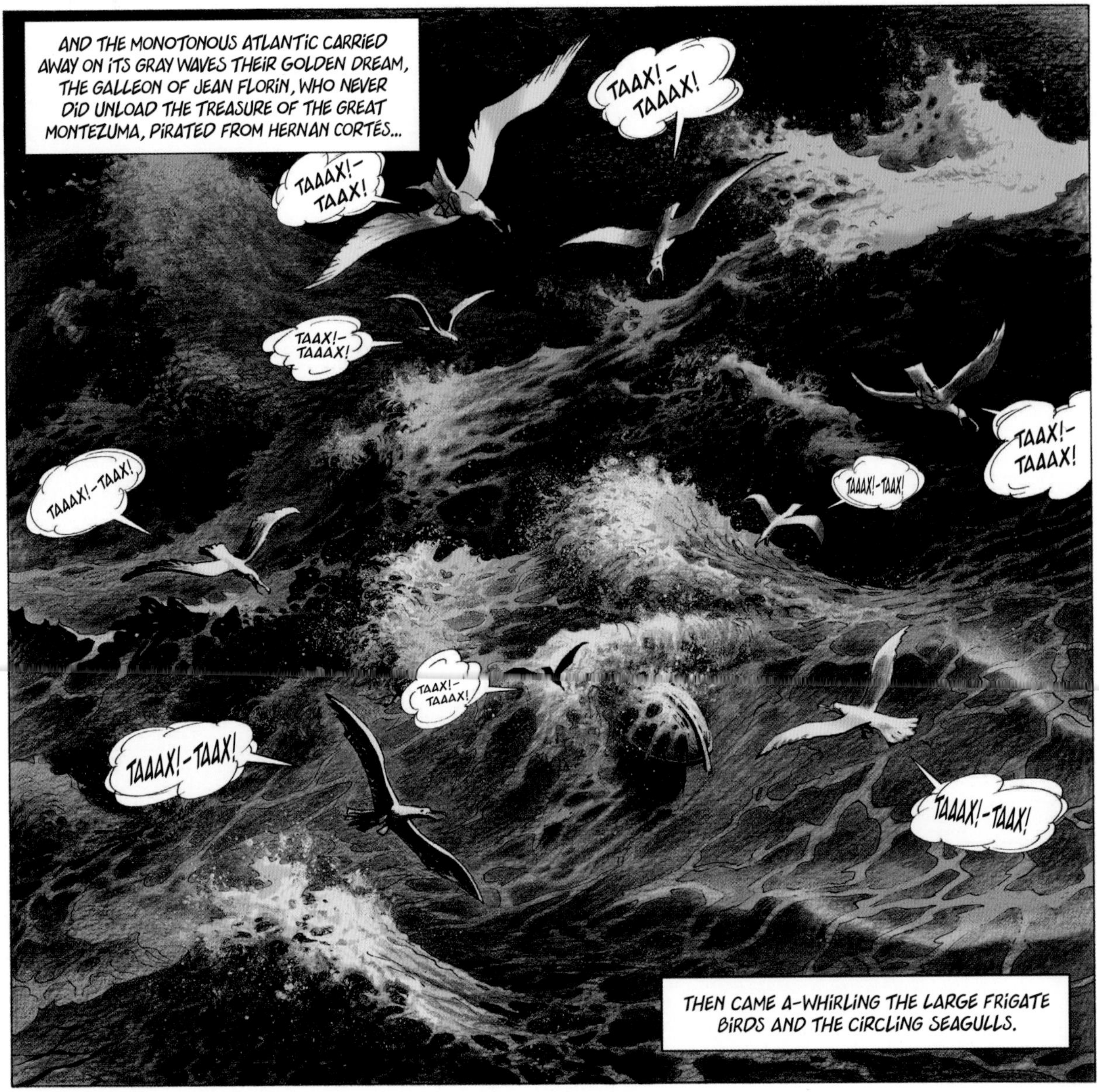
AND THE MONOTONOUS ATLANTIC CARRIED AWAY ON ITS GRAY WAVES THEIR GOLDEN DREAM, THE GALLEON OF JEAN FLORIN, WHO NEVER DID UNLOAD THE TREASURE OF THE GREAT MONTEZUMA, PIRATED FROM HERNAN CORTÉS...
TAAX!- TAAAX!
TAAAX!- TAAX!
TAAX!- TAAAX!
TAAX!- TAAAX!
TAAAX!-TAAX!
TAAAX!-TAAX!
TAAX!- TAAAX!
TAAAX!-TAAX!
TAAAX!-TAAX!
THEN CAME A-WHIRLING THE LARGE FRIGATE BIRDS AND THE CIRCLING SEAGULLS.

The End

The Death Ship

based on B. TRAVEN

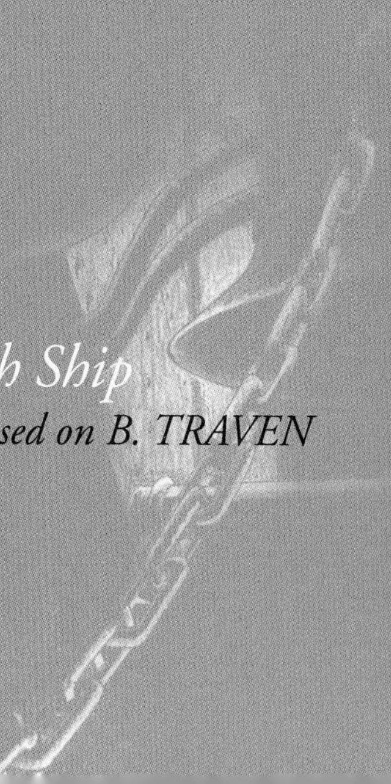

B. TRAVEN
The Death Ship

(Excerpt)

Morituri te salutant! Modern gladiators salute you, new Caesar, O Capitalism! We're ready to die for you, for the most holy and glorious Insurance Company. O the times! O morals! Once upon a time, gladiators clad in shining armor entered the arena to the sounds of fanfares and cymbals. Beauties seated above would signal to them and drop gold-embroidered kerchiefs into the arena. The gladiators would gather them, bear them to their lips, breathing in that intoxicating perfume, and a sweet smile thanked them. They died to the boos of the crowd, to the bursts of a somber music.

But we modern gladiators, we perish in grime, too tired to wash ourselves. Dying of hunger, we pass out in front of our plates. We're dying of hunger because the Company must economize to sustain competition. We die in rags, mute, in the depths of the boiler room, on a long-chosen reef. We see the water rising, hoping the boiler room explodes so that it won't take too long, because our hands are tied, the doors of the hearths torn off, our feet gnawed away by grit. The stoker? He's used to it: being burnt or scalded doesn't bother him anymore.

We die without fanfare, without smiling beauties, without applause. We die in silence and wretchedness for you, Caesar! We are nothing, nobody, the most faithful of your servants, those who are paid no retirement. Hail, Caesar! Those who are to die salute you.

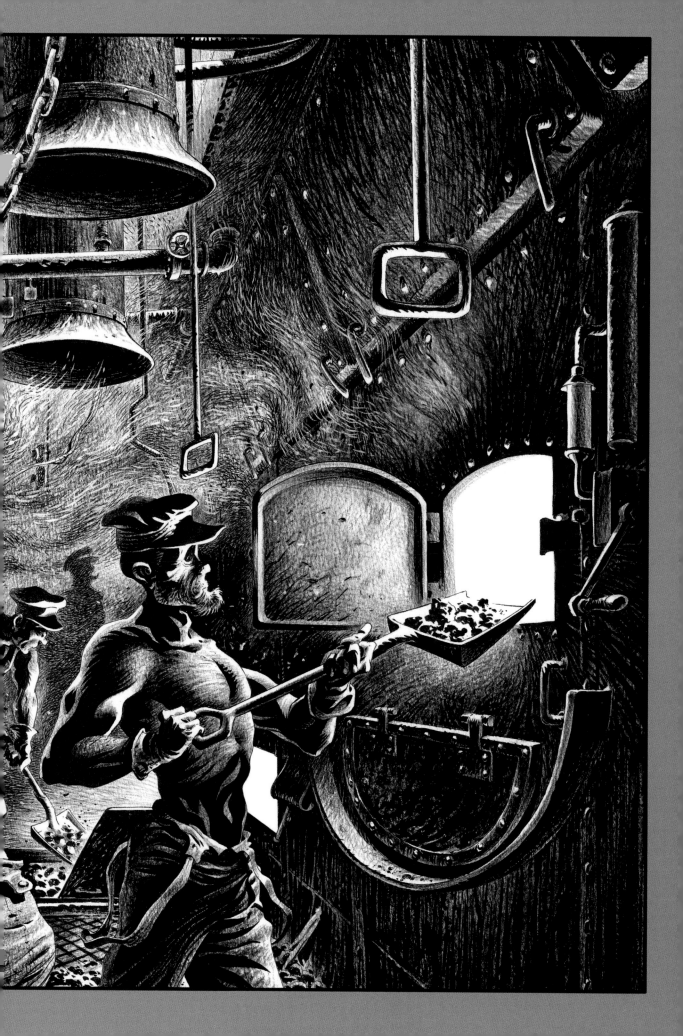

A Smile of Fortune

based on JOSEPH CONRAD

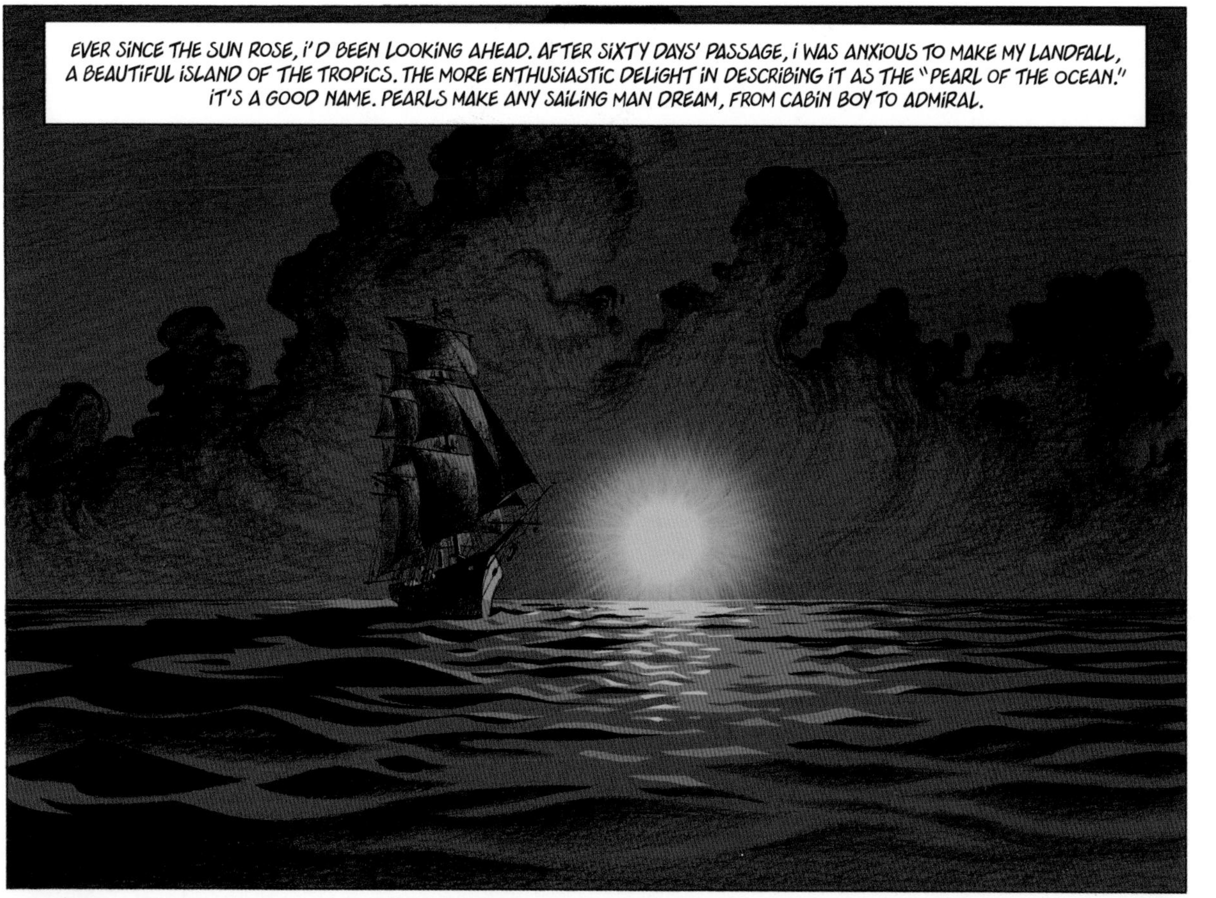
EVER SINCE THE SUN ROSE, I'D BEEN LOOKING AHEAD. AFTER SIXTY DAYS' PASSAGE, I WAS ANXIOUS TO MAKE MY LANDFALL, A BEAUTIFUL ISLAND OF THE TROPICS. THE MORE ENTHUSIASTIC DELIGHT IN DESCRIBING IT AS THE "PEARL OF THE OCEAN." IT'S A GOOD NAME. PEARLS MAKE ANY SAILING MAN DREAM, FROM CABIN BOY TO ADMIRAL.

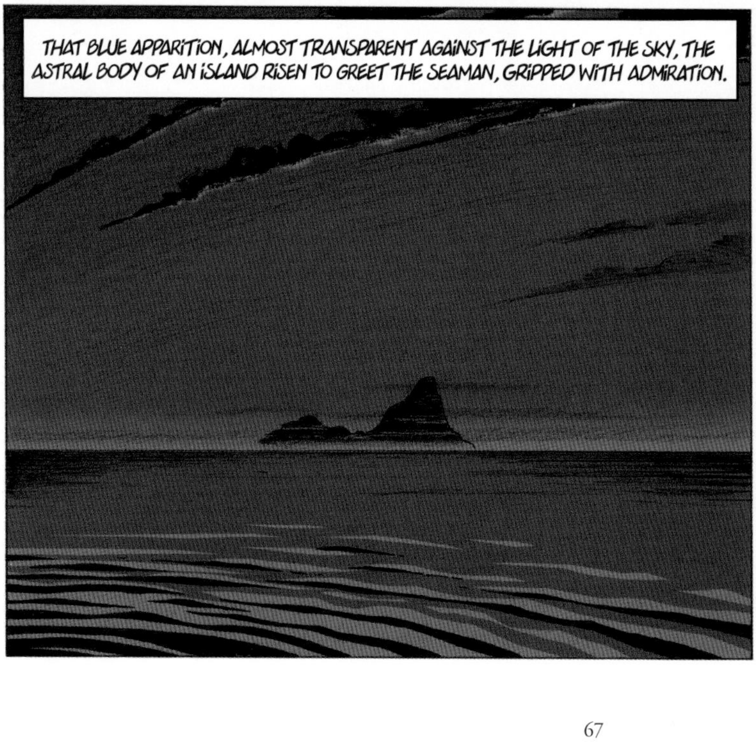
THAT BLUE APPARITION, ALMOST TRANSPARENT AGAINST THE LIGHT OF THE SKY, THE ASTRAL BODY OF AN ISLAND RISEN TO GREET THE SEAMAN, GRIPPED WITH ADMIRATION.

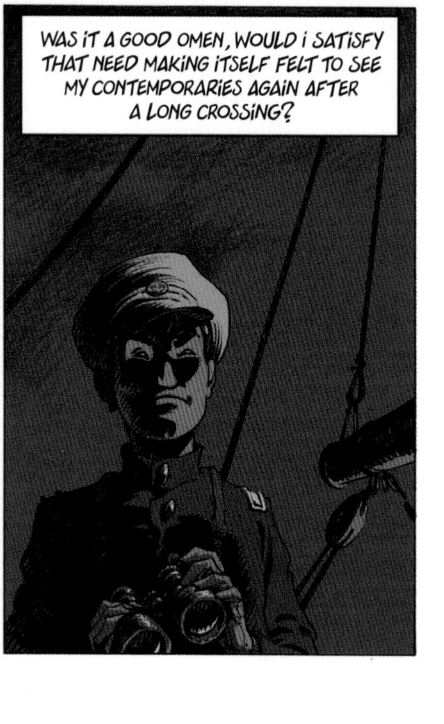
WAS IT A GOOD OMEN, WOULD I SATISFY THAT NEED MAKING ITSELF FELT TO SEE MY CONTEMPORARIES AGAIN AFTER A LONG CROSSING?

WE WERE LATE IN CLOSING IN WITH THE LAND. AN UNPLEASANT AND UNRESTFUL NIGHT FOLLOWED. THE WIND MADE A GREAT BULLYING NOISE IN OUR SPARS. AT TIMES A WILD GUST OF WIND STRUCK ON OUR RIGGING A HARSH AND PLAINTIVE NOTE LIKE THE WAIL OF A FORSAKEN SOUL.

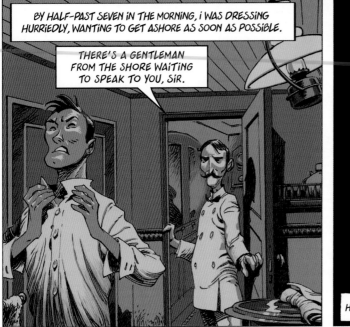

BY HALF-PAST SEVEN IN THE MORNING, I WAS DRESSING HURRIEDLY, WANTING TO GET ASHORE AS SOON AS POSSIBLE.

THERE'S A GENTLEMAN FROM THE SHORE WAITING TO SPEAK TO YOU, SIR.

SO EARLY! WHO'S HE?

HIS NAME'S JACOBUS, I BELIEVE.

GOOD MORNING, MR. JACOBUS. YOU ARE A MERCHANT, I SUPPOSE.

OH! EVERYONE MUST MAKE A LIVING, MUSTN'T THEY?!

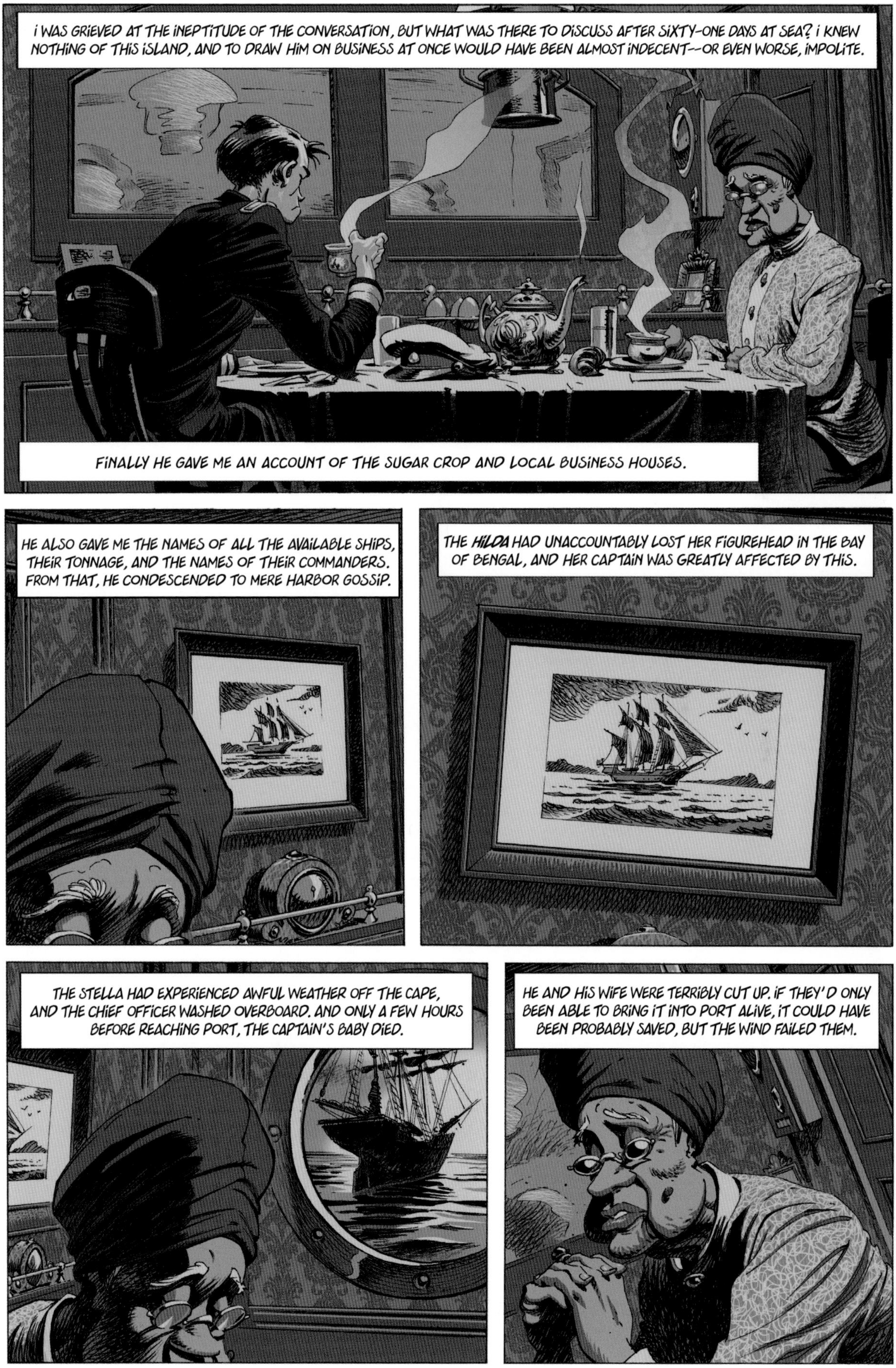
I WAS GRIEVED AT THE INEPTITUDE OF THE CONVERSATION, BUT WHAT WAS THERE TO DISCUSS AFTER SIXTY-ONE DAYS AT SEA? I KNEW NOTHING OF THIS ISLAND, AND TO DRAW HIM ON BUSINESS AT ONCE WOULD HAVE BEEN ALMOST INDECENT--OR EVEN WORSE, IMPOLITE.
FINALLY HE GAVE ME AN ACCOUNT OF THE SUGAR CROP AND LOCAL BUSINESS HOUSES.
HE ALSO GAVE ME THE NAMES OF ALL THE AVAILABLE SHIPS, THEIR TONNAGE, AND THE NAMES OF THEIR COMMANDERS. FROM THAT, HE CONDESCENDED TO MERE HARBOR GOSSIP.
THE *HILDA* HAD UNACCOUNTABLY LOST HER FIGUREHEAD IN THE BAY OF BENGAL, AND HER CAPTAIN WAS GREATLY AFFECTED BY THIS.
THE STELLA HAD EXPERIENCED AWFUL WEATHER OFF THE CAPE, AND THE CHIEF OFFICER WASHED OVERBOARD. AND ONLY A FEW HOURS BEFORE REACHING PORT, THE CAPTAIN'S BABY DIED.
HE AND HIS WIFE WERE TERRIBLY CUT UP. IF THEY'D ONLY BEEN ABLE TO BRING IT INTO PORT ALIVE, IT COULD HAVE BEEN PROBABLY SAVED, BUT THE WIND FAILED THEM.

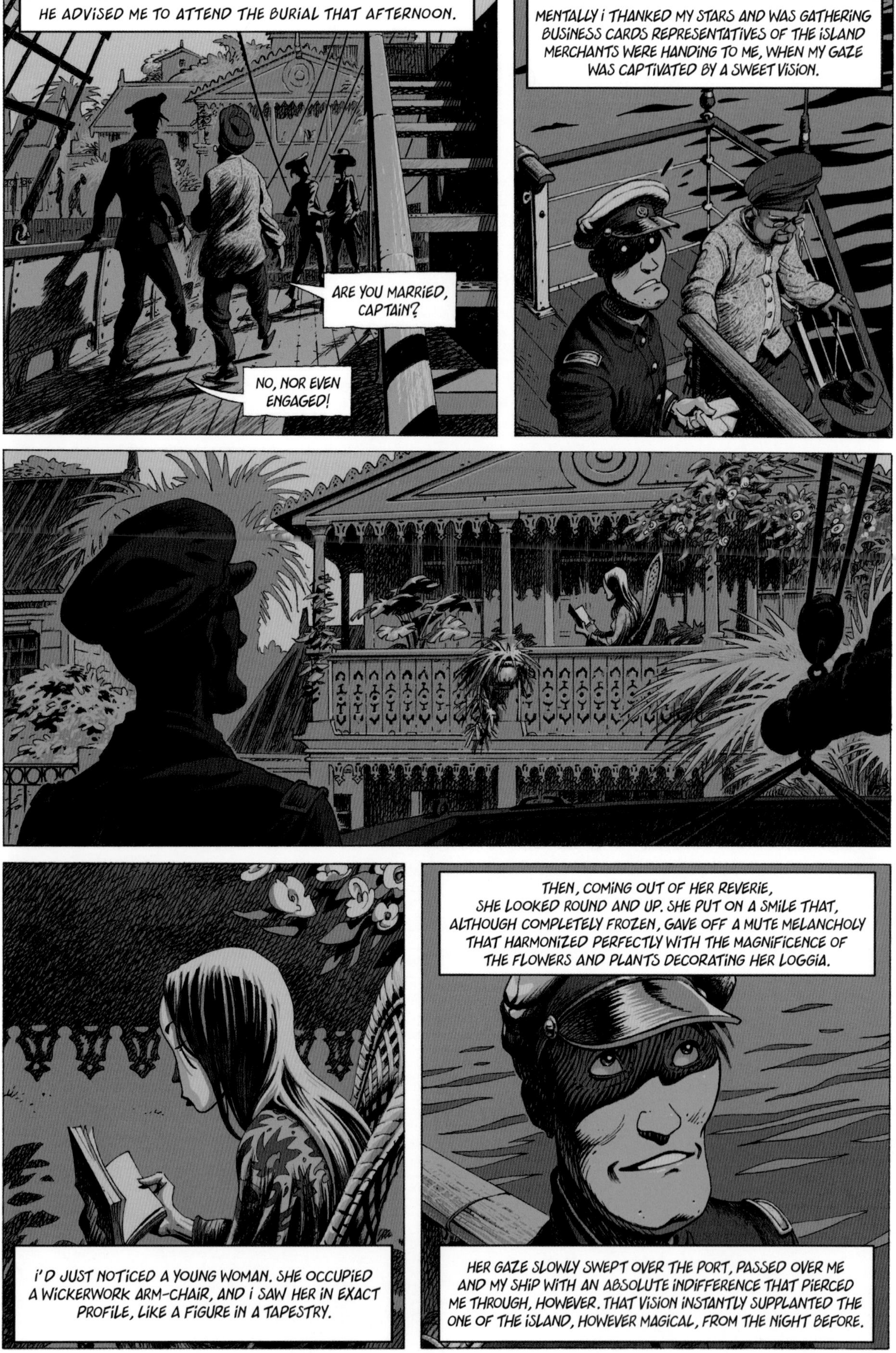
HE ADVISED ME TO ATTEND THE BURIAL THAT AFTERNOON.
ARE YOU MARRIED, CAPTAIN?
NO, NOR EVEN ENGAGED!
MENTALLY I THANKED MY STARS AND WAS GATHERING BUSINESS CARDS REPRESENTATIVES OF THE ISLAND MERCHANTS WERE HANDING TO ME, WHEN MY GAZE WAS CAPTIVATED BY A SWEET VISION.
I'D JUST NOTICED A YOUNG WOMAN. SHE OCCUPIED A WICKERWORK ARM-CHAIR, AND I SAW HER IN EXACT PROFILE, LIKE A FIGURE IN A TAPESTRY.
THEN, COMING OUT OF HER REVERIE, SHE LOOKED ROUND AND UP. SHE PUT ON A SMILE THAT, ALTHOUGH COMPLETELY FROZEN, GAVE OFF A MUTE MELANCHOLY THAT HARMONIZED PERFECTLY WITH THE MAGNIFICENCE OF THE FLOWERS AND PLANTS DECORATING HER LOGGIA.
HER GAZE SLOWLY SWEPT OVER THE PORT, PASSED OVER ME AND MY SHIP WITH AN ABSOLUTE INDIFFERENCE THAT PIERCED ME THROUGH, HOWEVER. THAT VISION INSTANTLY SUPPLANTED THE ONE OF THE ISLAND, HOWEVER MAGICAL, FROM THE NIGHT BEFORE.

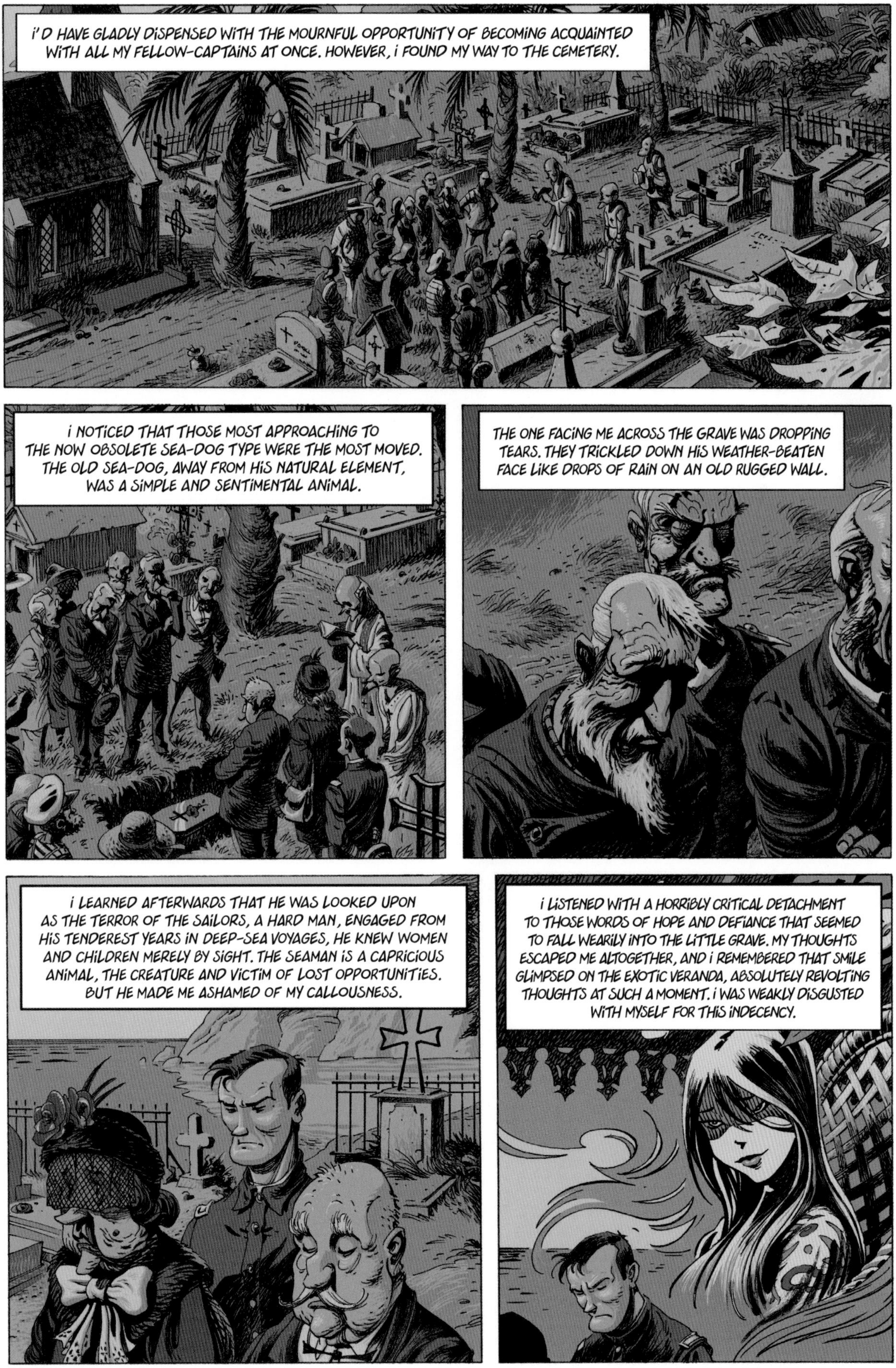
I'D HAVE GLADLY DISPENSED WITH THE MOURNFUL OPPORTUNITY OF BECOMING ACQUAINTED WITH ALL MY FELLOW-CAPTAINS AT ONCE. HOWEVER, I FOUND MY WAY TO THE CEMETERY.
I NOTICED THAT THOSE MOST APPROACHING TO THE NOW OBSOLETE SEA-DOG TYPE WERE THE MOST MOVED. THE OLD SEA-DOG, AWAY FROM HIS NATURAL ELEMENT, WAS A SIMPLE AND SENTIMENTAL ANIMAL.
THE ONE FACING ME ACROSS THE GRAVE WAS DROPPING TEARS. THEY TRICKLED DOWN HIS WEATHER-BEATEN FACE LIKE DROPS OF RAIN ON AN OLD RUGGED WALL.
I LEARNED AFTERWARDS THAT HE WAS LOOKED UPON AS THE TERROR OF THE SAILORS, A HARD MAN, ENGAGED FROM HIS TENDEREST YEARS IN DEEP-SEA VOYAGES, HE KNEW WOMEN AND CHILDREN MERELY BY SIGHT. THE SEAMAN IS A CAPRICIOUS ANIMAL, THE CREATURE AND VICTIM OF LOST OPPORTUNITIES. BUT HE MADE ME ASHAMED OF MY CALLOUSNESS.
I LISTENED WITH A HORRIBLY CRITICAL DETACHMENT TO THOSE WORDS OF HOPE AND DEFIANCE THAT SEEMED TO FALL WEARILY INTO THE LITTLE GRAVE. MY THOUGHTS ESCAPED ME ALTOGETHER, AND I REMEMBERED THAT SMILE GLIMPSED ON THE EXOTIC VERANDA, ABSOLUTELY REVOLTING THOUGHTS AT SUCH A MOMENT. I WAS WEAKLY DISGUSTED WITH MYSELF FOR THIS INDECENCY.

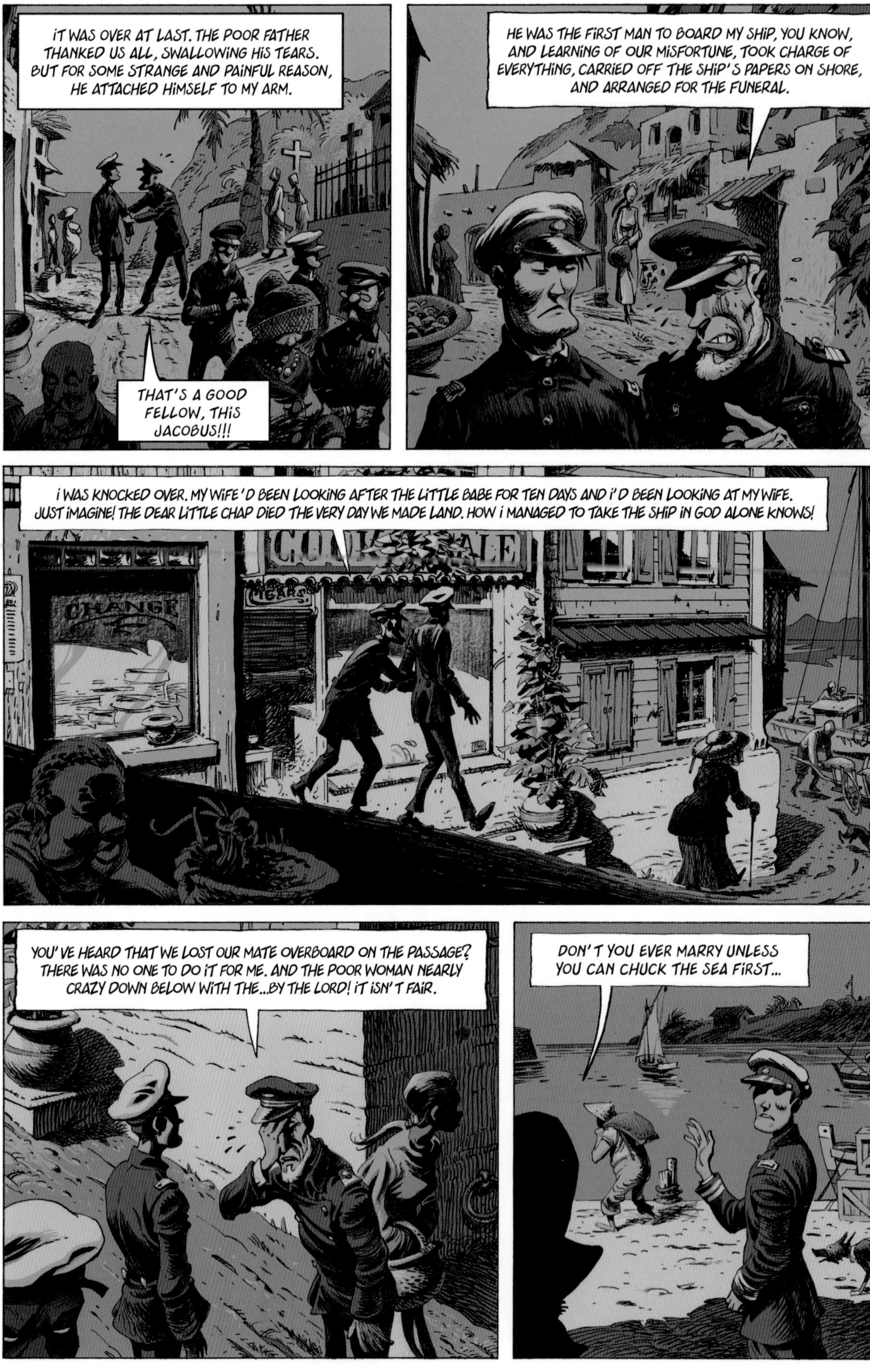
IT WAS OVER AT LAST. THE POOR FATHER THANKED US ALL, SWALLOWING HIS TEARS. BUT FOR SOME STRANGE AND PAINFUL REASON, HE ATTACHED HIMSELF TO MY ARM.
THAT'S A GOOD FELLOW, THIS JACOBUS!!!
HE WAS THE FIRST MAN TO BOARD MY SHIP, YOU KNOW, AND LEARNING OF OUR MISFORTUNE, TOOK CHARGE OF EVERYTHING, CARRIED OFF THE SHIP'S PAPERS ON SHORE, AND ARRANGED FOR THE FUNERAL.
I WAS KNOCKED OVER. MY WIFE'D BEEN LOOKING AFTER THE LITTLE BABE FOR TEN DAYS AND I'D BEEN LOOKING AT MY WIFE. JUST IMAGINE! THE DEAR LITTLE CHAP DIED THE VERY DAY WE MADE LAND. HOW I MANAGED TO TAKE THE SHIP IN GOD ALONE KNOWS!
CHANGE
YOU'VE HEARD THAT WE LOST OUR MATE OVERBOARD ON THE PASSAGE? THERE WAS NO ONE TO DO IT FOR ME. AND THE POOR WOMAN NEARLY CRAZY DOWN BELOW WITH THE...BY THE LORD! IT ISN'T FAIR.
DON'T YOU EVER MARRY UNLESS YOU CAN CHUCK THE SEA FIRST...

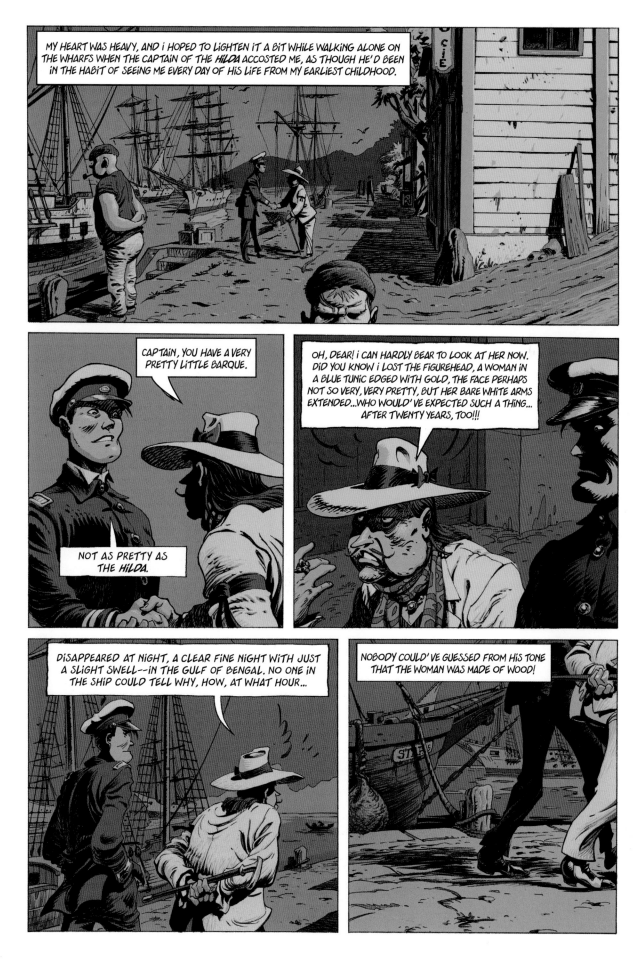

MY HEART WAS HEAVY, AND I HOPED TO LIGHTEN IT A BIT WHILE WALKING ALONE ON THE WHARFS WHEN THE CAPTAIN OF THE *HILDA* ACCOSTED ME, AS THOUGH HE'D BEEN IN THE HABIT OF SEEING ME EVERY DAY OF HIS LIFE FROM MY EARLIEST CHILDHOOD.

CAPTAIN, YOU HAVE A VERY PRETTY LITTLE BARQUE.

NOT AS PRETTY AS THE *HILDA*.

OH, DEAR! I CAN HARDLY BEAR TO LOOK AT HER NOW. DID YOU KNOW I LOST THE FIGUREHEAD, A WOMAN IN A BLUE TUNIC EDGED WITH GOLD, THE FACE PERHAPS NOT SO VERY, VERY PRETTY, BUT HER BARE WHITE ARMS EXTENDED...WHO WOULD'VE EXPECTED SUCH A THING... AFTER TWENTY YEARS, TOO!!!

DISAPPEARED AT NIGHT, A CLEAR FINE NIGHT WITH JUST A SLIGHT SWELL--IN THE GULF OF BENGAL. NO ONE IN THE SHIP COULD TELL WHY, HOW, AT WHAT HOUR...

NOBODY COULD'VE GUESSED FROM HIS TONE THAT THE WOMAN WAS MADE OF WOOD!

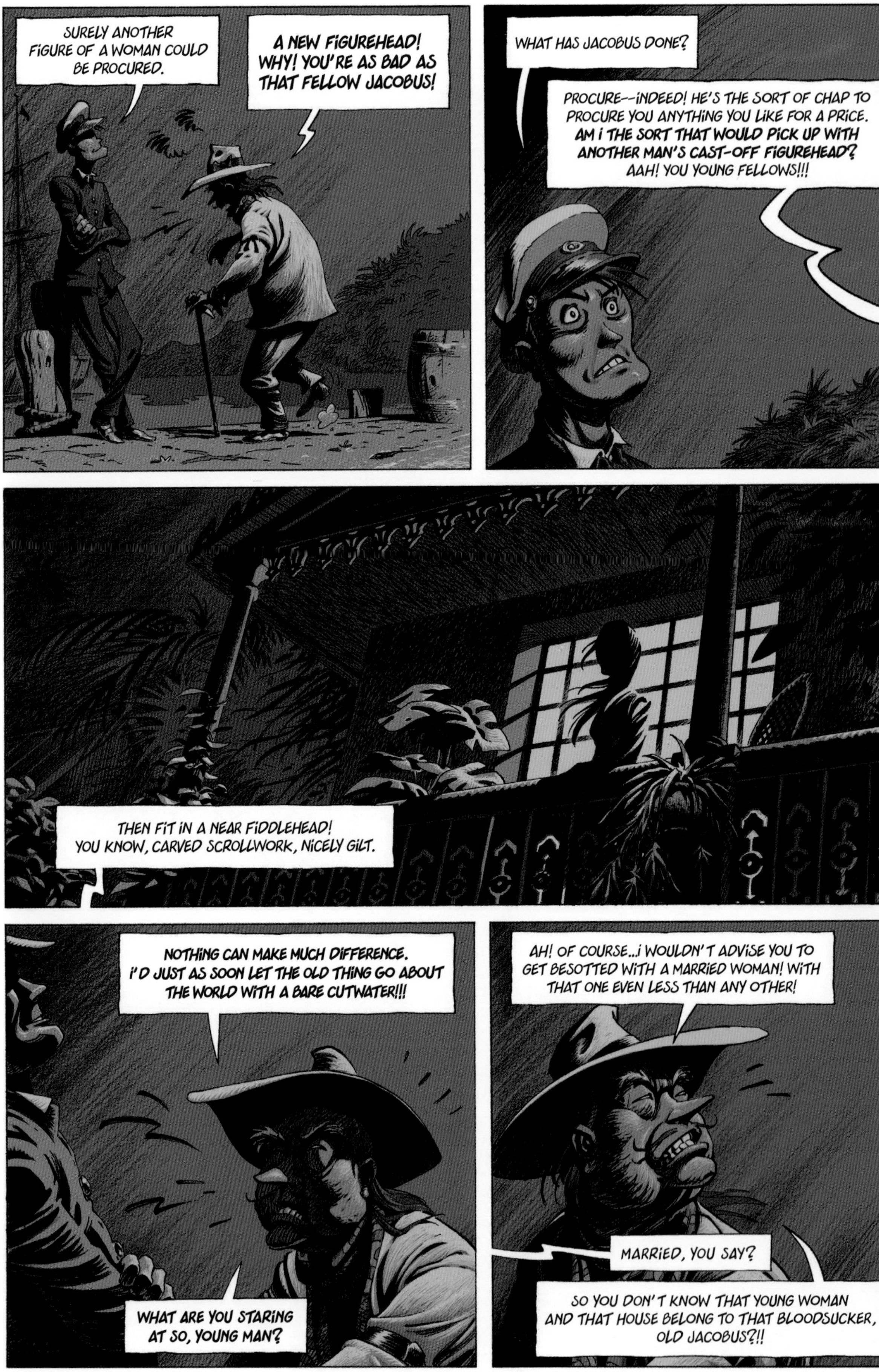
SURELY ANOTHER FIGURE OF A WOMAN COULD BE PROCURED.
A NEW FIGUREHEAD! WHY! YOU'RE AS BAD AS THAT FELLOW JACOBUS!
WHAT HAS JACOBUS DONE?
PROCURE--INDEED! HE'S THE SORT OF CHAP TO PROCURE YOU ANYTHING YOU LIKE FOR A PRICE. AM I THE SORT THAT WOULD PICK UP WITH ANOTHER MAN'S CAST-OFF FIGUREHEAD? AAH! YOU YOUNG FELLOWS!!!
THEN FIT IN A NEAR FIDDLEHEAD! YOU KNOW, CARVED SCROLLWORK, NICELY GILT.
NOTHING CAN MAKE MUCH DIFFERENCE. I'D JUST AS SOON LET THE OLD THING GO ABOUT THE WORLD WITH A BARE CUTWATER!!!
WHAT ARE YOU STARING AT SO, YOUNG MAN?
AH! OF COURSE...I WOULDN'T ADVISE YOU TO GET BESOTTED WITH A MARRIED WOMAN! WITH THAT ONE EVEN LESS THAN ANY OTHER!
MARRIED, YOU SAY?
SO YOU DON'T KNOW THAT YOUNG WOMAN AND THAT HOUSE BELONG TO THAT BLOODSUCKER, OLD JACOBUS?!!

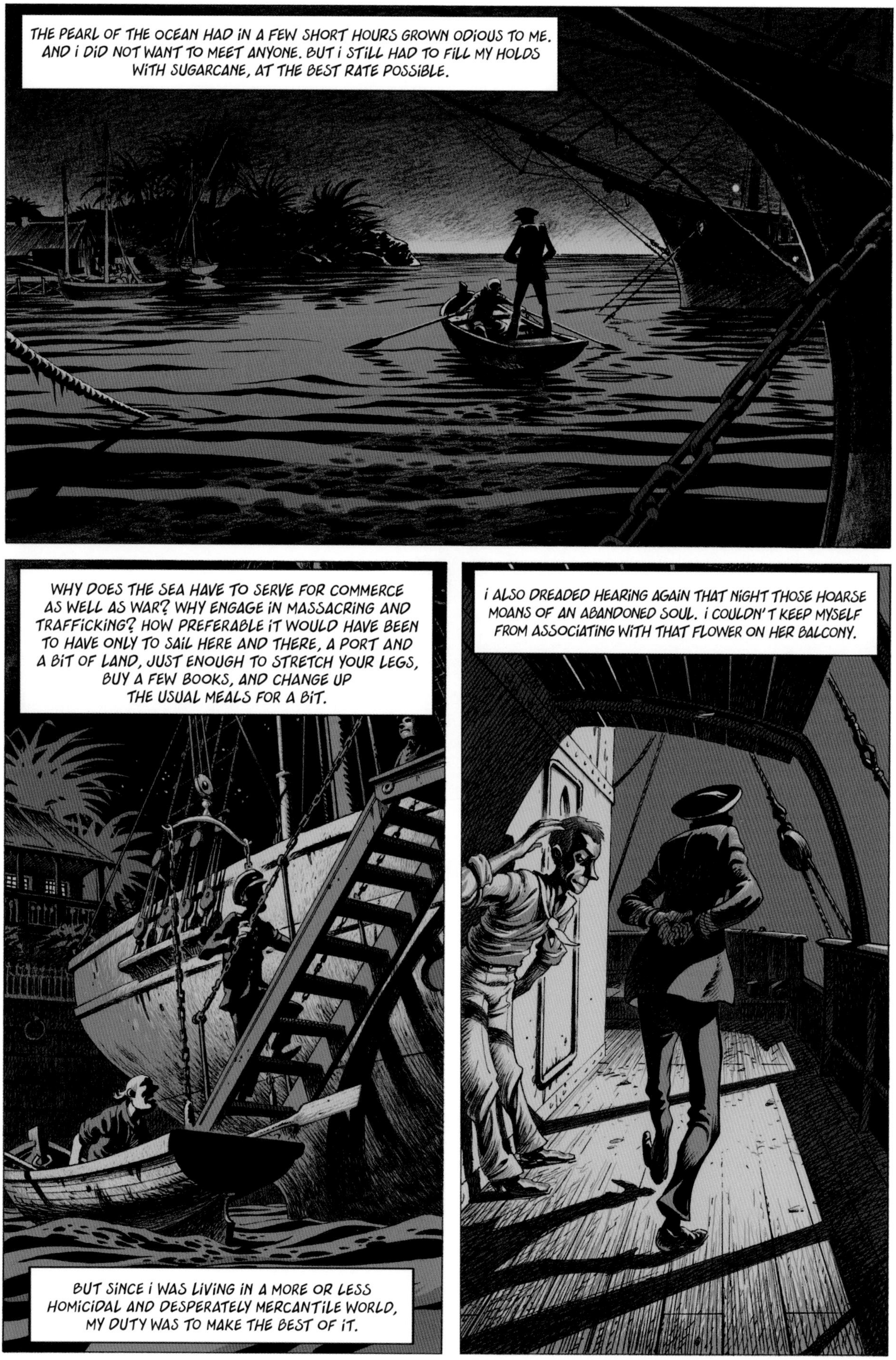
THE PEARL OF THE OCEAN HAD IN A FEW SHORT HOURS GROWN ODIOUS TO ME. AND I DID NOT WANT TO MEET ANYONE. BUT I STILL HAD TO FILL MY HOLDS WITH SUGARCANE, AT THE BEST RATE POSSIBLE.
WHY DOES THE SEA HAVE TO SERVE FOR COMMERCE AS WELL AS WAR? WHY ENGAGE IN MASSACRING AND TRAFFICKING? HOW PREFERABLE IT WOULD HAVE BEEN TO HAVE ONLY TO SAIL HERE AND THERE, A PORT AND A BIT OF LAND, JUST ENOUGH TO STRETCH YOUR LEGS, BUY A FEW BOOKS, AND CHANGE UP THE USUAL MEALS FOR A BIT.
BUT SINCE I WAS LIVING IN A MORE OR LESS HOMICIDAL AND DESPERATELY MERCANTILE WORLD, MY DUTY WAS TO MAKE THE BEST OF IT.
I ALSO DREADED HEARING AGAIN THAT NIGHT THOSE HOARSE MOANS OF AN ABANDONED SOUL. I COULDN'T KEEP MYSELF FROM ASSOCIATING WITH THAT FLOWER ON HER BALCONY.

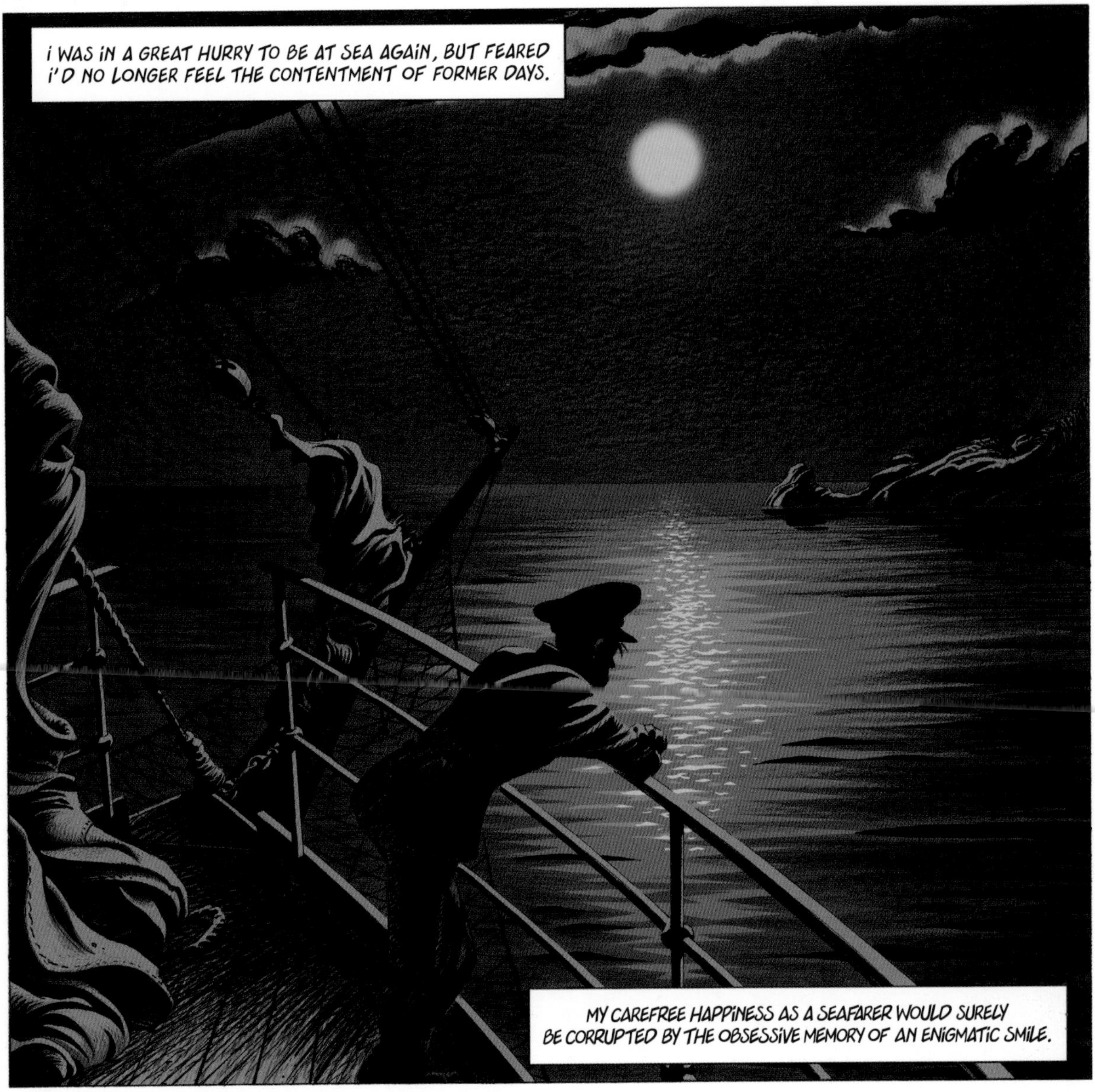
I WAS IN A GREAT HURRY TO BE AT SEA AGAIN, BUT FEARED I'D NO LONGER FEEL THE CONTENTMENT OF FORMER DAYS.
MY CAREFREE HAPPINESS AS A SEAFARER WOULD SURELY BE CORRUPTED BY THE OBSESSIVE MEMORY OF AN ENIGMATIC SMILE.

The End

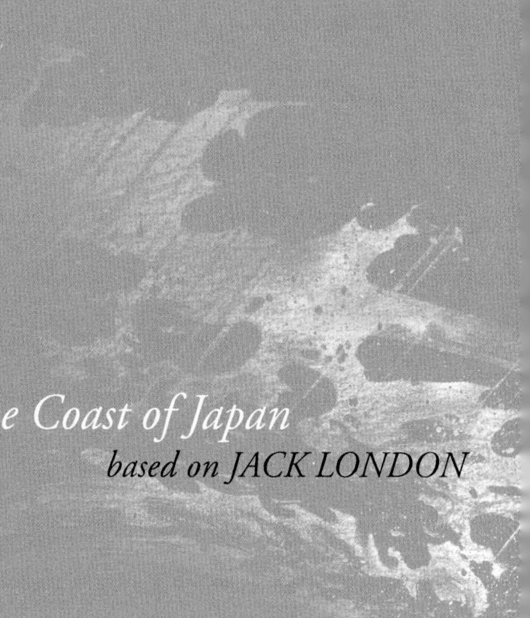

Typhoon off the Coast of Japan

based on JACK LONDON

JACK LONDON
Typhoon off the Coast of Japan

(Excerpt)

We had the first watch from eight to midnight. The wind was soon blowing half a gale, and our sailing-master expected little sleep that night as he paced up and down the poop. The topsails were soon furled up, then the flying jib run down and furled. Quite a sea was rolling by this time, occasionally breaking over the decks, flooding them and threatening to smash the boats. At six bells, we were ordered to turn them over and put on the storm lashings. This occupied us till eight bells, when we were relieved by the mid-watch. I was the last to go below, doing so just as the watch on deck was furling the spanker. Below all were asleep except our green hand, the "bricklayer," who was dying of consumption. The wildly dancing movements of the sea lamp cast a pale, flickering light through the fo'castle and turned to golden honey the drops of water on the yellow oilskins. In all corners dark shadows seemed to come and go, while up in the eyes of her, beyond the pall bits, descending from deck to deck, where they seemed to lurk like some dragon at the cavern's mouth, it was as dark as Erebus. Now and again, the light seemed to penetrate for a moment as the schooner rolled heavier than usually, only to recede, leaving it darker and blacker than before. The roar of the wind through the rigging came to the ear muffled like the distant rumble of a train crossing a trestle or the surf on the beach, while the loud crash of the seas on her weather bow seemed almost to rend the beams and planking asunder as it resounded through the fo'castle. The creaking and groaning of the timbers, stanchions, and bulkheads, as the strain the vessel was undergoing was felt, served to drown the groans of the dying man as he tossed uneasily in his bunk. The working of the foremast against the deck beams caused a shower of flaky powder to fall, and sent another sound mingling with the tumultuous storm. Small cascades of water streamed from the pall bits from the fo'castle head above, and, joining issue with the streams from the wet oilskins, ran along the floor and disappeared aft into the main hold. [...]

Below, a couple of men were sewing the bricklayer's body in canvas preparatory to the sea burial.

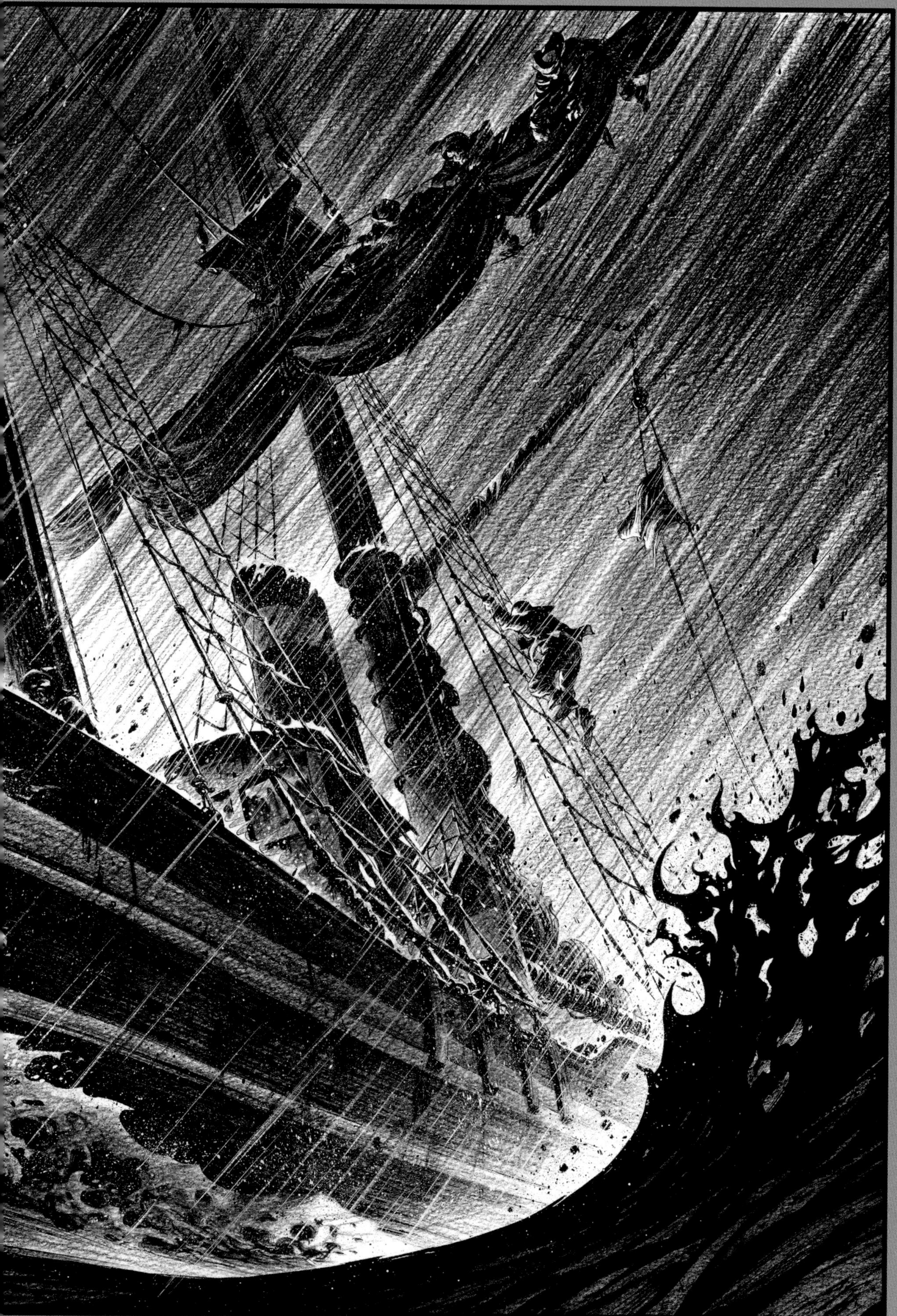

The Sinking Ship

based on ROBERT LOUIS STEVENSON

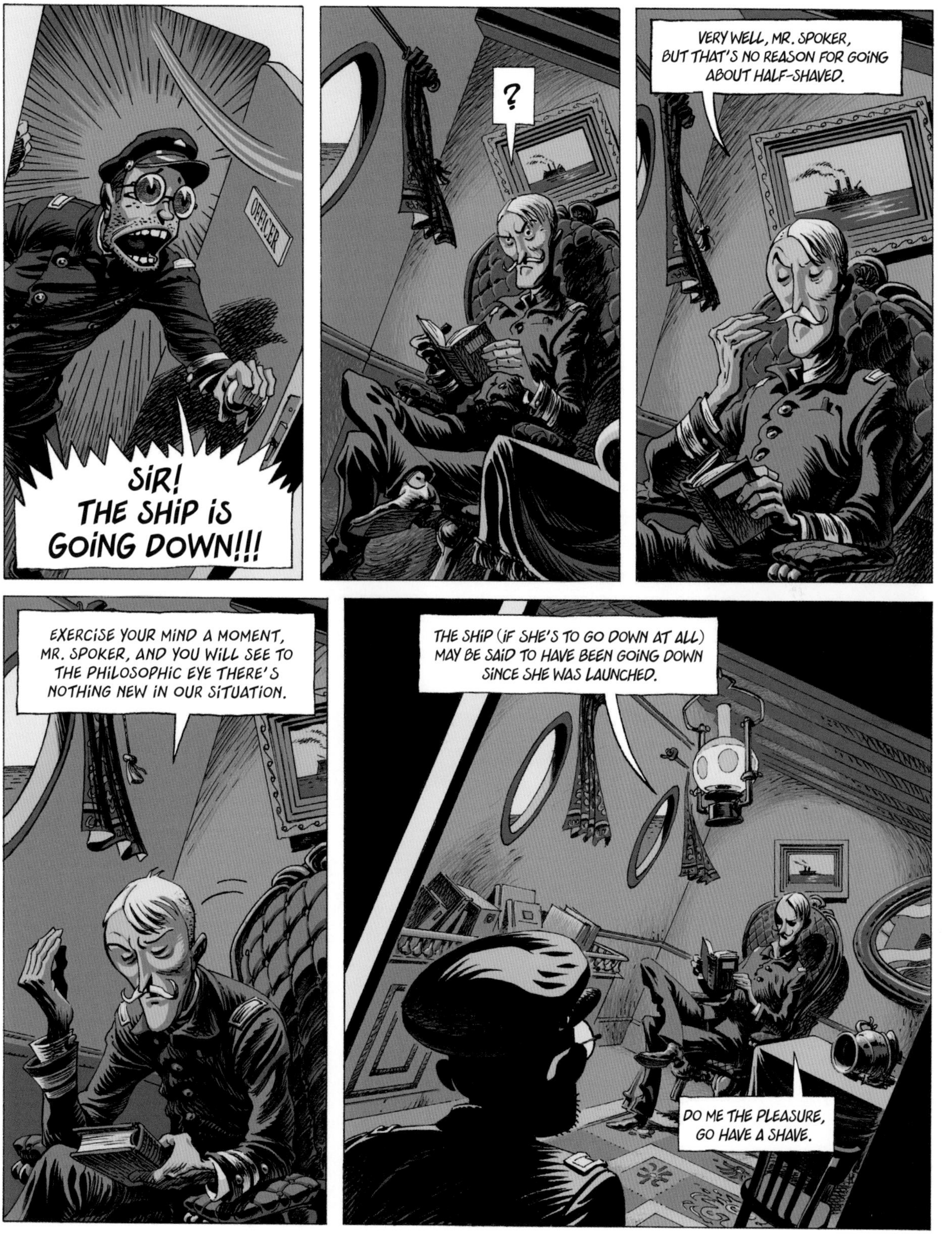
OFFICER
SIR! THE SHIP IS GOING DOWN!!!
?
VERY WELL, MR. SPOKER, BUT THAT'S NO REASON FOR GOING ABOUT HALF-SHAVED.
EXERCISE YOUR MIND A MOMENT, MR. SPOKER, AND YOU WILL SEE TO THE PHILOSOPHIC EYE THERE'S NOTHING NEW IN OUR SITUATION.
THE SHIP (IF SHE'S TO GO DOWN AT ALL) MAY BE SAID TO HAVE BEEN GOING DOWN SINCE SHE WAS LAUNCHED.
DO ME THE PLEASURE, GO HAVE A SHAVE.

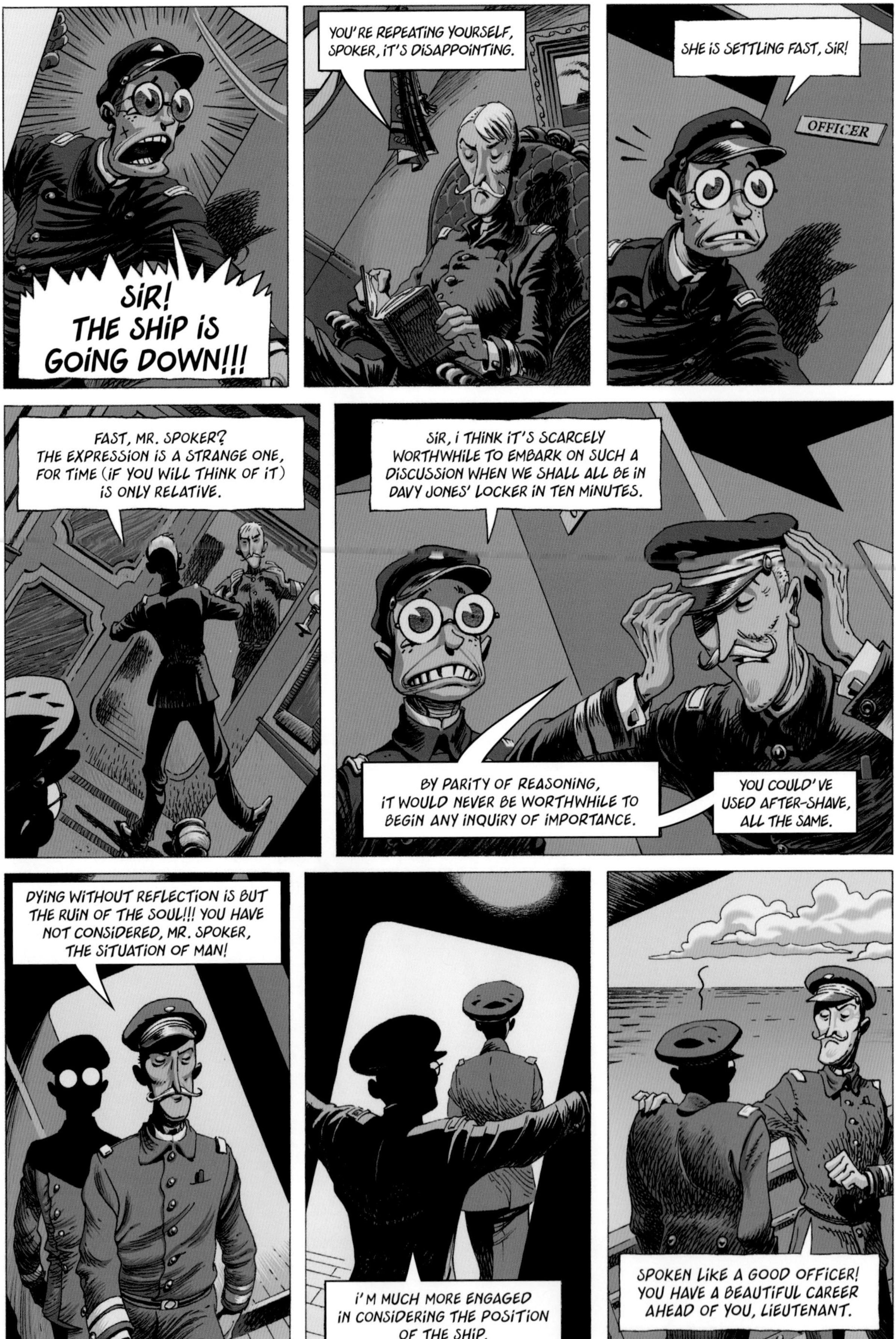
SIR! THE SHIP IS GOING DOWN!!!
YOU'RE REPEATING YOURSELF, SPOKER, IT'S DISAPPOINTING.
SHE IS SETTLING FAST, SIR!
OFFICER
FAST, MR. SPOKER? THE EXPRESSION IS A STRANGE ONE, FOR TIME (IF YOU WILL THINK OF IT) IS ONLY RELATIVE.
SIR, I THINK IT'S SCARCELY WORTHWHILE TO EMBARK ON SUCH A DISCUSSION WHEN WE SHALL ALL BE IN DAVY JONES' LOCKER IN TEN MINUTES.
BY PARITY OF REASONING, IT WOULD NEVER BE WORTHWHILE TO BEGIN ANY INQUIRY OF IMPORTANCE.
YOU COULD'VE USED AFTER-SHAVE, ALL THE SAME.
DYING WITHOUT REFLECTION IS BUT THE RUIN OF THE SOUL!!! YOU HAVE NOT CONSIDERED, MR. SPOKER, THE SITUATION OF MAN!
I'M MUCH MORE ENGAGED IN CONSIDERING THE POSITION OF THE SHIP.
SPOKEN LIKE A GOOD OFFICER! YOU HAVE A BEAUTIFUL CAREER AHEAD OF YOU, LIEUTENANT.

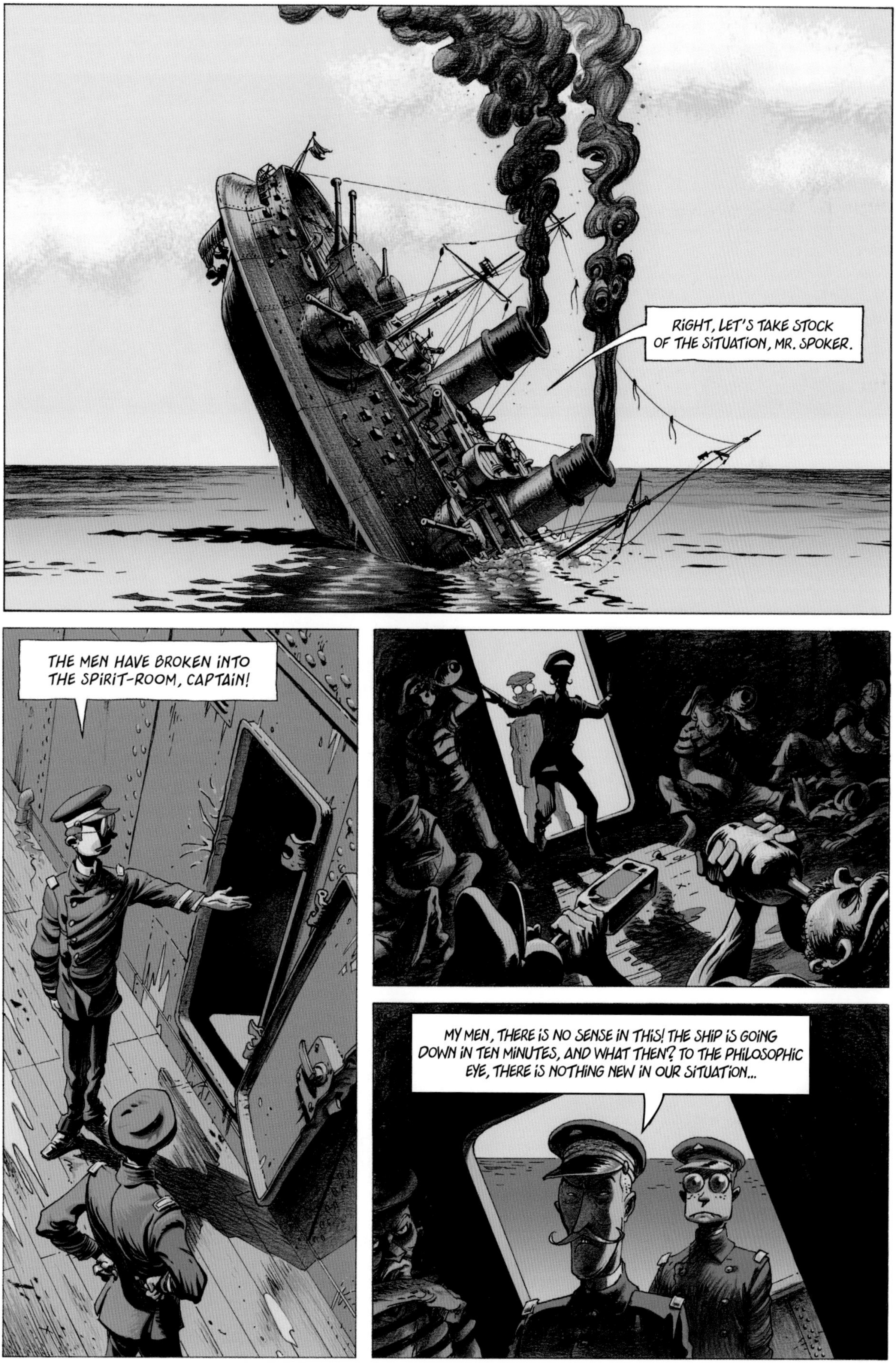
RIGHT, LET'S TAKE STOCK OF THE SITUATION, MR. SPOKER.
THE MEN HAVE BROKEN INTO THE SPIRIT-ROOM, CAPTAIN!
MY MEN, THERE IS NO SENSE IN THIS! THE SHIP IS GOING DOWN IN TEN MINUTES, AND WHAT THEN? TO THE PHILOSOPHIC EYE, THERE IS NOTHING NEW IN OUR SITUATION...

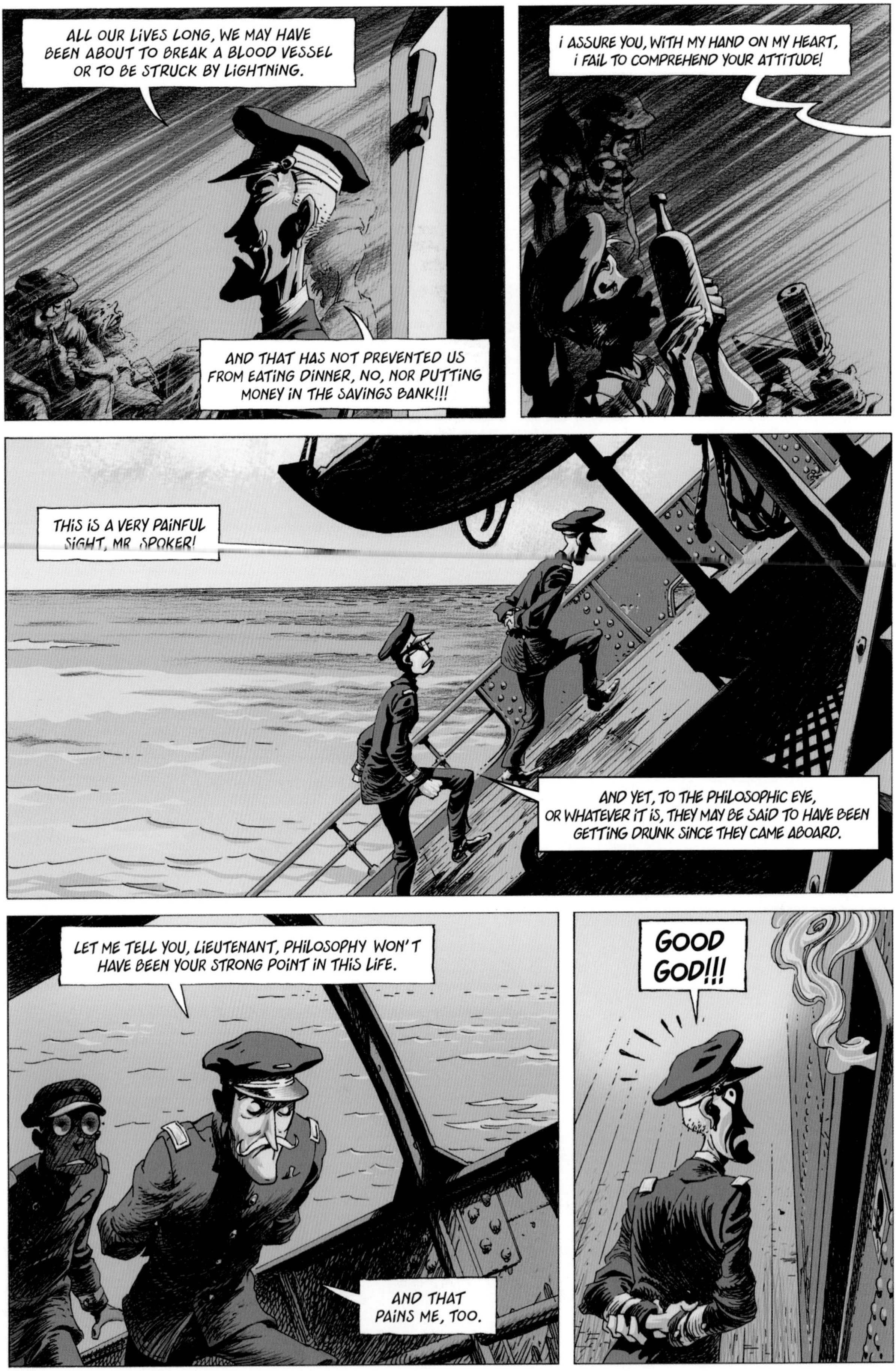
ALL OUR LIVES LONG, WE MAY HAVE BEEN ABOUT TO BREAK A BLOOD VESSEL OR TO BE STRUCK BY LIGHTNING.
AND THAT HAS NOT PREVENTED US FROM EATING DINNER, NO, NOR PUTTING MONEY IN THE SAVINGS BANK!!!
I ASSURE YOU, WITH MY HAND ON MY HEART, I FAIL TO COMPREHEND YOUR ATTITUDE!
THIS IS A VERY PAINFUL SIGHT, MR SPOKER!
AND YET, TO THE PHILOSOPHIC EYE, OR WHATEVER IT IS, THEY MAY BE SAID TO HAVE BEEN GETTING DRUNK SINCE THEY CAME ABOARD.
LET ME TELL YOU, LIEUTENANT, PHILOSOPHY WON'T HAVE BEEN YOUR STRONG POINT IN THIS LIFE.
AND THAT PAINS ME, TOO.
GOOD GOD!!!

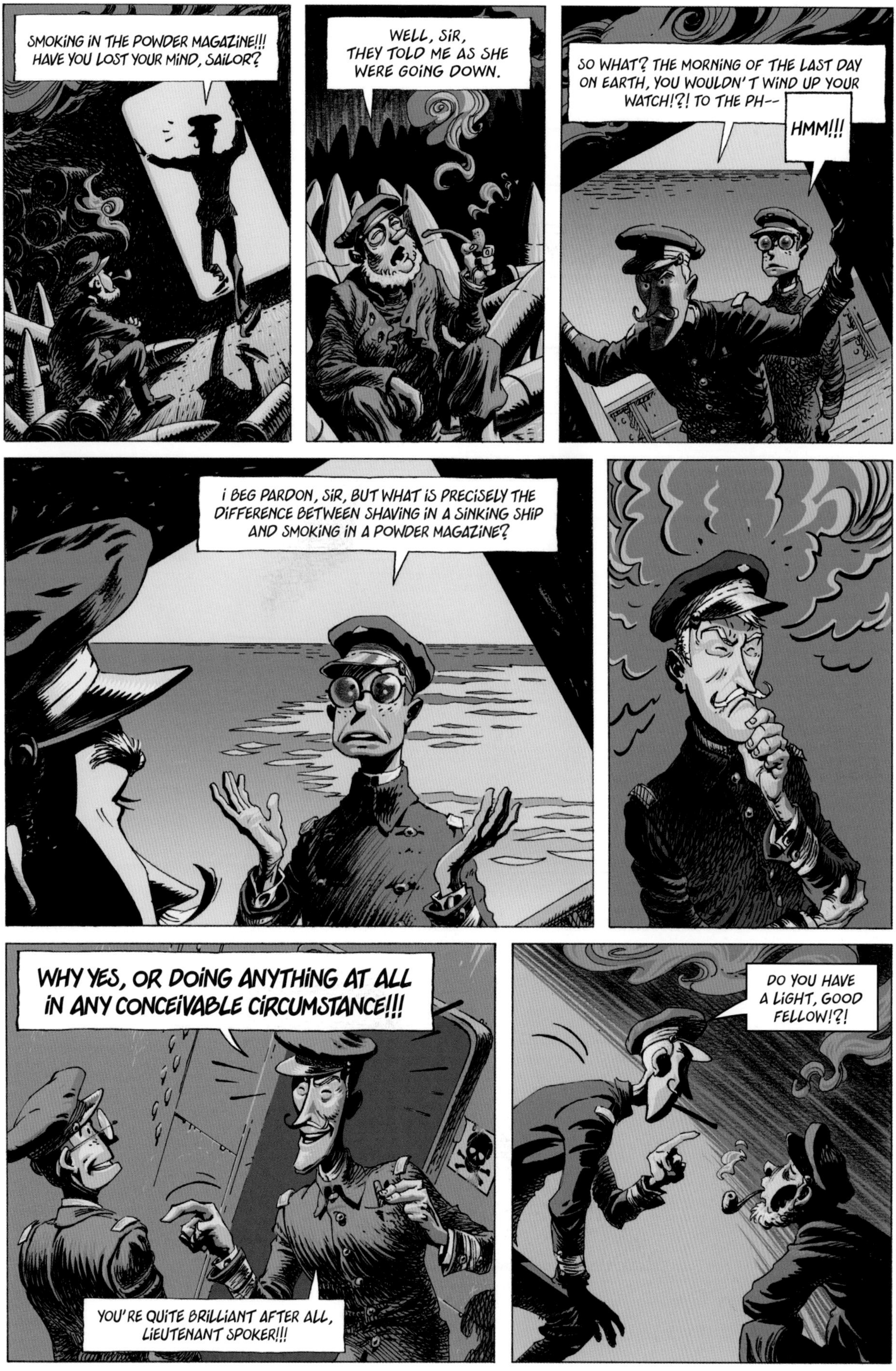
SMOKING IN THE POWDER MAGAZINE!!! HAVE YOU LOST YOUR MIND, SAILOR?
WELL, SIR, THEY TOLD ME AS SHE WERE GOING DOWN.
SO WHAT? THE MORNING OF THE LAST DAY ON EARTH, YOU WOULDN'T WIND UP YOUR WATCH!?! TO THE PH--
HMM!!!
I BEG PARDON, SIR, BUT WHAT IS PRECISELY THE DIFFERENCE BETWEEN SHAVING IN A SINKING SHIP AND SMOKING IN A POWDER MAGAZINE?
WHY YES, OR DOING ANYTHING AT ALL IN ANY CONCEIVABLE CIRCUMSTANCE!!!
YOU'RE QUITE BRILLIANT AFTER ALL, LIEUTENANT SPOKER!!!
DO YOU HAVE A LIGHT, GOOD FELLOW!?!

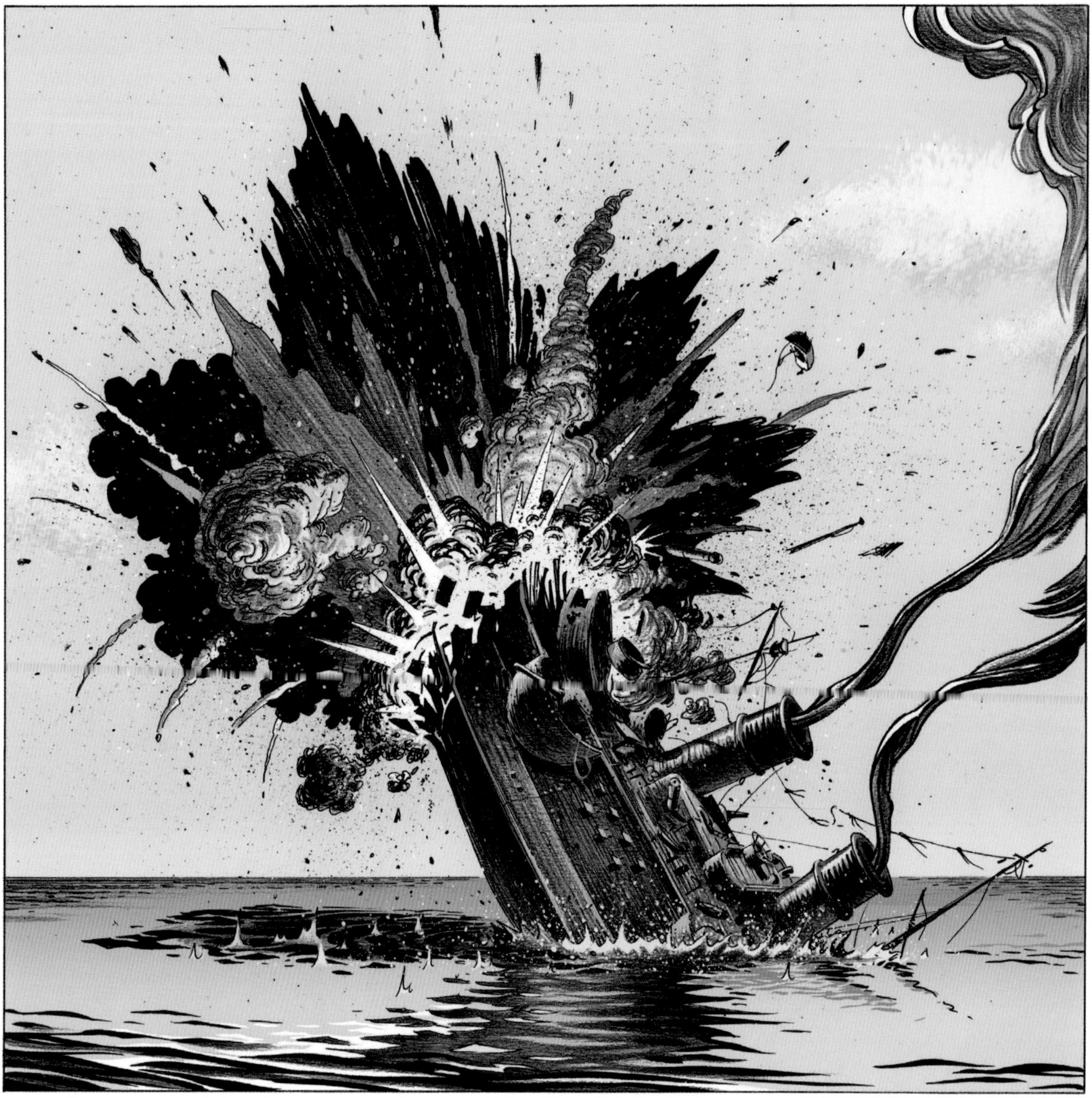

The End

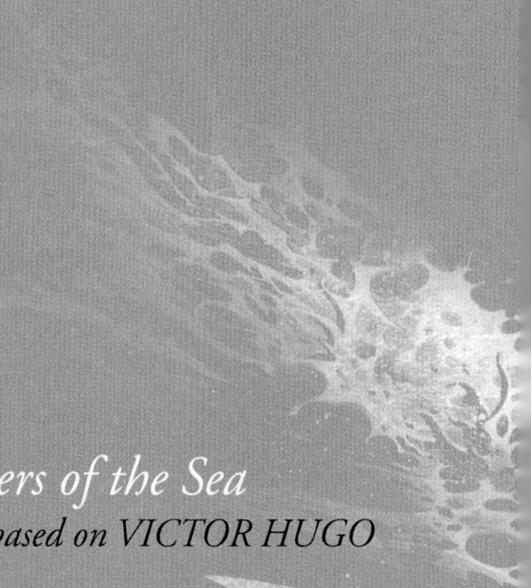

The Toilers of the Sea

based on VICTOR HUGO

VICTOR HUGO
The Toilers of the Sea

(Excerpt)

You must have seen the octopus to believe in it. Compared to it, ancient hydras are laughable.

At certain moments, one would be tempted to think, the elusive shape that floats in our dreams encounters in the possible attractive forces to which its lineaments get caught, and from these obscure fixations of dreaming, creatures emerge. The unknown has the miraculous at its disposal and makes use of it to compose the monster. Orpheus, Homer, and Hesiod could create only the Chimera; God made the octopus.

When God wishes, He excels in the execrable.

The reason for this desire
is the fear of the religious minded.
All ideals being admitted, if terror
were the goal, the octopus is a masterpiece. [...]

In the reefs of the open sea, there where the water spreads out and hides all its splendors, in the hollows of unfrequented rocks, in unknown caves where vegetation, crustaceans, and shellfish abound, beneath the deep portals of the ocean, the swimmer who ventures there, drawn by the beauty of the place, risks an encounter. If this should be you, don't be curious, flee. One enters bedazzled, one leaves terrified.

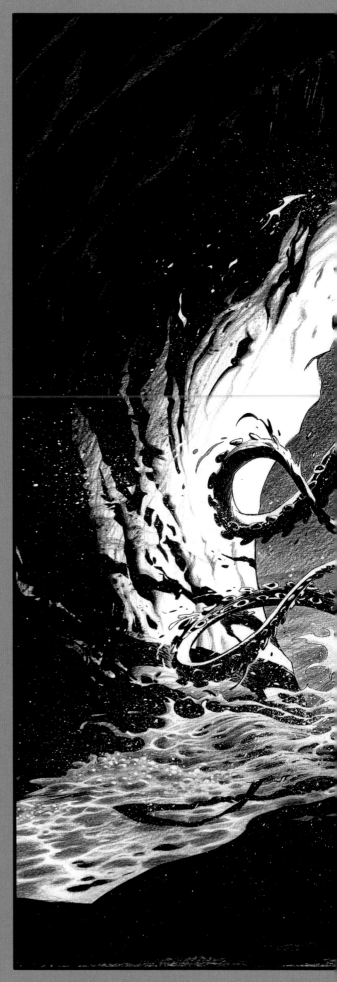

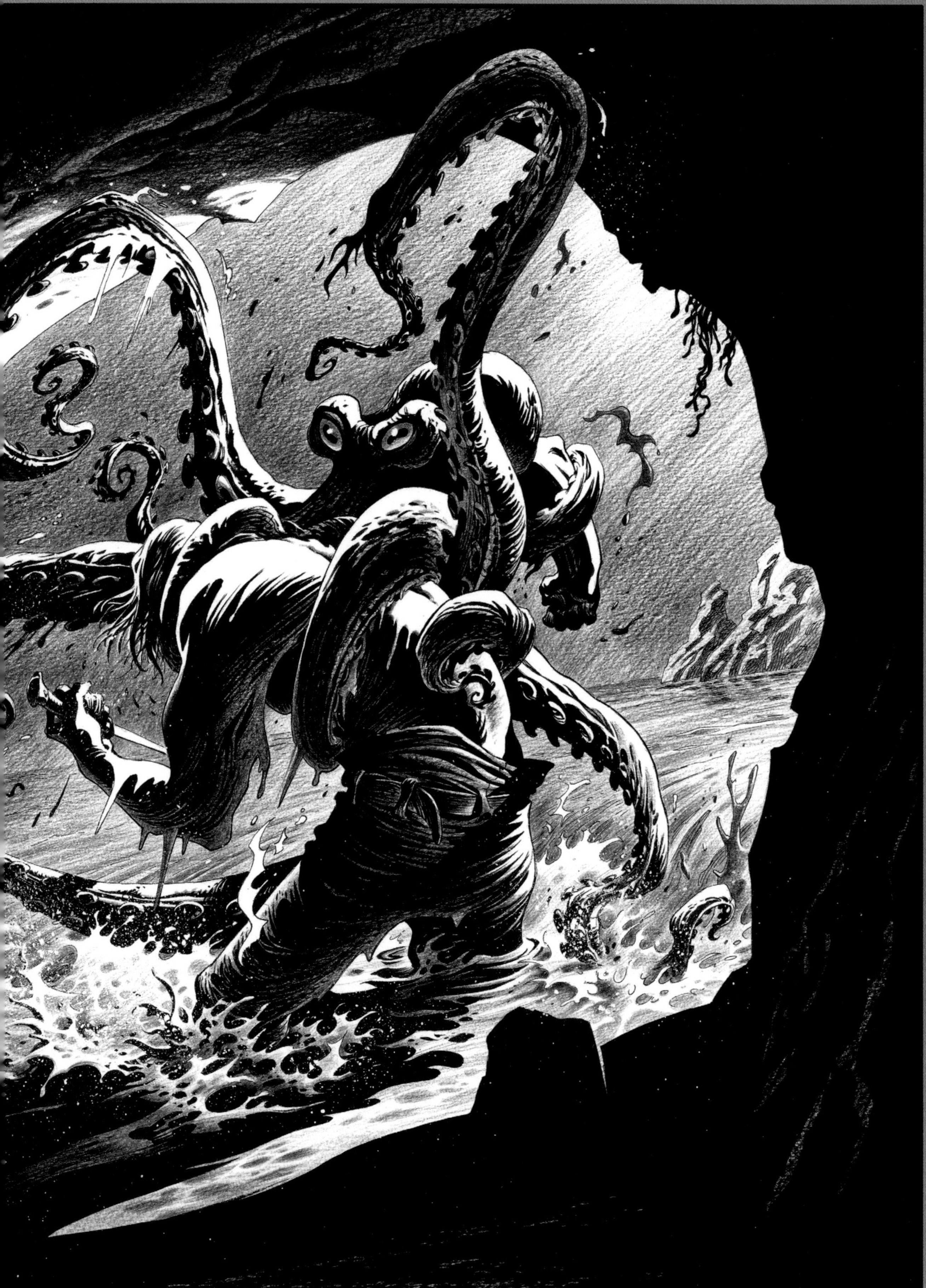

A Descent into the Maelström

based on EDGAR ALLAN POE

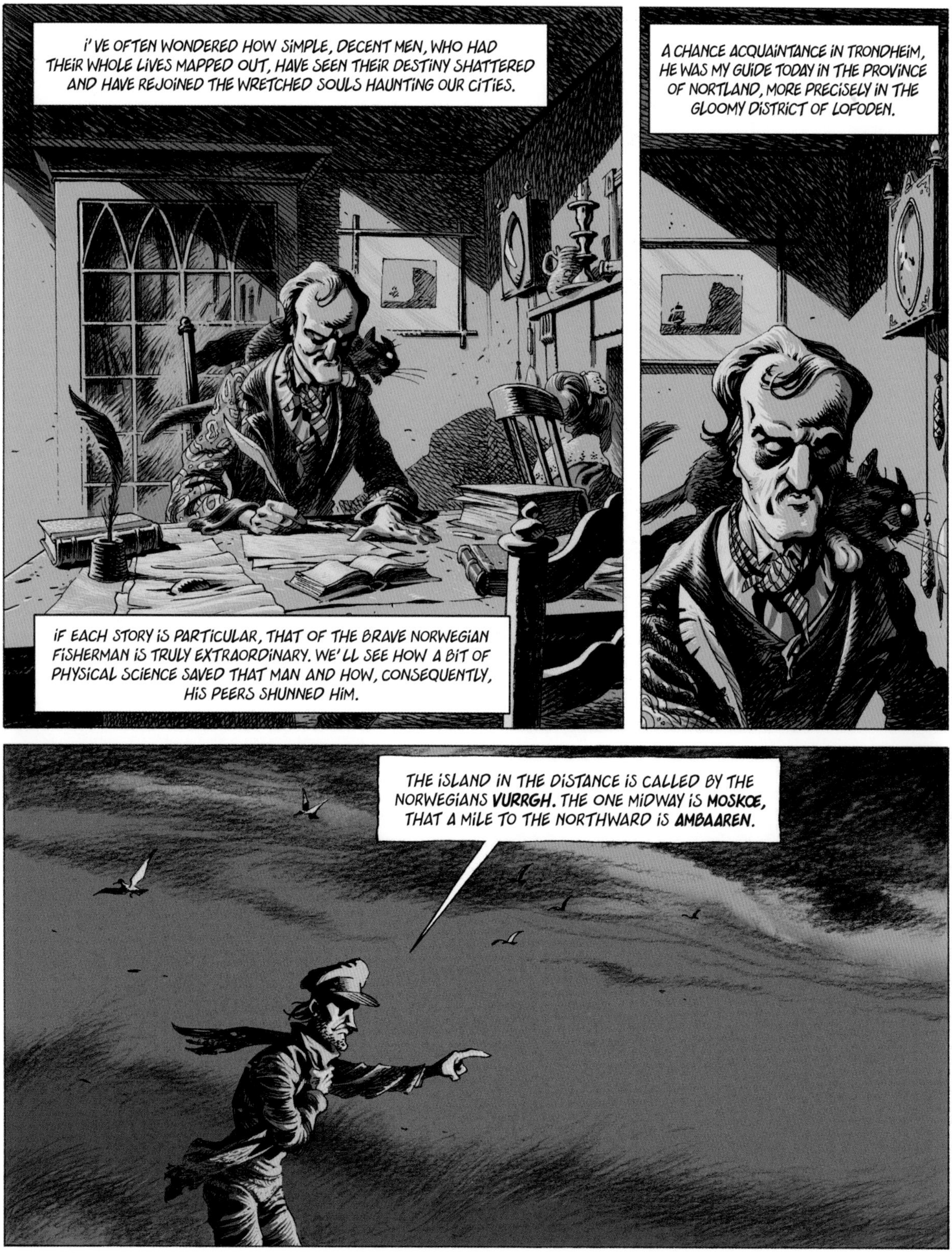

I'VE OFTEN WONDERED HOW SIMPLE, DECENT MEN, WHO HAD THEIR WHOLE LIVES MAPPED OUT, HAVE SEEN THEIR DESTINY SHATTERED AND HAVE REJOINED THE WRETCHED SOULS HAUNTING OUR CITIES.
IF EACH STORY IS PARTICULAR, THAT OF THE BRAVE NORWEGIAN FISHERMAN IS TRULY EXTRAORDINARY. WE'LL SEE HOW A BIT OF PHYSICAL SCIENCE SAVED THAT MAN AND HOW, CONSEQUENTLY, HIS PEERS SHUNNED HIM.
A CHANCE ACQUAINTANCE IN TRONDHEIM, HE WAS MY GUIDE TODAY IN THE PROVINCE OF NORTLAND, MORE PRECISELY IN THE GLOOMY DISTRICT OF LOFODEN.
THE ISLAND IN THE DISTANCE IS CALLED BY THE NORWEGIANS **VURRGH**. THE ONE MIDWAY IS **MOSKOE**, THAT A MILE TO THE NORTHWARD IS **AMBAAREN**.

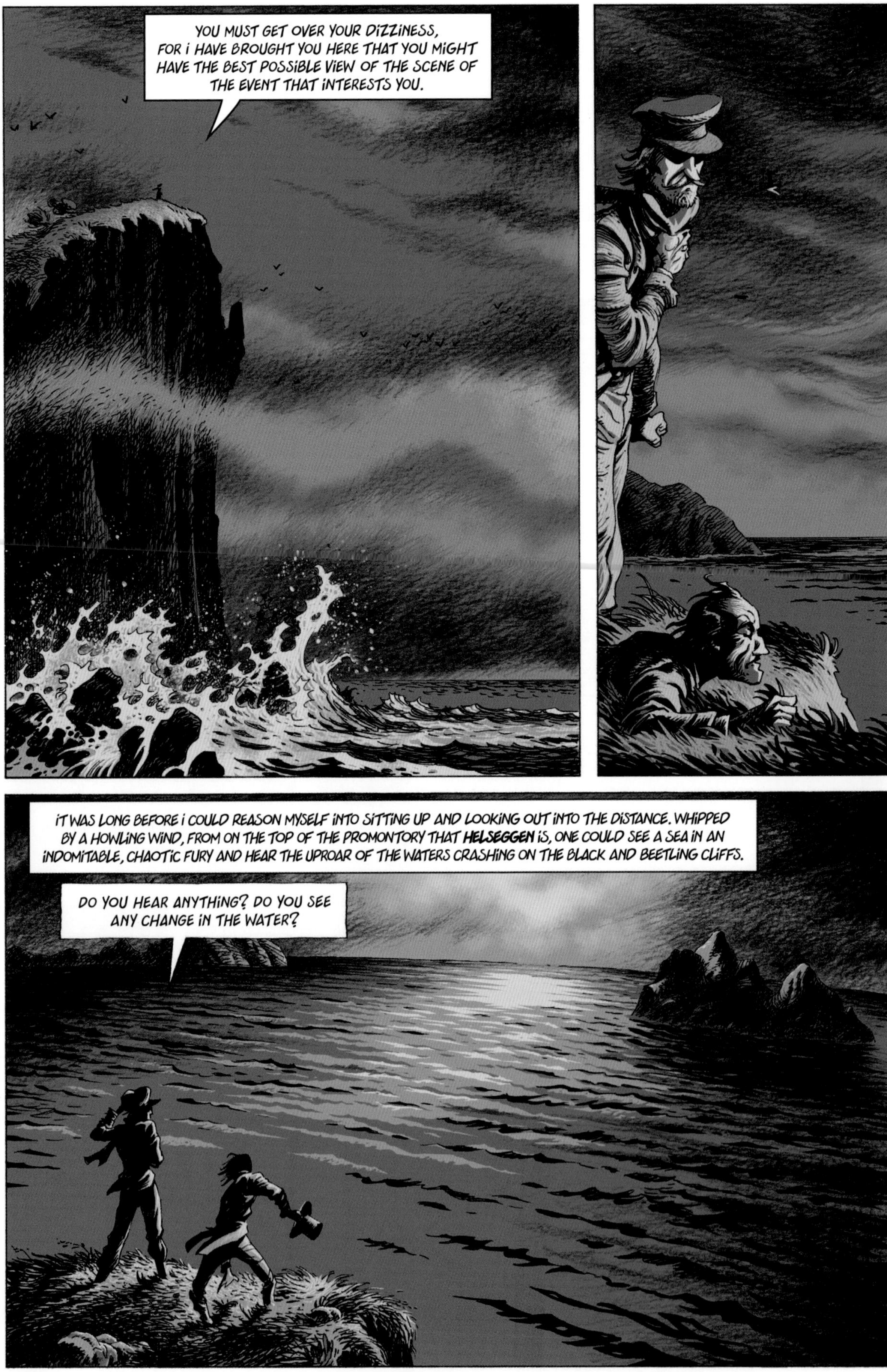
YOU MUST GET OVER YOUR DIZZINESS, FOR I HAVE BROUGHT YOU HERE THAT YOU MIGHT HAVE THE BEST POSSIBLE VIEW OF THE SCENE OF THE EVENT THAT INTERESTS YOU.
IT WAS LONG BEFORE I COULD REASON MYSELF INTO SITTING UP AND LOOKING OUT INTO THE DISTANCE. WHIPPED BY A HOWLING WIND, FROM ON THE TOP OF THE PROMONTORY THAT **HELSEGGEN** IS, ONE COULD SEE A SEA IN AN INDOMITABLE, CHAOTIC FURY AND HEAR THE UPROAR OF THE WATERS CRASHING ON THE BLACK AND BEETLING CLIFFS.
DO YOU HEAR ANYTHING? DO YOU SEE ANY CHANGE IN THE WATER?

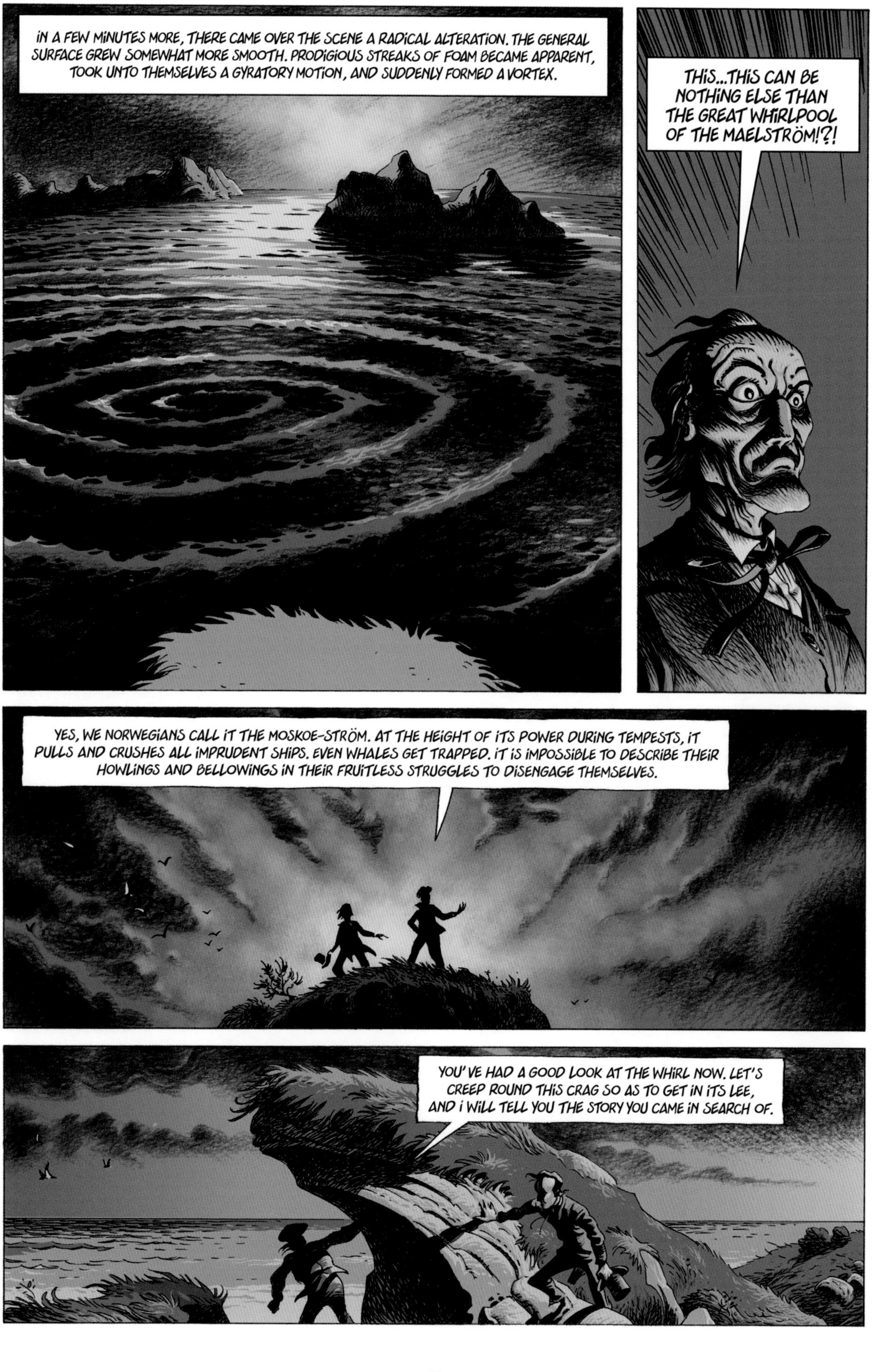
IN A FEW MINUTES MORE, THERE CAME OVER THE SCENE A RADICAL ALTERATION. THE GENERAL SURFACE GREW SOMEWHAT MORE SMOOTH. PRODIGIOUS STREAKS OF FOAM BECAME APPARENT, TOOK UNTO THEMSELVES A GYRATORY MOTION, AND SUDDENLY FORMED A VORTEX.
THIS...THIS CAN BE NOTHING ELSE THAN THE GREAT WHIRLPOOL OF THE MAELSTRÖM!?!
YES, WE NORWEGIANS CALL IT THE MOSKOE-STRÖM. AT THE HEIGHT OF ITS POWER DURING TEMPESTS, IT PULLS AND CRUSHES ALL IMPRUDENT SHIPS. EVEN WHALES GET TRAPPED. IT IS IMPOSSIBLE TO DESCRIBE THEIR HOWLINGS AND BELLOWINGS IN THEIR FRUITLESS STRUGGLES TO DISENGAGE THEMSELVES.
YOU'VE HAD A GOOD LOOK AT THE WHIRL NOW. LET'S CREEP ROUND THIS CRAG SO AS TO GET IN ITS LEE, AND I WILL TELL YOU THE STORY YOU CAME IN SEARCH OF.

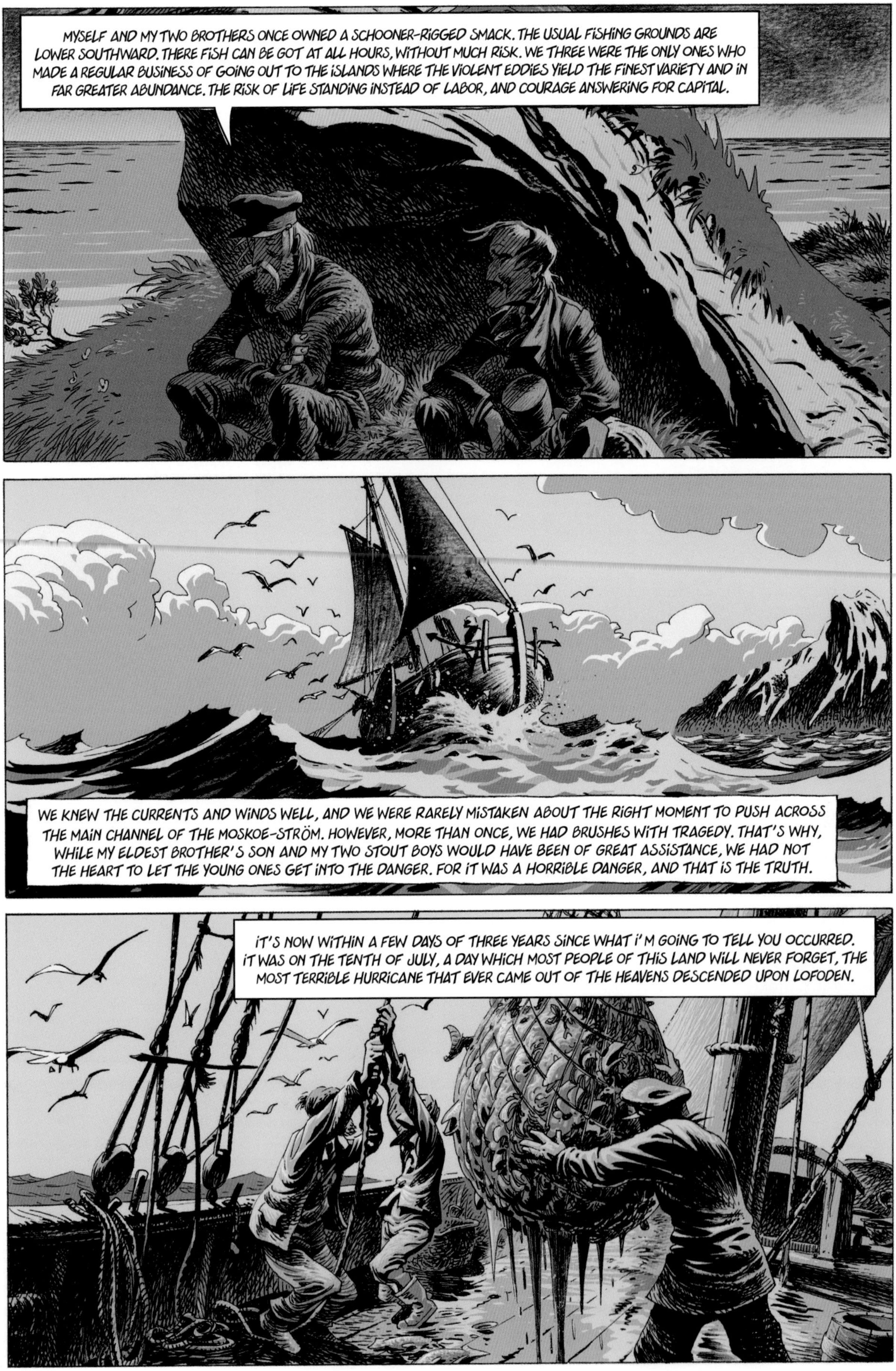
MYSELF AND MY TWO BROTHERS ONCE OWNED A SCHOONER-RIGGED SMACK. THE USUAL FISHING GROUNDS ARE LOWER SOUTHWARD. THERE FISH CAN BE GOT AT ALL HOURS, WITHOUT MUCH RISK. WE THREE WERE THE ONLY ONES WHO MADE A REGULAR BUSINESS OF GOING OUT TO THE ISLANDS WHERE THE VIOLENT EDDIES YIELD THE FINEST VARIETY AND IN FAR GREATER ABUNDANCE. THE RISK OF LIFE STANDING INSTEAD OF LABOR, AND COURAGE ANSWERING FOR CAPITAL.
WE KNEW THE CURRENTS AND WINDS WELL, AND WE WERE RARELY MISTAKEN ABOUT THE RIGHT MOMENT TO PUSH ACROSS THE MAIN CHANNEL OF THE MOSKOE-STRÖM. HOWEVER, MORE THAN ONCE, WE HAD BRUSHES WITH TRAGEDY. THAT'S WHY, WHILE MY ELDEST BROTHER'S SON AND MY TWO STOUT BOYS WOULD HAVE BEEN OF GREAT ASSISTANCE, WE HAD NOT THE HEART TO LET THE YOUNG ONES GET INTO THE DANGER. FOR IT WAS A HORRIBLE DANGER, AND THAT IS THE TRUTH.
IT'S NOW WITHIN A FEW DAYS OF THREE YEARS SINCE WHAT I'M GOING TO TELL YOU OCCURRED. IT WAS ON THE TENTH OF JULY, A DAY WHICH MOST PEOPLE OF THIS LAND WILL NEVER FORGET, THE MOST TERRIBLE HURRICANE THAT EVER CAME OUT OF THE HEAVENS DESCENDED UPON LOFODEN.

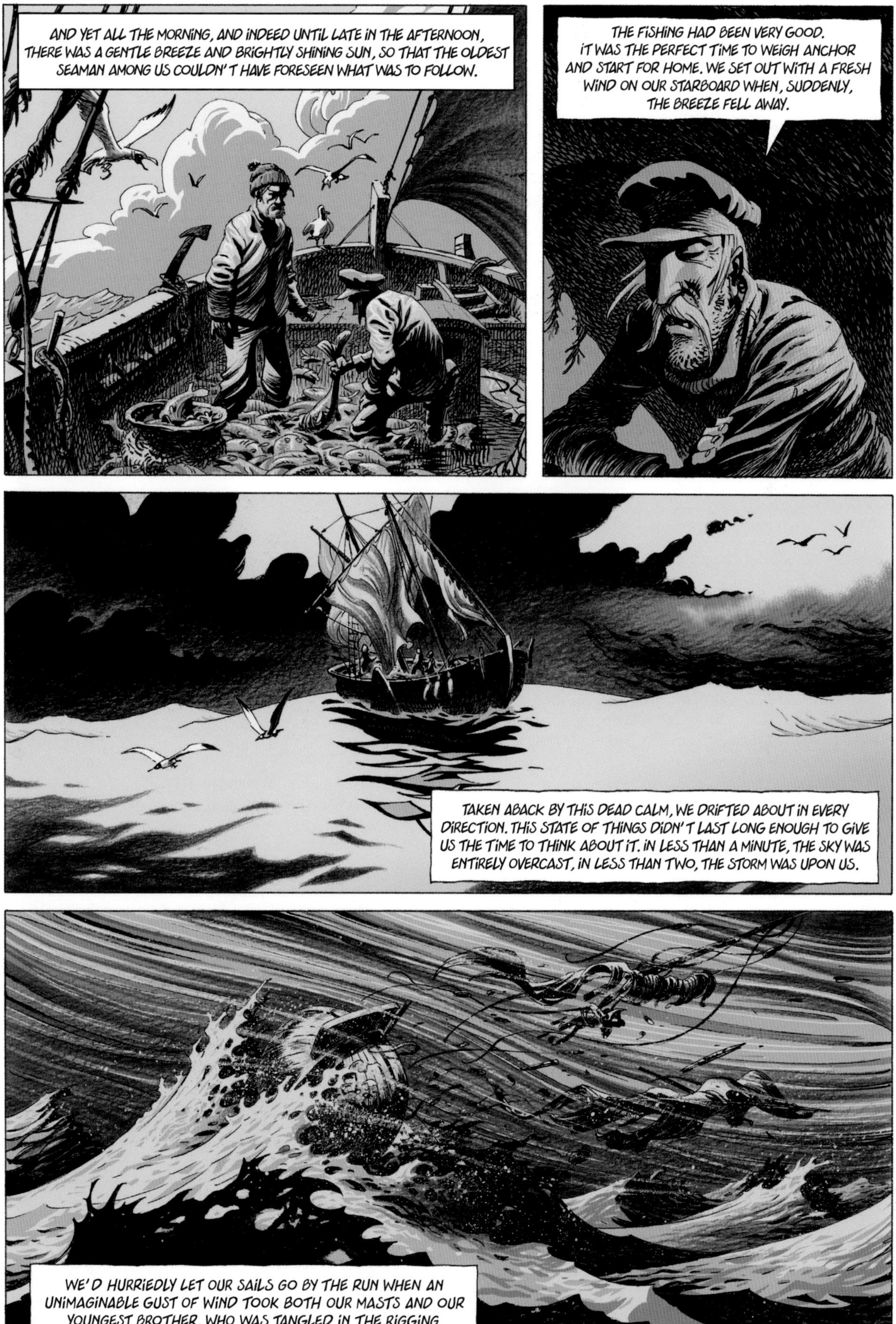
AND YET ALL THE MORNING, AND INDEED UNTIL LATE IN THE AFTERNOON, THERE WAS A GENTLE BREEZE AND BRIGHTLY SHINING SUN, SO THAT THE OLDEST SEAMAN AMONG US COULDN'T HAVE FORESEEN WHAT WAS TO FOLLOW.
THE FISHING HAD BEEN VERY GOOD. IT WAS THE PERFECT TIME TO WEIGH ANCHOR AND START FOR HOME. WE SET OUT WITH A FRESH WIND ON OUR STARBOARD WHEN, SUDDENLY, THE BREEZE FELL AWAY.
TAKEN ABACK BY THIS DEAD CALM, WE DRIFTED ABOUT IN EVERY DIRECTION. THIS STATE OF THINGS DIDN'T LAST LONG ENOUGH TO GIVE US THE TIME TO THINK ABOUT IT. IN LESS THAN A MINUTE, THE SKY WAS ENTIRELY OVERCAST, IN LESS THAN TWO, THE STORM WAS UPON US.
WE'D HURRIEDLY LET OUR SAILS GO BY THE RUN WHEN AN UNIMAGINABLE GUST OF WIND TOOK BOTH OUR MASTS AND OUR YOUNGEST BROTHER, WHO WAS TANGLED IN THE RIGGING.

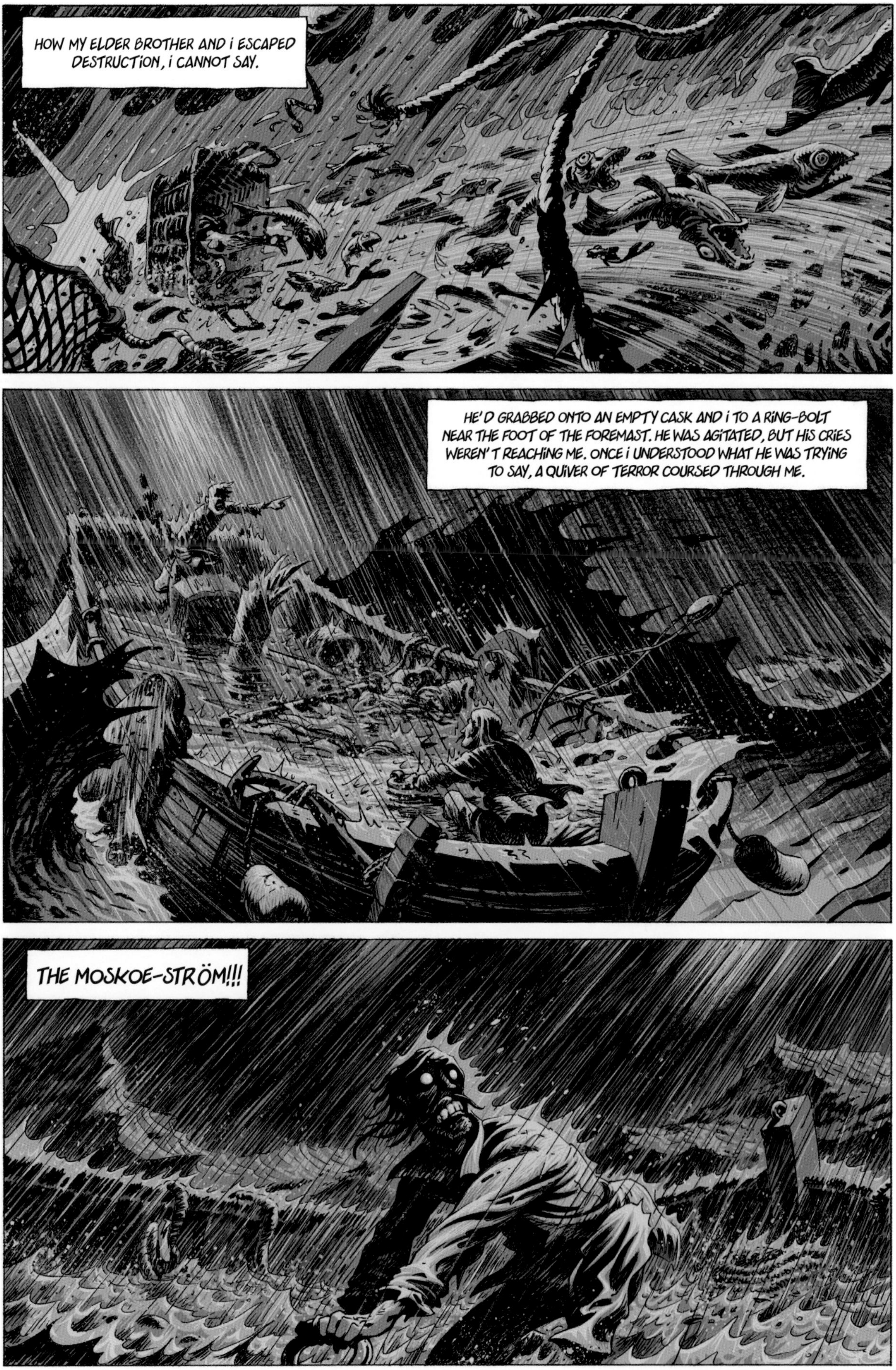
HOW MY ELDER BROTHER AND I ESCAPED DESTRUCTION, I CANNOT SAY.
HE'D GRABBED ONTO AN EMPTY CASK AND I TO A RING-BOLT NEAR THE FOOT OF THE FOREMAST. HE WAS AGITATED, BUT HIS CRIES WEREN'T REACHING ME. ONCE I UNDERSTOOD WHAT HE WAS TRYING TO SAY, A QUIVER OF TERROR COURSED THROUGH ME.
THE MOSKOE-STRÖM!!!

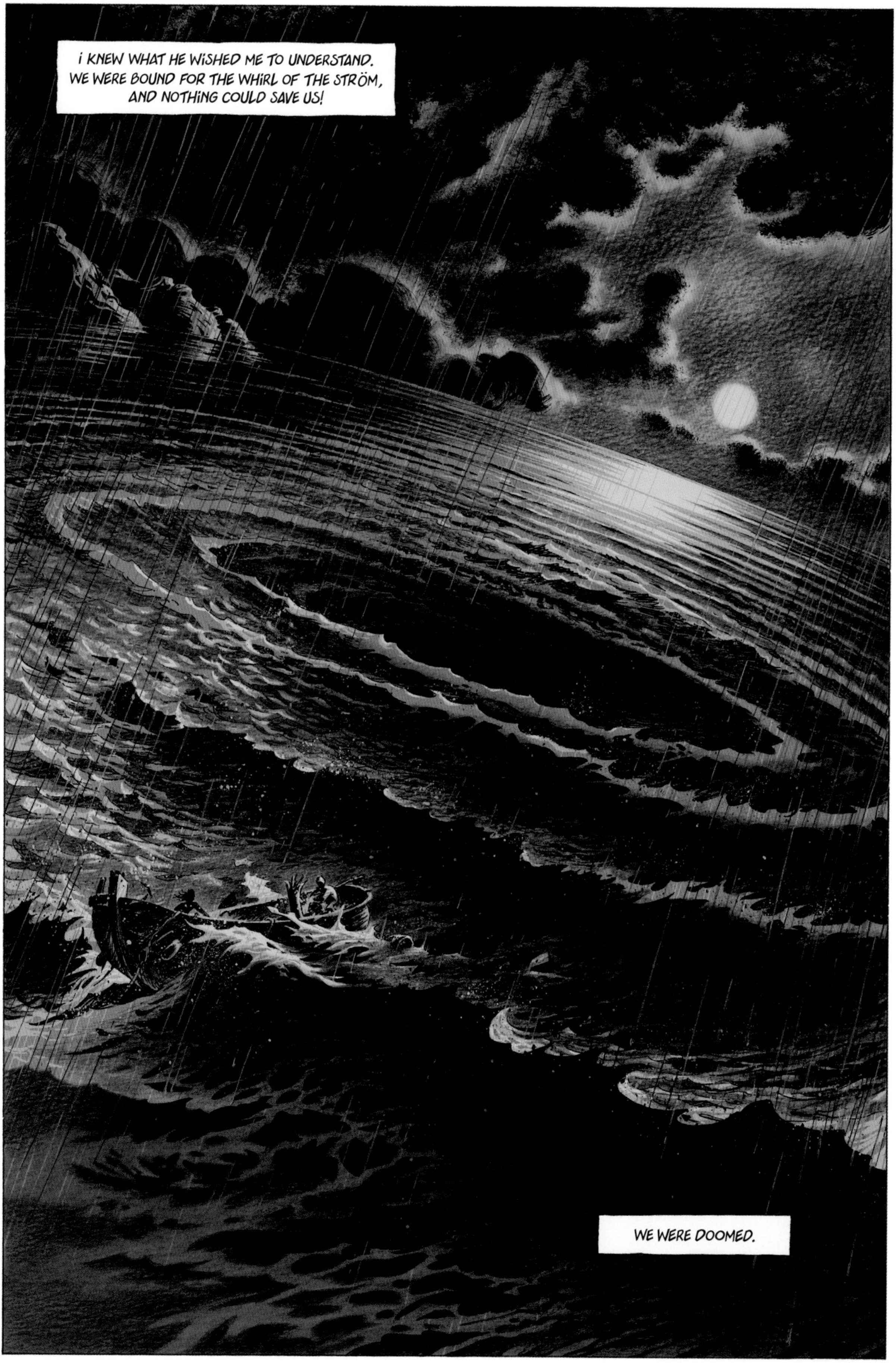
I KNEW WHAT HE WISHED ME TO UNDERSTAND. WE WERE BOUND FOR THE WHIRL OF THE STRÖM, AND NOTHING COULD SAVE US!
WE WERE DOOMED.

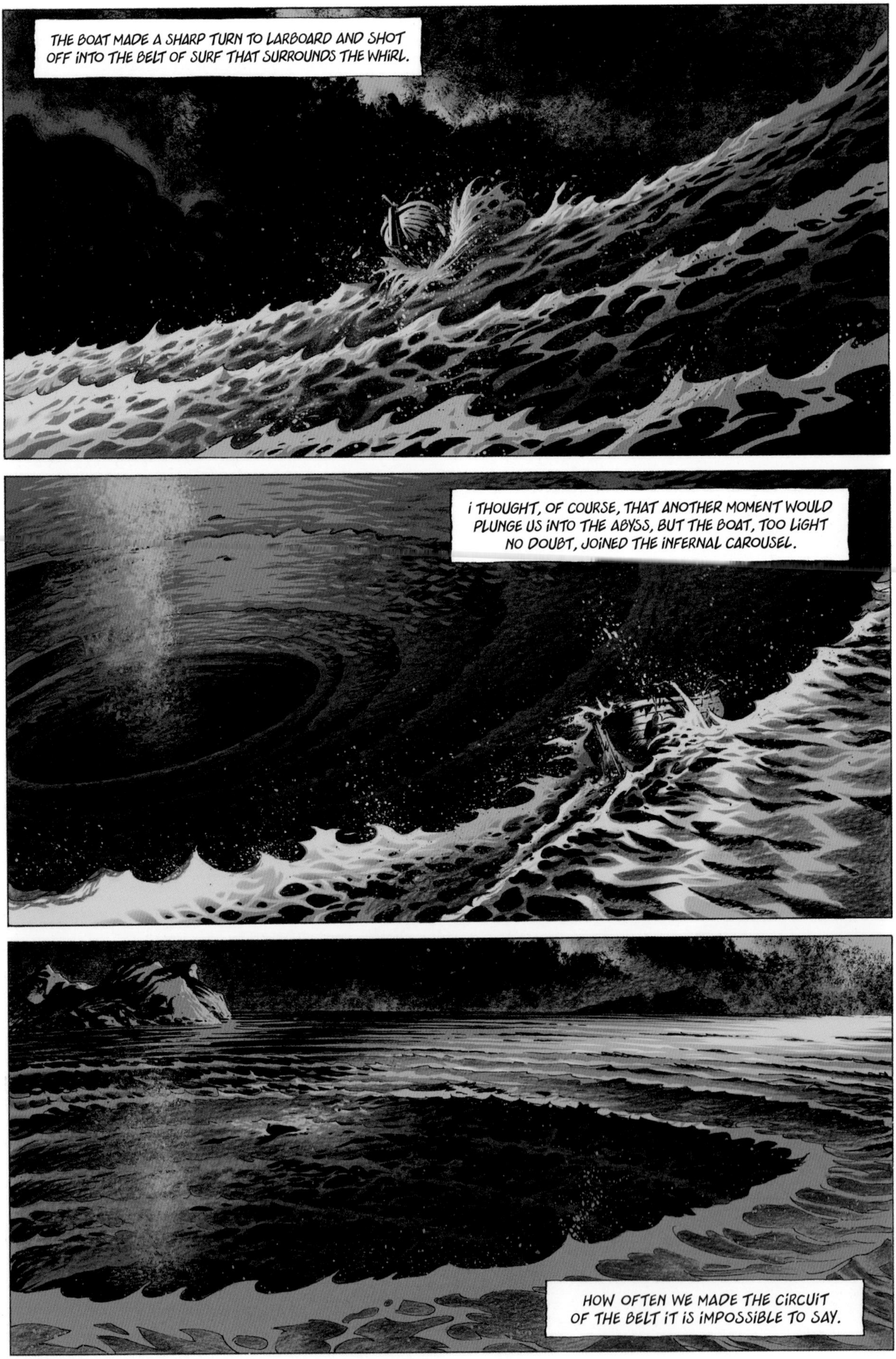
THE BOAT MADE A SHARP TURN TO LARBOARD AND SHOT OFF INTO THE BELT OF SURF THAT SURROUNDS THE WHIRL.
I THOUGHT, OF COURSE, THAT ANOTHER MOMENT WOULD PLUNGE US INTO THE ABYSS, BUT THE BOAT, TOO LIGHT NO DOUBT, JOINED THE INFERNAL CAROUSEL.
HOW OFTEN WE MADE THE CIRCUIT OF THE BELT IT IS IMPOSSIBLE TO SAY.

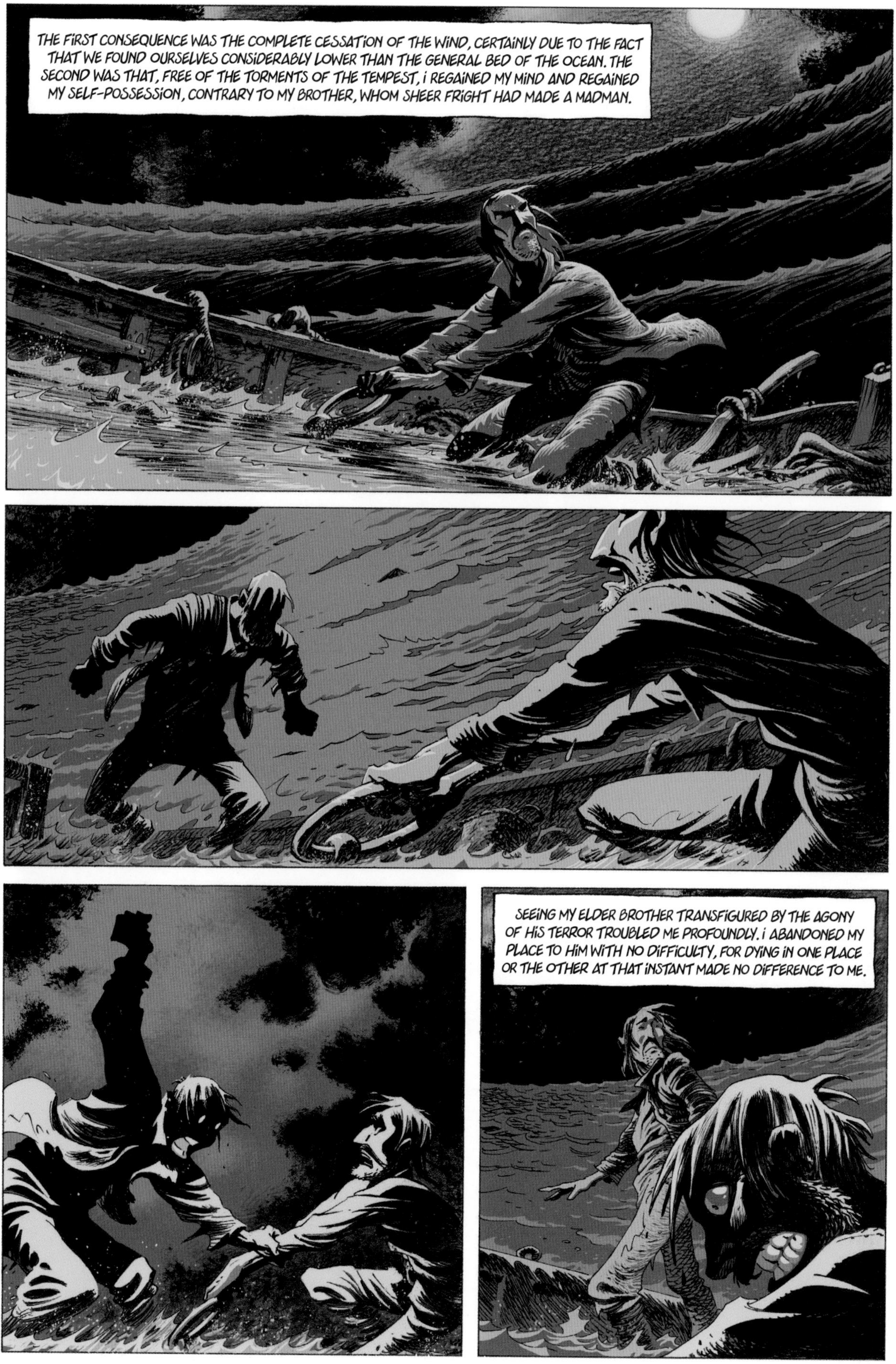
THE FIRST CONSEQUENCE WAS THE COMPLETE CESSATION OF THE WIND, CERTAINLY DUE TO THE FACT THAT WE FOUND OURSELVES CONSIDERABLY LOWER THAN THE GENERAL BED OF THE OCEAN. THE SECOND WAS THAT, FREE OF THE TORMENTS OF THE TEMPEST, I REGAINED MY MIND AND REGAINED MY SELF-POSSESSION, CONTRARY TO MY BROTHER, WHOM SHEER FRIGHT HAD MADE A MADMAN.
SEEING MY ELDER BROTHER TRANSFIGURED BY THE AGONY OF HIS TERROR TROUBLED ME PROFOUNDLY. I ABANDONED MY PLACE TO HIM WITH NO DIFFICULTY, FOR DYING IN ONE PLACE OR THE OTHER AT THAT INSTANT MADE NO DIFFERENCE TO ME.

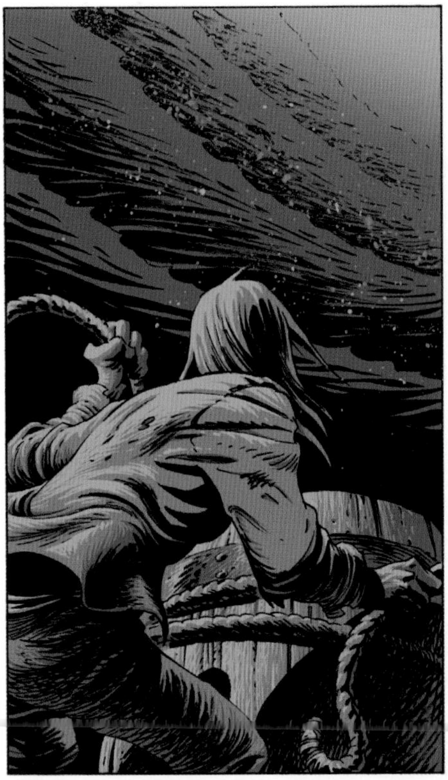

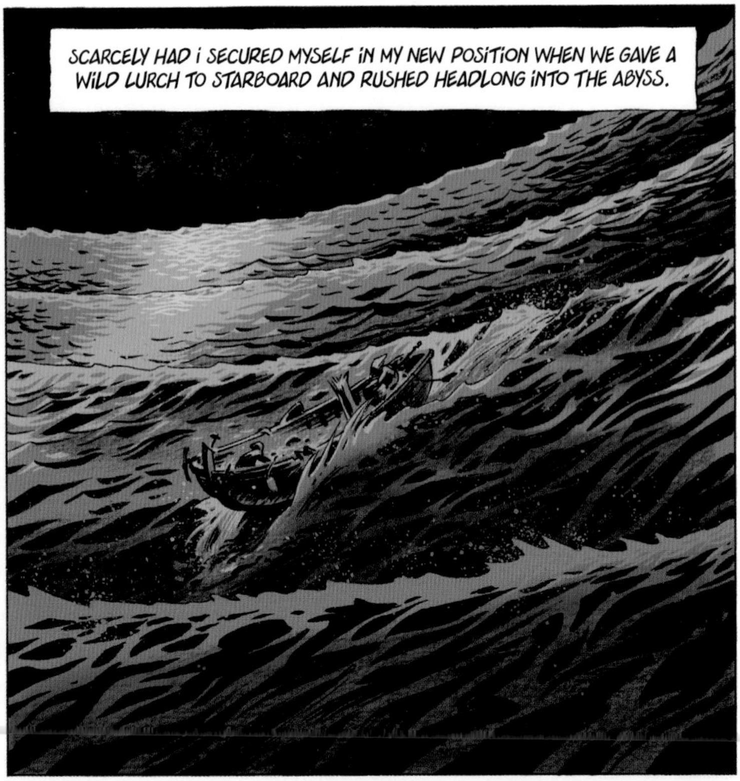
SCARCELY HAD I SECURED MYSELF IN MY NEW POSITION WHEN WE GAVE A WILD LURCH TO STARBOARD AND RUSHED HEADLONG INTO THE ABYSS.

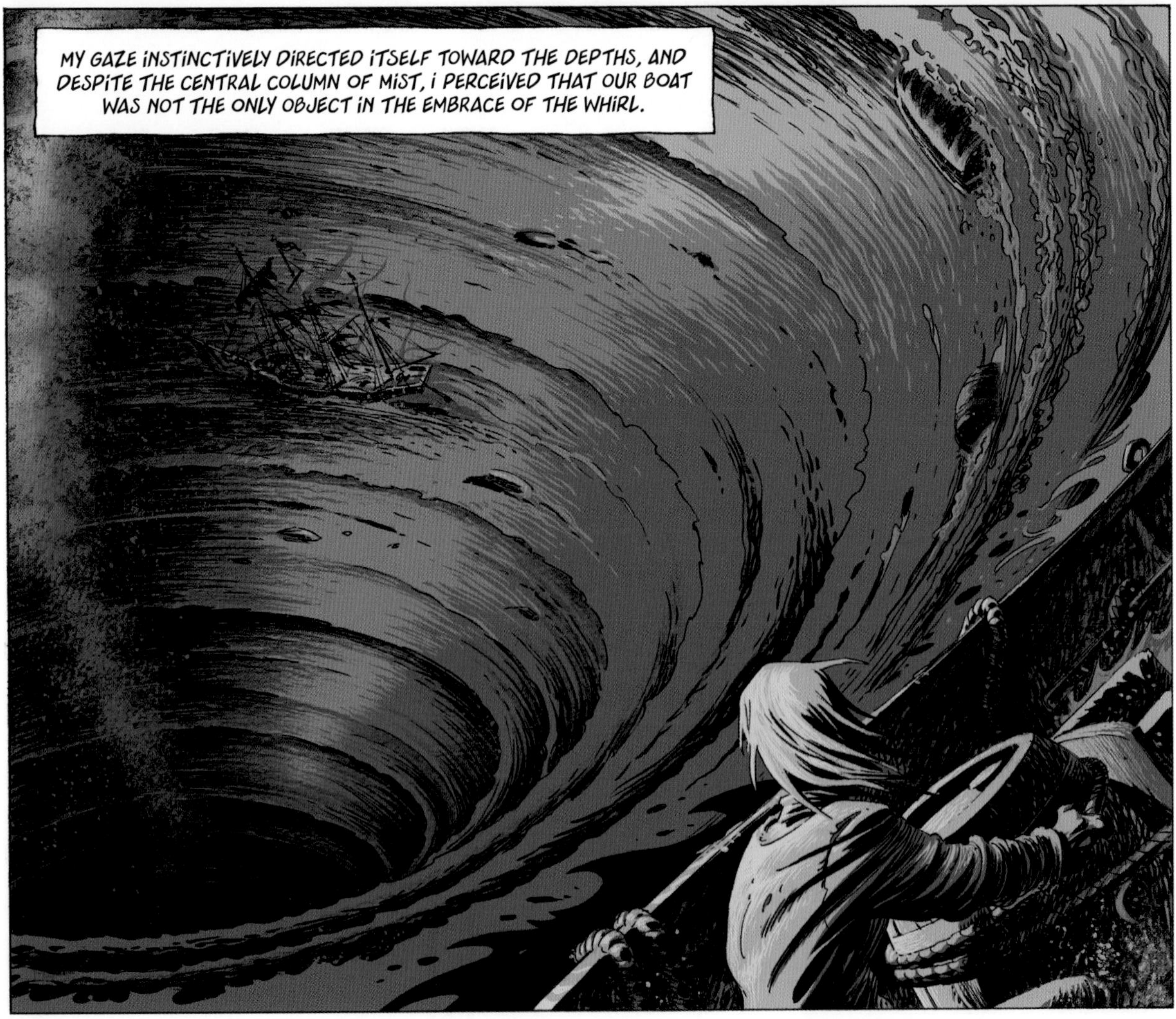
MY GAZE INSTINCTIVELY DIRECTED ITSELF TOWARD THE DEPTHS, AND DESPITE THE CENTRAL COLUMN OF MIST, I PERCEIVED THAT OUR BOAT WAS NOT THE ONLY OBJECT IN THE EMBRACE OF THE WHIRL.

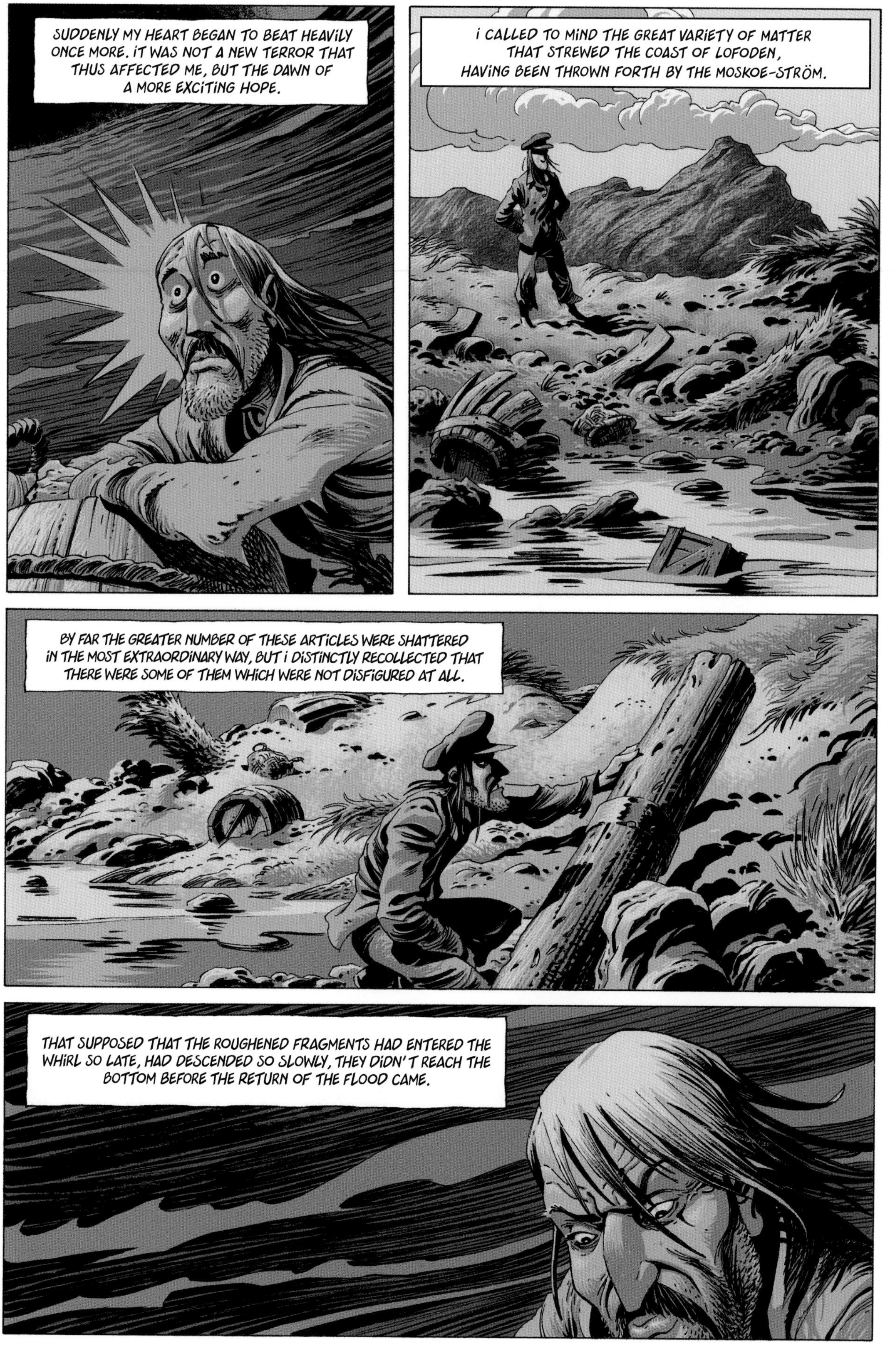
SUDDENLY MY HEART BEGAN TO BEAT HEAVILY ONCE MORE. IT WAS NOT A NEW TERROR THAT THUS AFFECTED ME, BUT THE DAWN OF A MORE EXCITING HOPE.
I CALLED TO MIND THE GREAT VARIETY OF MATTER THAT STREWED THE COAST OF LOFODEN, HAVING BEEN THROWN FORTH BY THE MOSKOE-STRÖM.
BY FAR THE GREATER NUMBER OF THESE ARTICLES WERE SHATTERED IN THE MOST EXTRAORDINARY WAY, BUT I DISTINCTLY RECOLLECTED THAT THERE WERE SOME OF THEM WHICH WERE NOT DISFIGURED AT ALL.
THAT SUPPOSED THAT THE ROUGHENED FRAGMENTS HAD ENTERED THE WHIRL SO LATE, HAD DESCENDED SO SLOWLY, THEY DIDN'T REACH THE BOTTOM BEFORE THE RETURN OF THE FLOOD CAME.

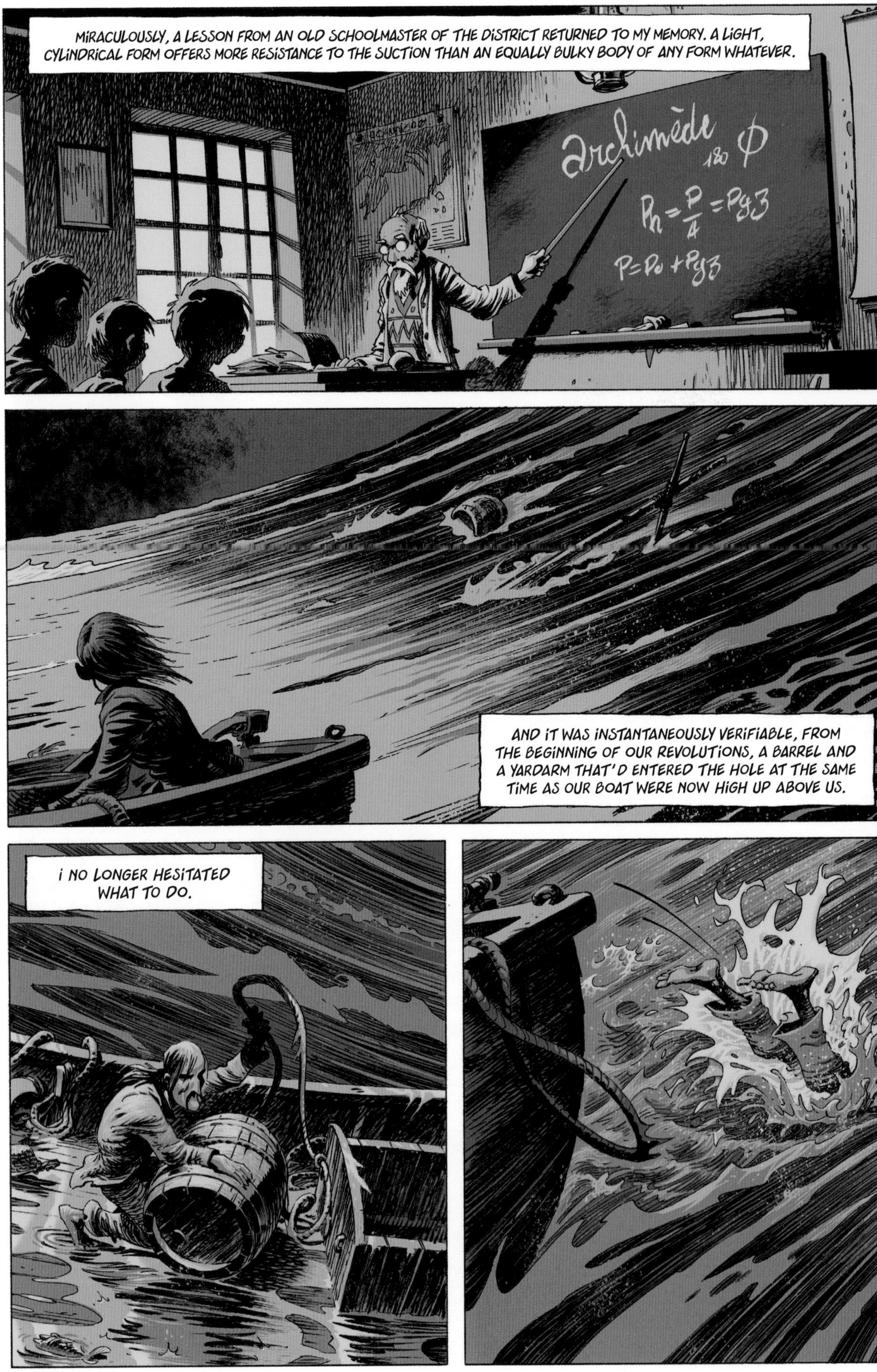
MIRACULOUSLY, A LESSON FROM AN OLD SCHOOLMASTER OF THE DISTRICT RETURNED TO MY MEMORY. A LIGHT, CYLINDRICAL FORM OFFERS MORE RESISTANCE TO THE SUCTION THAN AN EQUALLY BULKY BODY OF ANY FORM WHATEVER.
archimède
AND IT WAS INSTANTANEOUSLY VERIFIABLE, FROM THE BEGINNING OF OUR REVOLUTIONS, A BARREL AND A YARDARM THAT'D ENTERED THE HOLE AT THE SAME TIME AS OUR BOAT WERE NOW HIGH UP ABOVE US.
I NO LONGER HESITATED WHAT TO DO.

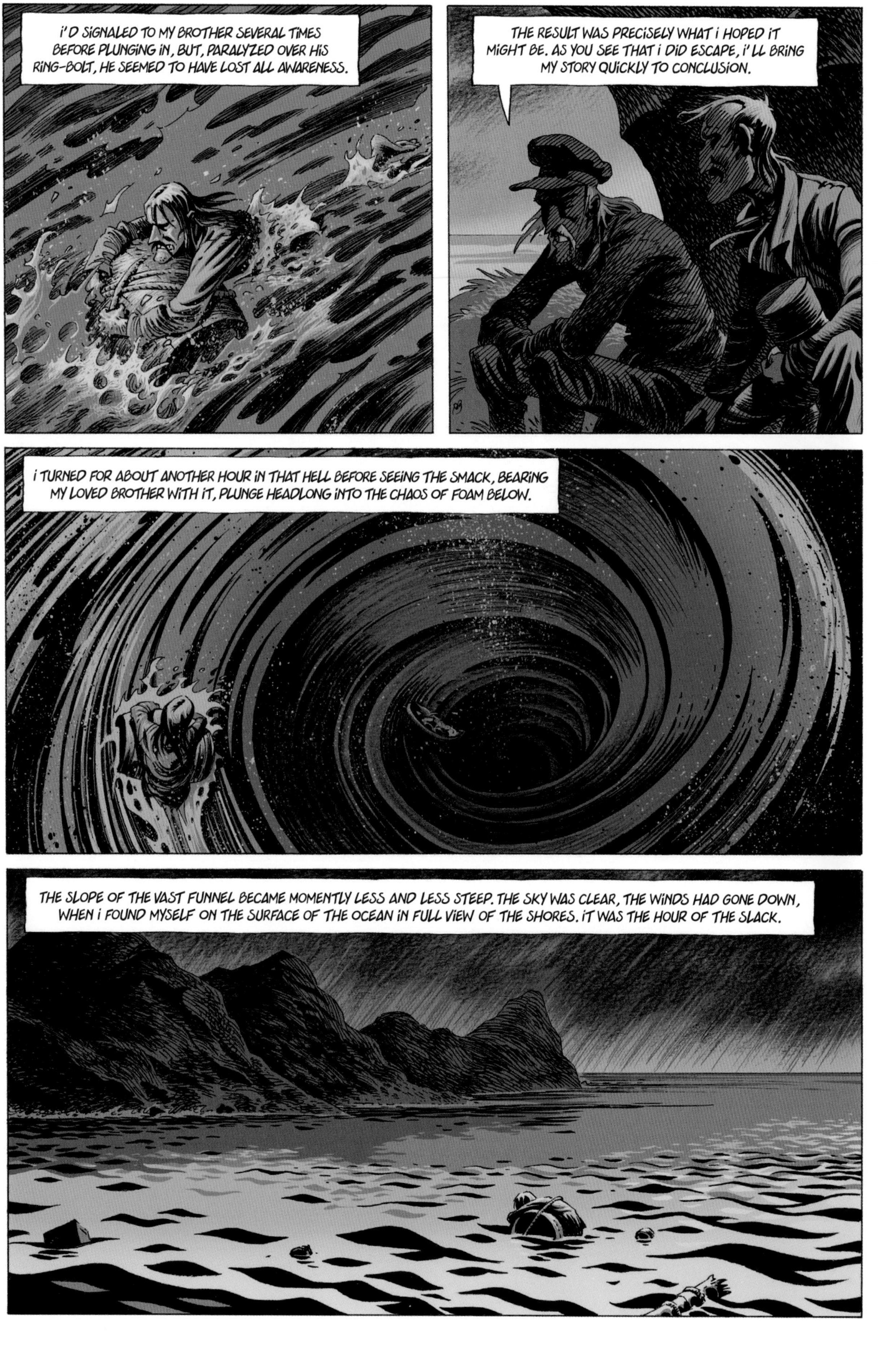
I'D SIGNALED TO MY BROTHER SEVERAL TIMES BEFORE PLUNGING IN, BUT, PARALYZED OVER HIS RING-BOLT, HE SEEMED TO HAVE LOST ALL AWARENESS.
THE RESULT WAS PRECISELY WHAT I HOPED IT MIGHT BE. AS YOU SEE THAT I DID ESCAPE, I'LL BRING MY STORY QUICKLY TO CONCLUSION.
I TURNED FOR ABOUT ANOTHER HOUR IN THAT HELL BEFORE SEEING THE SMACK, BEARING MY LOVED BROTHER WITH IT, PLUNGE HEADLONG INTO THE CHAOS OF FOAM BELOW.
THE SLOPE OF THE VAST FUNNEL BECAME MOMENTLY LESS AND LESS STEEP. THE SKY WAS CLEAR, THE WINDS HAD GONE DOWN, WHEN I FOUND MYSELF ON THE SURFACE OF THE OCEAN IN FULL VIEW OF THE SHORES. IT WAS THE HOUR OF THE SLACK.

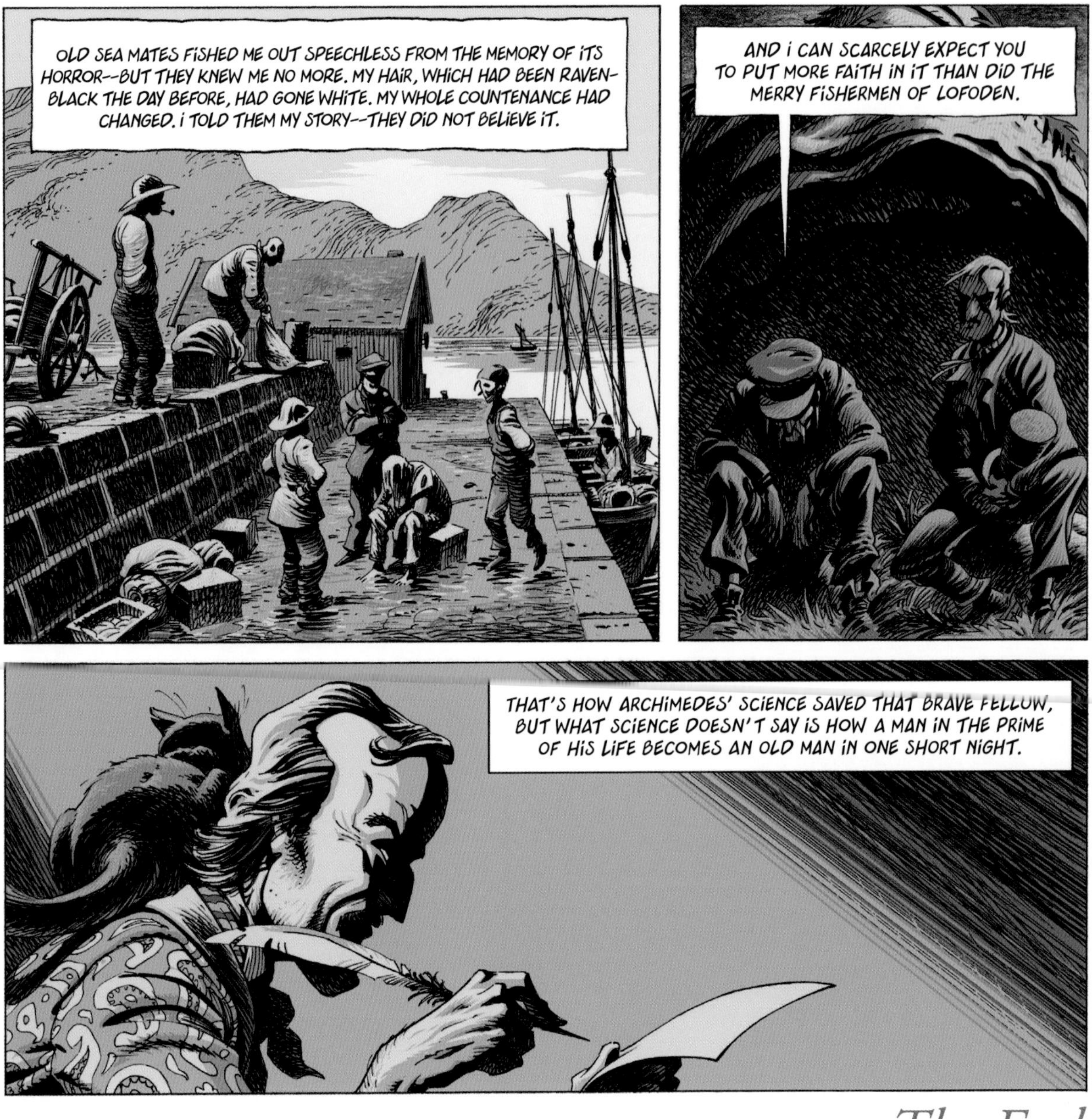
OLD SEA MATES FISHED ME OUT SPEECHLESS FROM THE MEMORY OF ITS HORROR--BUT THEY KNEW ME NO MORE. MY HAIR, WHICH HAD BEEN RAVEN-BLACK THE DAY BEFORE, HAD GONE WHITE. MY WHOLE COUNTENANCE HAD CHANGED. I TOLD THEM MY STORY--THEY DID NOT BELIEVE IT.
AND I CAN SCARCELY EXPECT YOU TO PUT MORE FAITH IN IT THAN DID THE MERRY FISHERMEN OF LOFODEN.
THAT'S HOW ARCHIMEDES' SCIENCE SAVED THAT BRAVE FELLOW, BUT WHAT SCIENCE DOESN'T SAY IS HOW A MAN IN THE PRIME OF HIS LIFE BECOMES AN OLD MAN IN ONE SHORT NIGHT.

The End

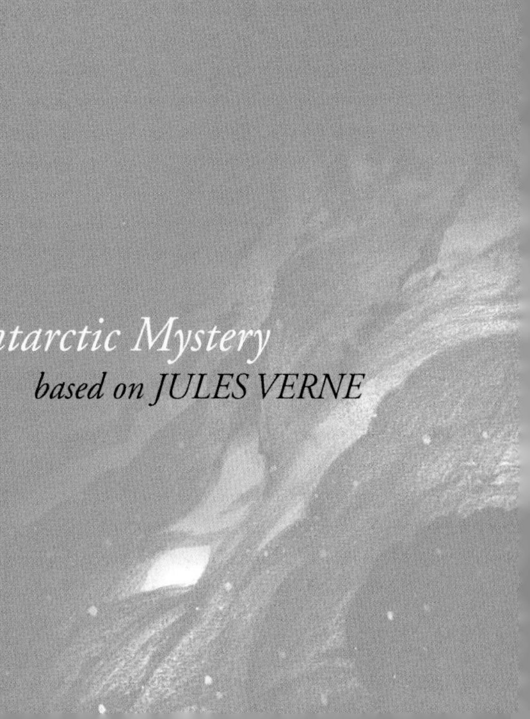

An Antarctic Mystery

based on JULES VERNE

JULES VERNE
An Antarctic Mystery

(Excerpt)

"An iceberg, bosun?"

"Yes, an iceberg, which has chosen this
moment to turn head over heels!"

While turning over, it encountered the *Halbrane* and
lifted it up like a racket captures a shuttlecock, and
now here we are, stranded a good hundred feet above
the level of the Antarctic Sea.

Could one have imagined a more terrible ending to
the *Halbrane's* adventurous undertaking?

In the midst of these distant waters, our sole means of
transportation had just been snatched from its natural
element, carried off by the flipping of an iceberg
surpassing a height of a hundred feet!...

Yes! I repeat, what an ending!
Sinking during a tempest, being destroyed by an
attack of savages, being crushed by the ice, those are
the dangers to which every ship plying the polar seas
is exposed!...

But for the *Halbrane* to have been lifted aloft by a
floating mountain at the instant when this mountain
turned over, and for the ship, at this hour, to be
stranded almost at its peak, no! It was beyond the
bounds of belief!

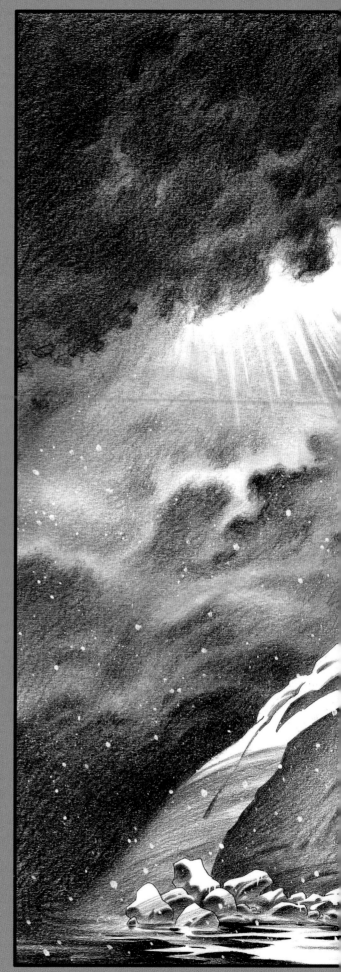

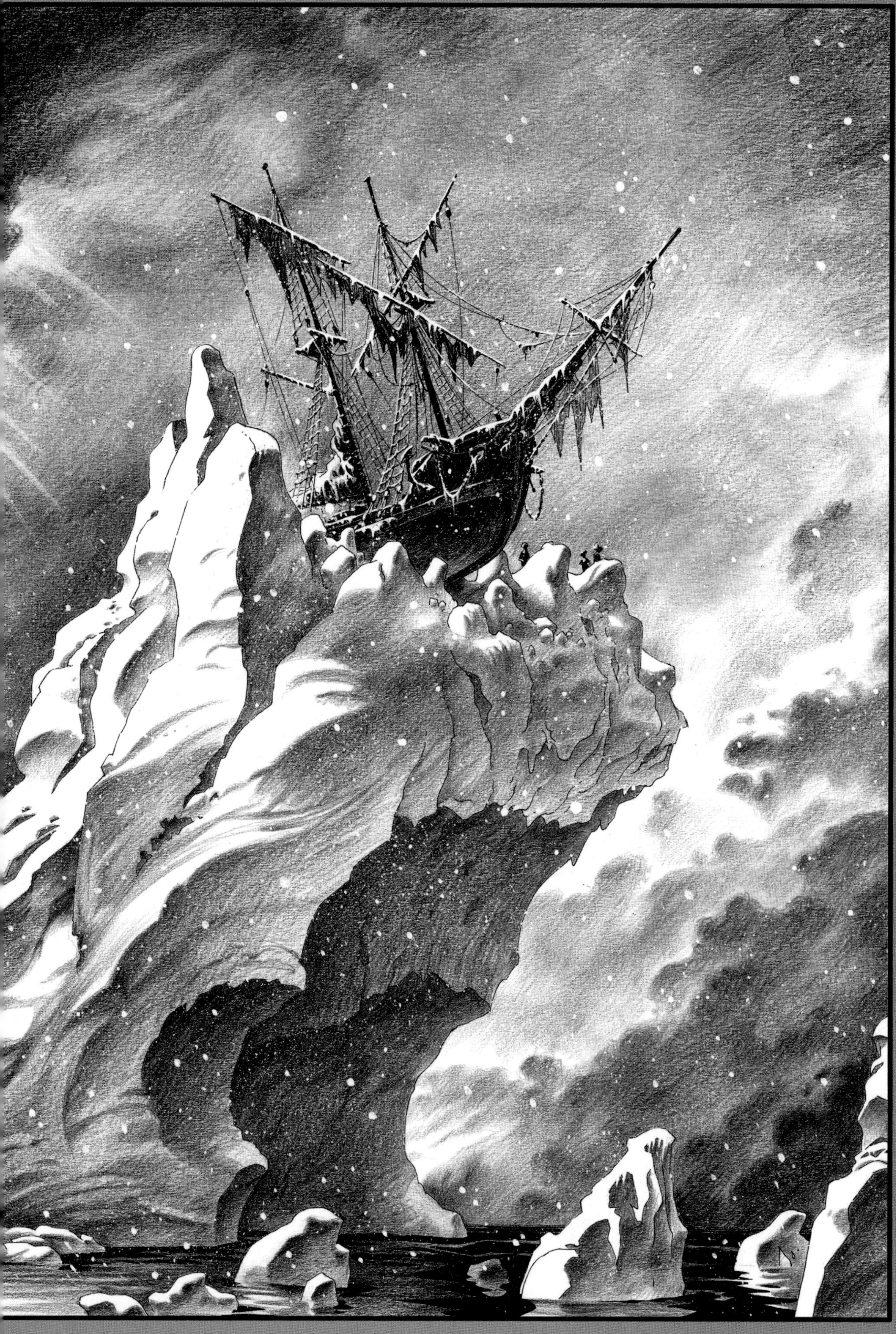

The Shamraken Homeward-Bounder

based on WILLIAM HOPE HODGSON

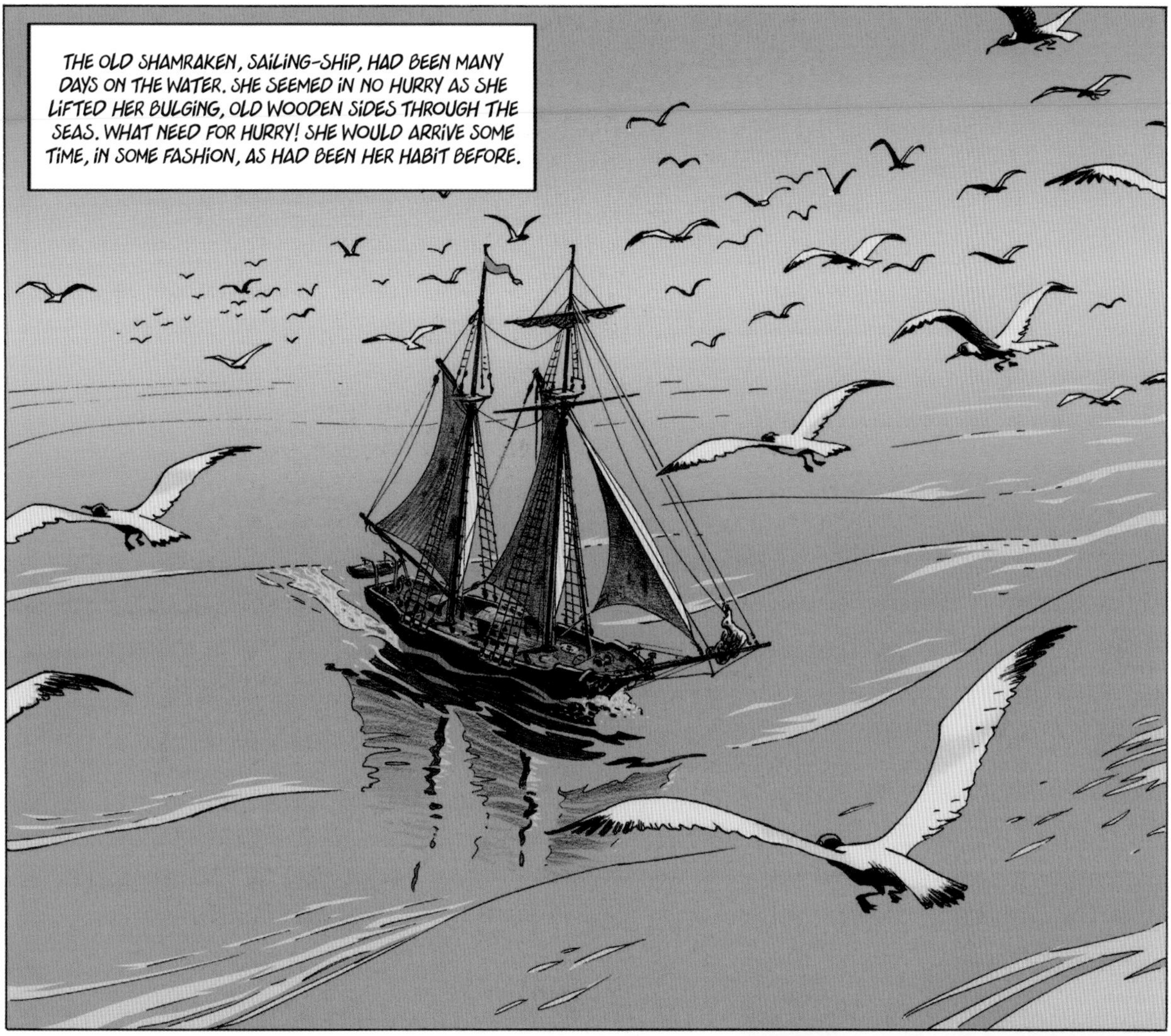
THE OLD SHAMRAKEN, SAILING-SHIP, HAD BEEN MANY DAYS ON THE WATER. SHE SEEMED IN NO HURRY AS SHE LIFTED HER BULGING, OLD WOODEN SIDES THROUGH THE SEAS. WHAT NEED FOR HURRY! SHE WOULD ARRIVE SOME TIME, IN SOME FASHION, AS HAD BEEN HER HABIT BEFORE.

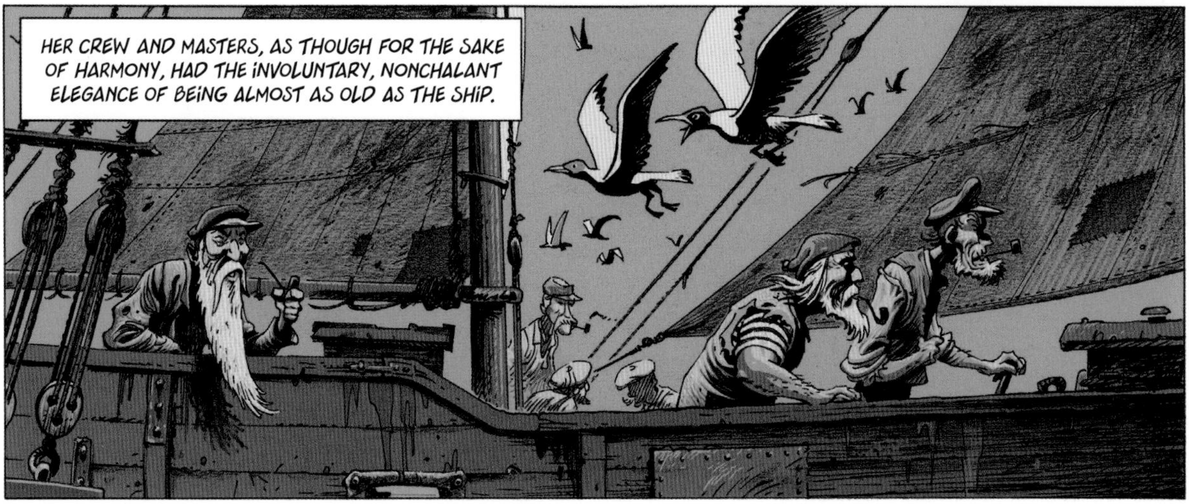
HER CREW AND MASTERS, AS THOUGH FOR THE SAKE OF HARMONY, HAD THE INVOLUNTARY, NONCHALANT ELEGANCE OF BEING ALMOST AS OLD AS THE SHIP.

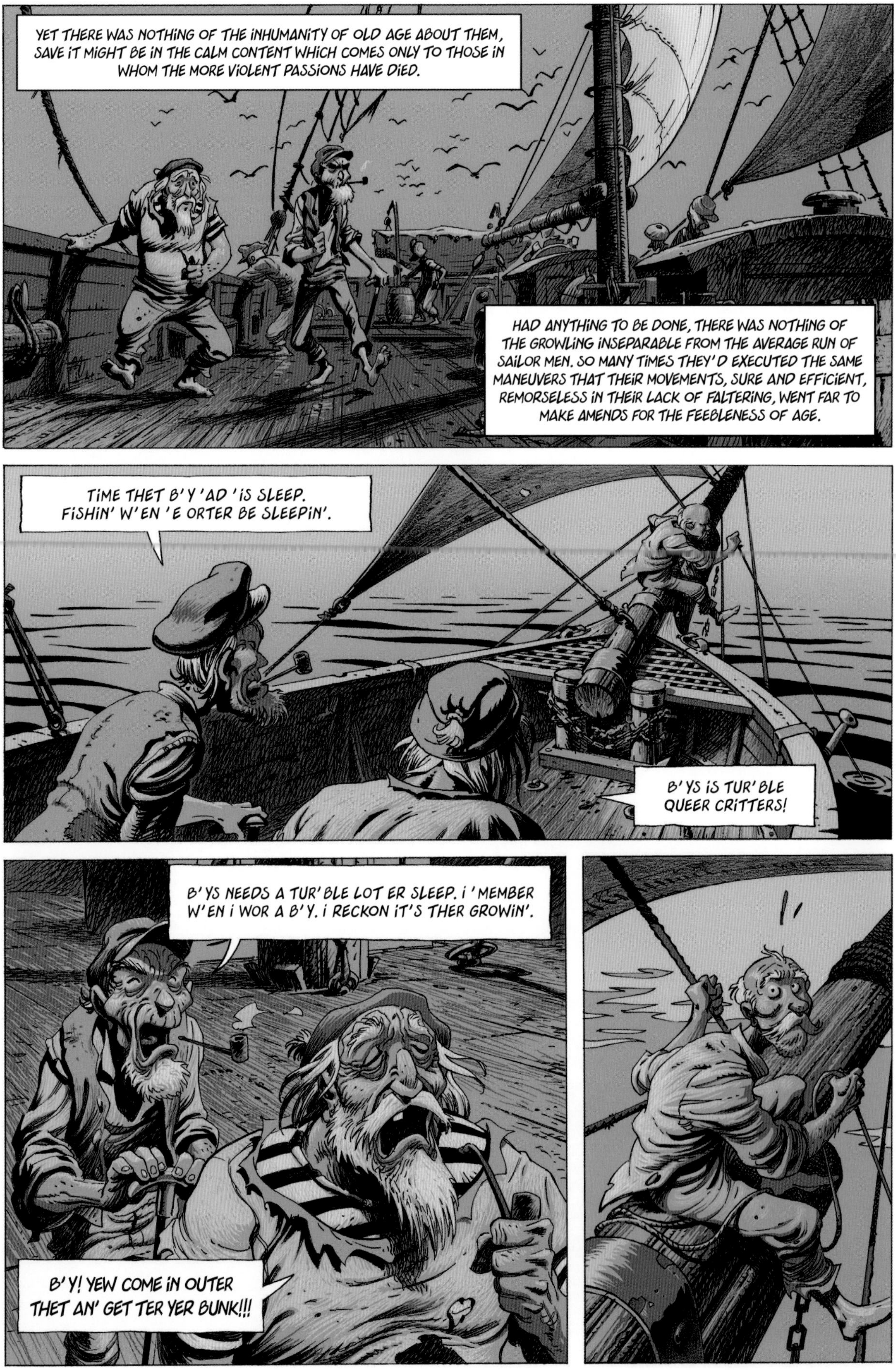
YET THERE WAS NOTHING OF THE INHUMANITY OF OLD AGE ABOUT THEM, SAVE IT MIGHT BE IN THE CALM CONTENT WHICH COMES ONLY TO THOSE IN WHOM THE MORE VIOLENT PASSIONS HAVE DIED.
HAD ANYTHING TO BE DONE, THERE WAS NOTHING OF THE GROWLING INSEPARABLE FROM THE AVERAGE RUN OF SAILOR MEN. SO MANY TIMES THEY'D EXECUTED THE SAME MANEUVERS THAT THEIR MOVEMENTS, SURE AND EFFICIENT, REMORSELESS IN THEIR LACK OF FALTERING, WENT FAR TO MAKE AMENDS FOR THE FEEBLENESS OF AGE.
TIME THET B'Y 'AD 'IS SLEEP. FISHIN' W'EN 'E ORTER BE SLEEPIN'.
B'YS IS TUR'BLE QUEER CRITTERS!
B'YS NEEDS A TUR'BLE LOT ER SLEEP. I 'MEMBER W'EN I WOR A B'Y. I RECKON IT'S THER GROWIN'.
B'Y! YEW COME IN OUTER THET AN' GET TER YER BUNK!!!

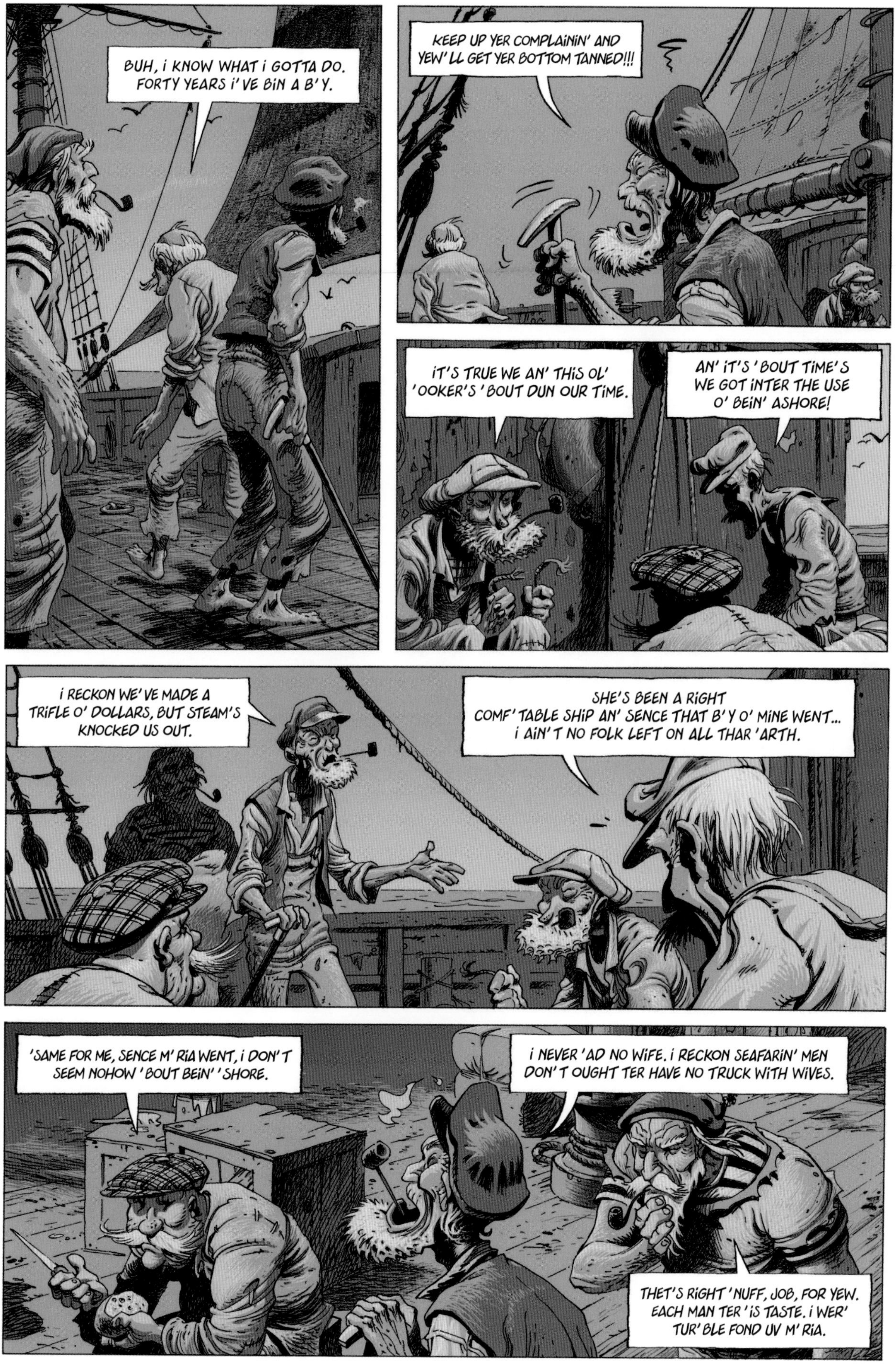
BUH, I KNOW WHAT I GOTTA DO. FORTY YEARS I'VE BIN A B'Y.
KEEP UP YER COMPLAININ' AND YEW'LL GET YER BOTTOM TANNED!!!
IT'S TRUE WE AN' THIS OL' 'OOKER'S 'BOUT DUN OUR TIME.
AN' IT'S 'BOUT TIME'S WE GOT INTER THE USE O' BEIN' ASHORE!
I RECKON WE'VE MADE A TRIFLE O' DOLLARS, BUT STEAM'S KNOCKED US OUT.
SHE'S BEEN A RIGHT COMF'TABLE SHIP AN' SENCE THAT B'Y O' MINE WENT... I AIN'T NO FOLK LEFT ON ALL THAR 'ARTH.
'SAME FOR ME, SENCE M'RIA WENT, I DON'T SEEM NOHOW 'BOUT BEIN' 'SHORE.
I NEVER 'AD NO WIFE. I RECKON SEAFARIN' MEN DON'T OUGHT TER HAVE NO TRUCK WITH WIVES.
THET'S RIGHT 'NUFF, JOB, FOR YEW. EACH MAN TER 'IS TASTE. I WER' TUR'BLE FOND UV M'RIA.

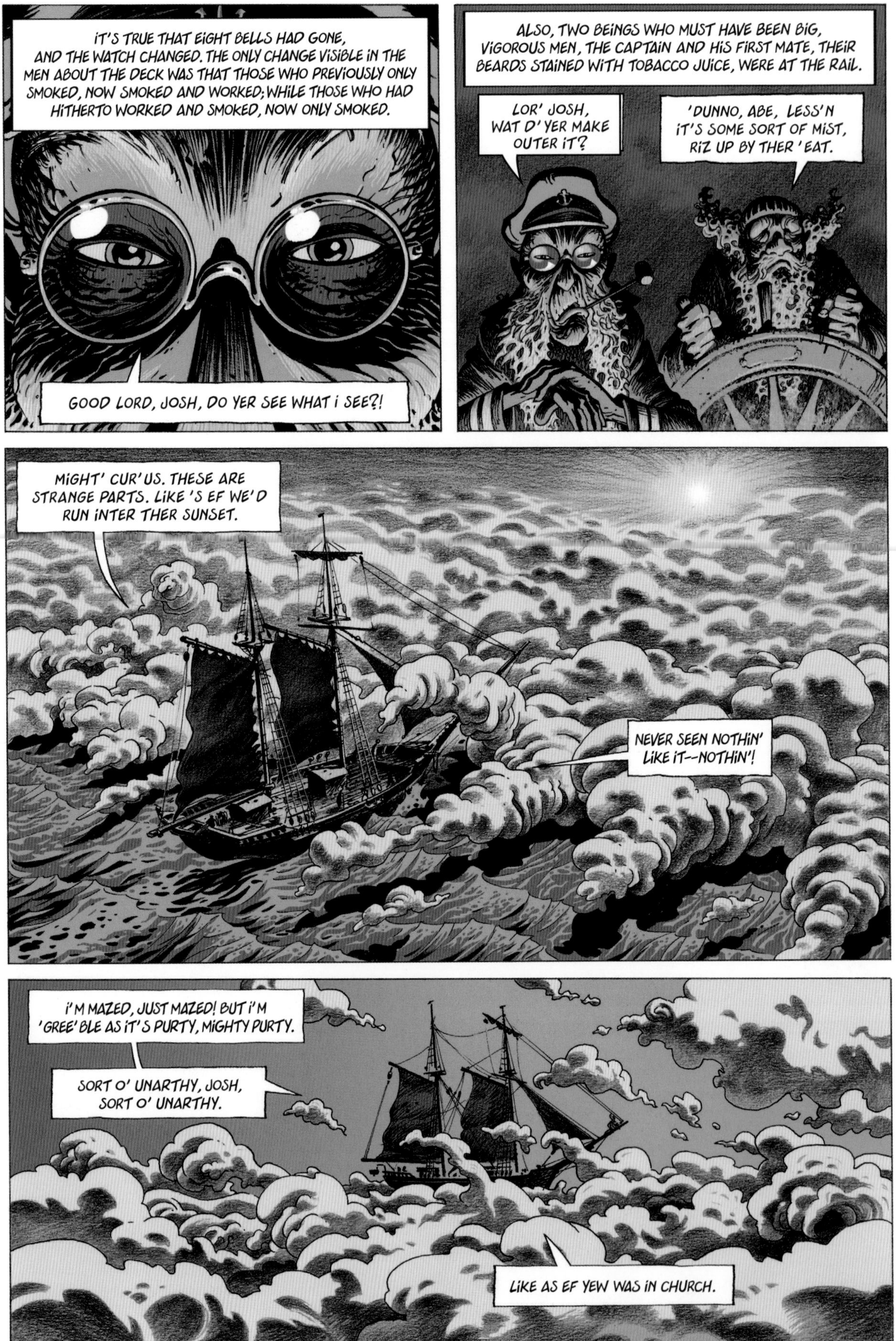
IT'S TRUE THAT EIGHT BELLS HAD GONE, AND THE WATCH CHANGED. THE ONLY CHANGE VISIBLE IN THE MEN ABOUT THE DECK WAS THAT THOSE WHO PREVIOUSLY ONLY SMOKED, NOW SMOKED AND WORKED; WHILE THOSE WHO HAD HITHERTO WORKED AND SMOKED, NOW ONLY SMOKED.
GOOD LORD, JOSH, DO YER SEE WHAT I SEE?!
ALSO, TWO BEINGS WHO MUST HAVE BEEN BIG, VIGOROUS MEN, THE CAPTAIN AND HIS FIRST MATE, THEIR BEARDS STAINED WITH TOBACCO JUICE, WERE AT THE RAIL.
LOR' JOSH, WAT D' YER MAKE OUTER IT?
'DUNNO, ABE, LESS'N IT'S SOME SORT OF MIST, RIZ UP BY THER 'EAT.
MIGHT' CUR' US. THESE ARE STRANGE PARTS. LIKE 'S EF WE'D RUN INTER THER SUNSET.
NEVER SEEN NOTHIN' LIKE IT--NOTHIN'!
I'M MAZED, JUST MAZED! BUT I'M 'GREE' BLE AS IT'S PURTY, MIGHTY PURTY.
SORT O' UNARTHY, JOSH, SORT O' UNARTHY.
LIKE AS EF YEW WAS IN CHURCH.

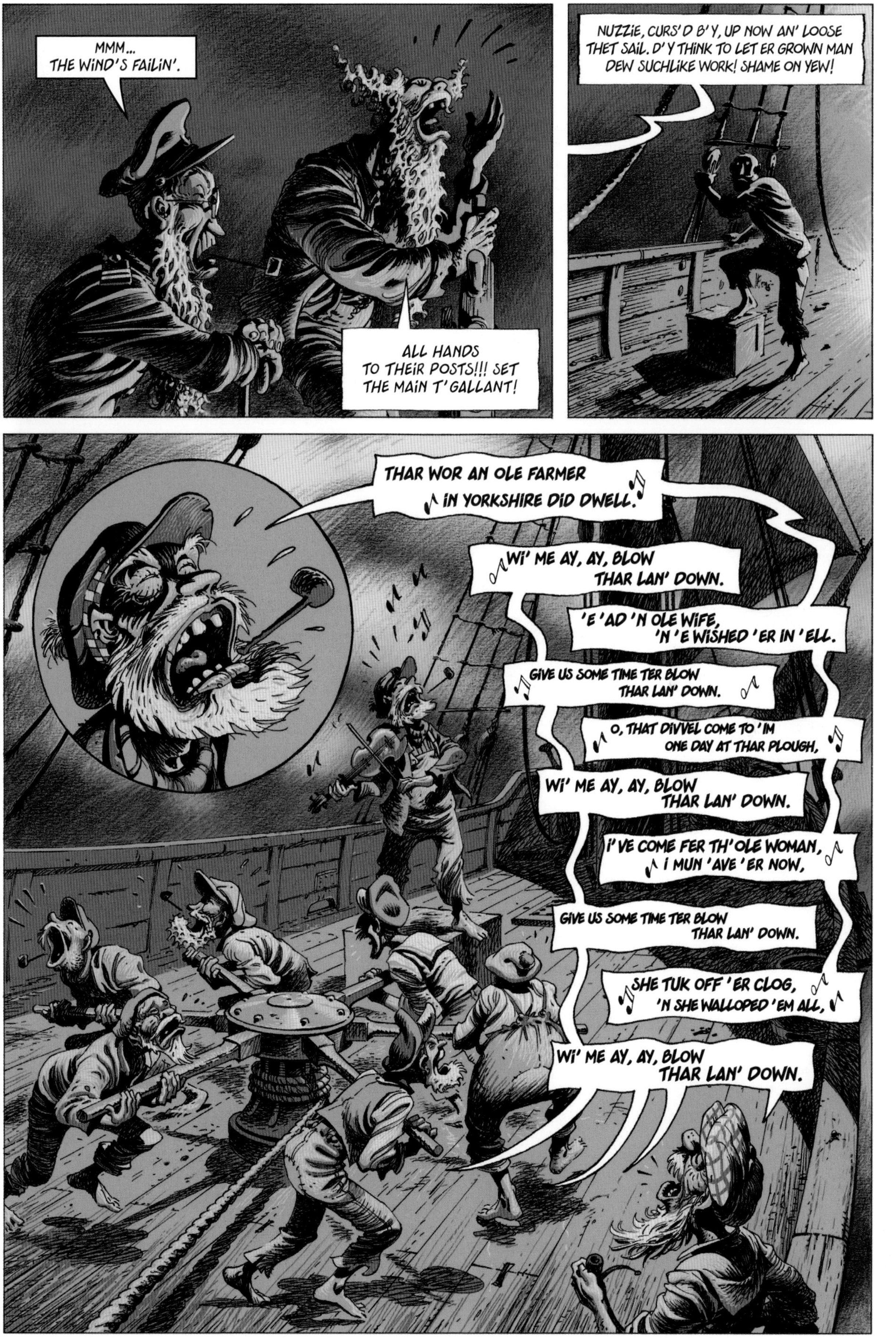
MMM...
THE WIND'S FAILIN'.
ALL HANDS
TO THEIR POSTS!!! SET
THE MAIN T'GALLANT!
NUZZIE, CURS'D B'Y, UP NOW AN' LOOSE
THET SAIL. D'Y THINK TO LET ER GROWN MAN
DEW SUCHLIKE WORK! SHAME ON YEW!
THAR WOR AN OLE FARMER
IN YORKSHIRE DID DWELL.
WI' ME AY, AY, BLOW
THAR LAN' DOWN.
'E 'AD 'N OLE WIFE,
'N 'E WISHED 'ER IN 'ELL.
GIVE US SOME TIME TER BLOW
THAR LAN' DOWN.
O, THAT DIVVEL COME TO 'IM
ONE DAY AT THAR PLOUGH,
WI' ME AY, AY, BLOW
THAR LAN' DOWN.
I'VE COME FER TH' OLE WOMAN,
I MUN 'AVE 'ER NOW,
GIVE US SOME TIME TER BLOW
THAR LAN' DOWN.
SHE TUK OFF 'ER CLOG,
'N SHE WALLOPED 'EM ALL,
WI' ME AY, AY, BLOW
THAR LAN' DOWN.

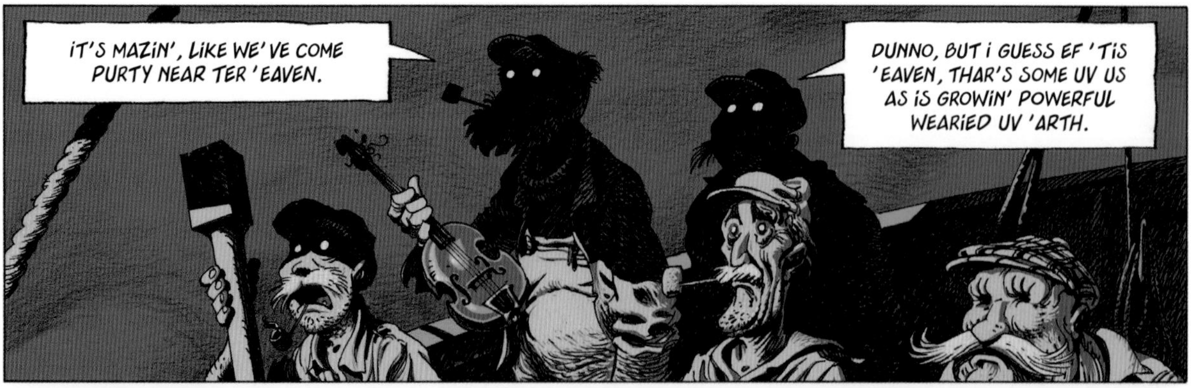
IT'S MAZIN', LIKE WE'VE COME PURTY NEAR TER 'EAVEN.
DUNNO, BUT I GUESS EF 'TIS 'EAVEN, THAR'S SOME UV US AS IS GROWIN' POWERFUL WEARIED UV 'ARTH.

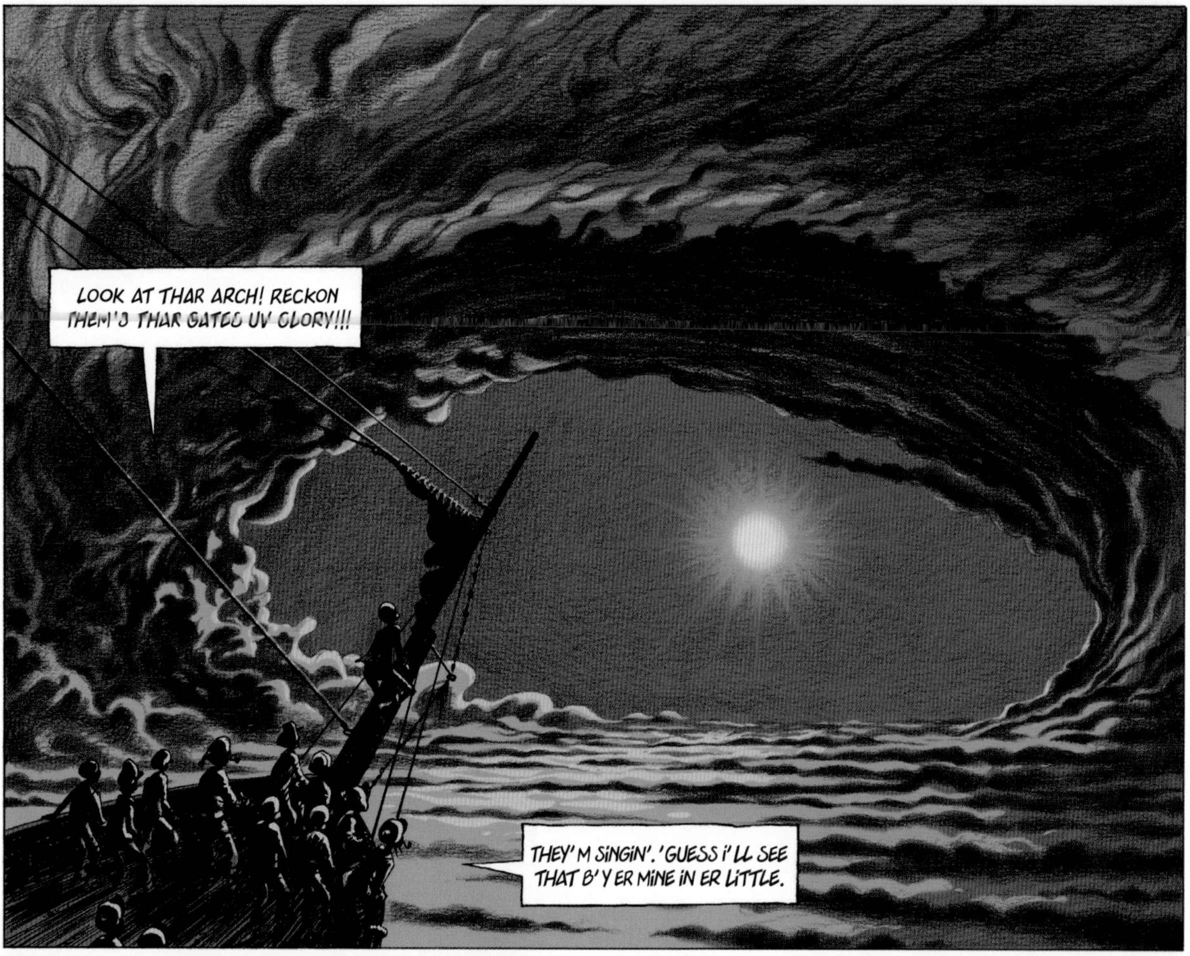
LOOK AT THAR ARCH! RECKON THEM'S THAR GATES UV GLORY!!!
THEY'M SINGIN'. 'GUESS I'LL SEE THAT B'Y ER MINE IN ER LITTLE.

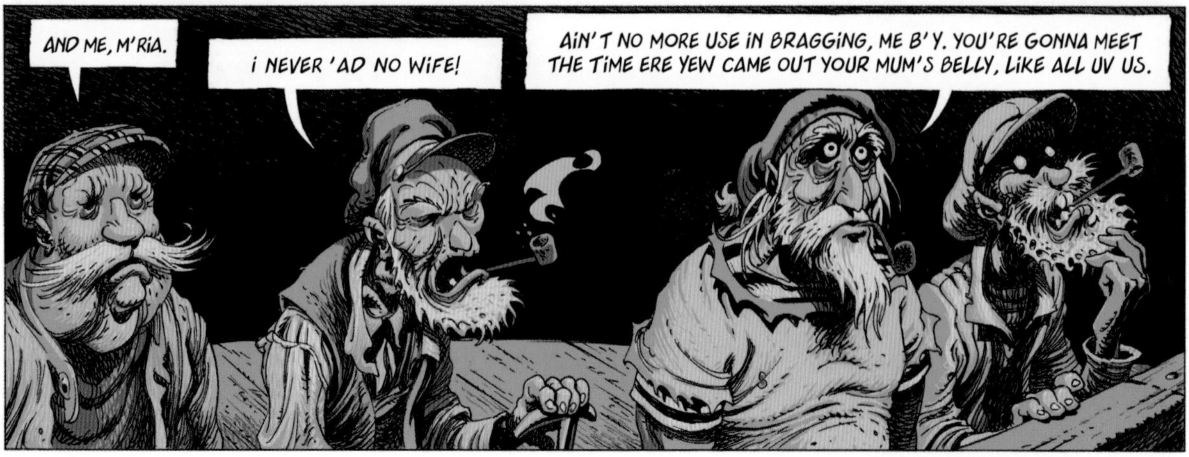
AND ME, M'RIA.
I NEVER 'AD NO WIFE!
AIN'T NO MORE USE IN BRAGGING, ME B'Y. YOU'RE GONNA MEET THE TIME ERE YEW CAME OUT YOUR MUM'S BELLY, LIKE ALL UV US.

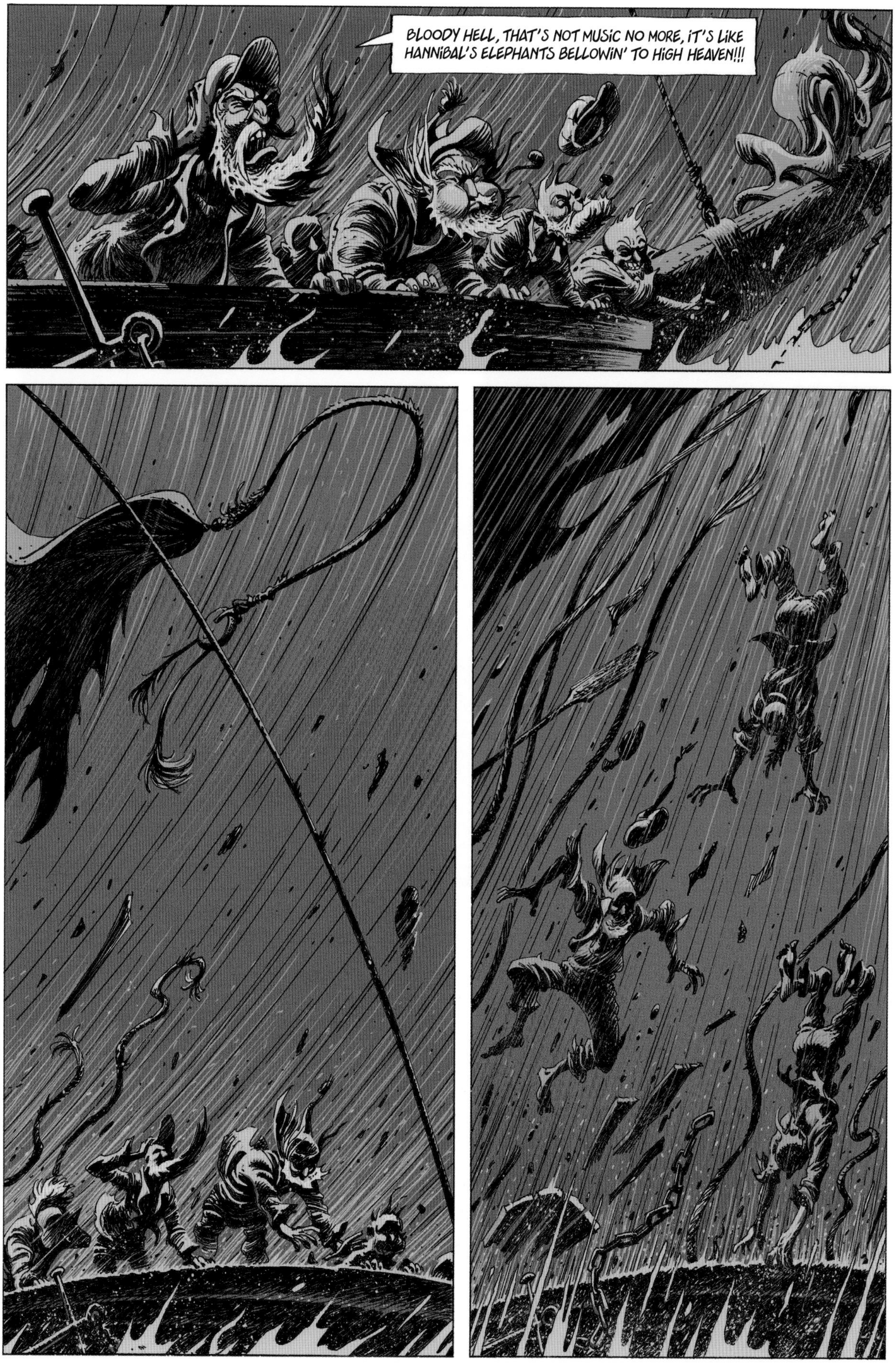
BLOODY HELL, THAT'S NOT MUSIC NO MORE, IT'S LIKE HANNIBAL'S ELEPHANTS BELLOWIN' TO HIGH HEAVEN!!!

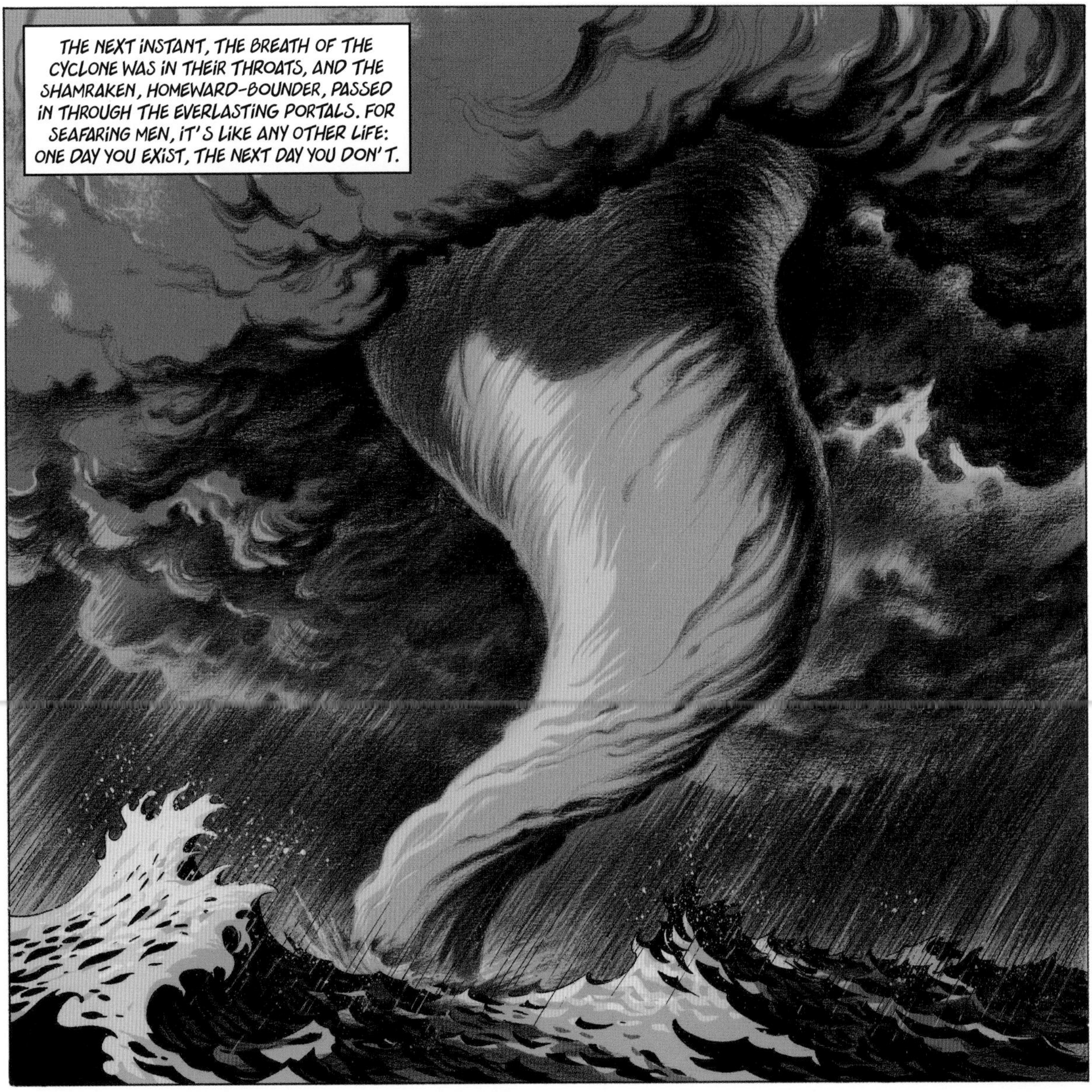
THE NEXT INSTANT, THE BREATH OF THE CYCLONE WAS IN THEIR THROATS, AND THE SHAMRAKEN, HOMEWARD-BOUNDER, PASSED IN THROUGH THE EVERLASTING PORTALS. FOR SEAFARING MEN, IT'S LIKE ANY OTHER LIFE: ONE DAY YOU EXIST, THE NEXT DAY YOU DON'T.

The End

Discussion with
the Author

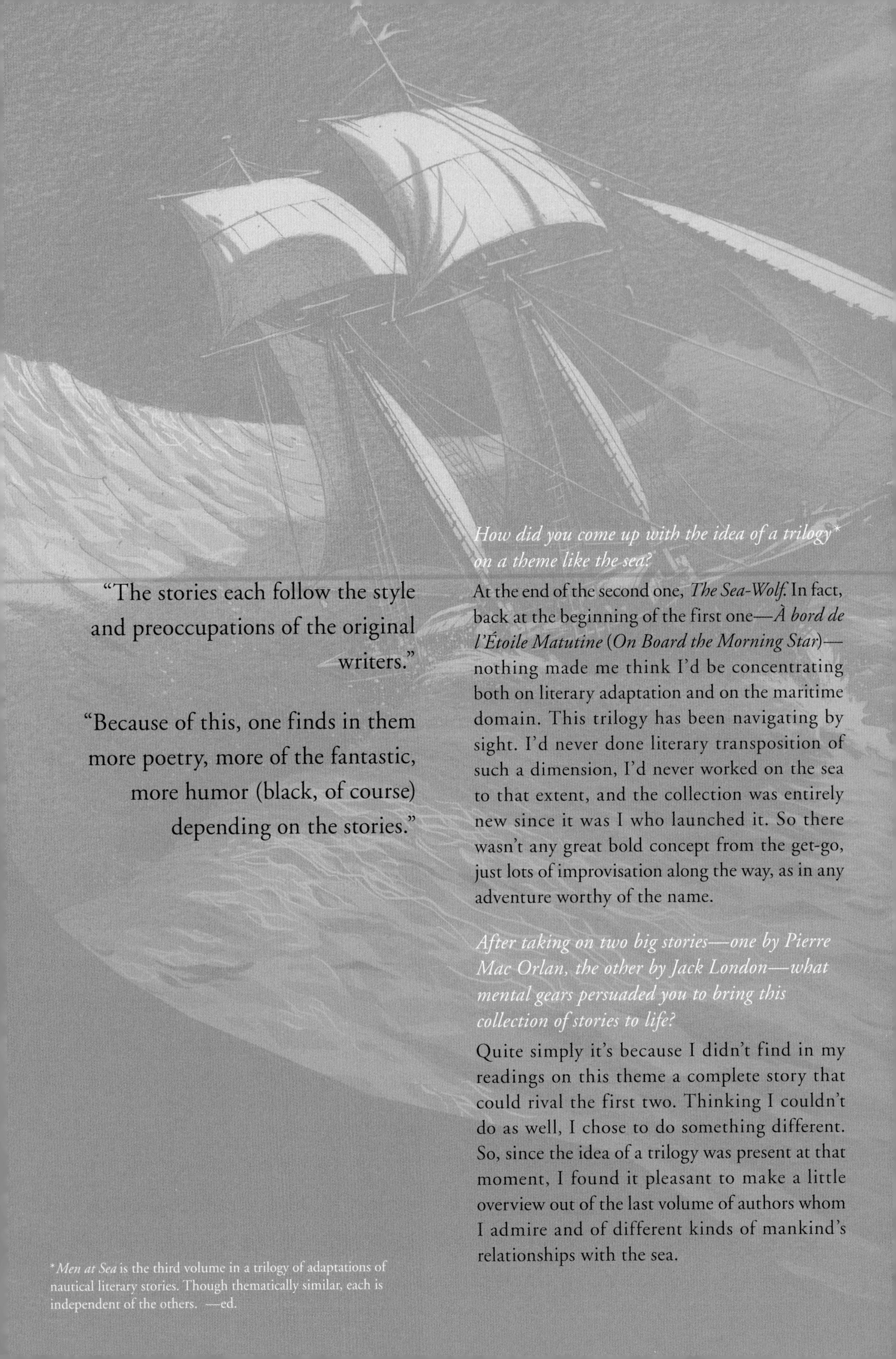

"The stories each follow the style and preoccupations of the original writers."

"Because of this, one finds in them more poetry, more of the fantastic, more humor (black, of course) depending on the stories."

How did you come up with the idea of a trilogy on a theme like the sea?*

At the end of the second one, *The Sea-Wolf.* In fact, back at the beginning of the first one—*À bord de l'Étoile Matutine* (*On Board the Morning Star*)—nothing made me think I'd be concentrating both on literary adaptation and on the maritime domain. This trilogy has been navigating by sight. I'd never done literary transposition of such a dimension, I'd never worked on the sea to that extent, and the collection was entirely new since it was I who launched it. So there wasn't any great bold concept from the get-go, just lots of improvisation along the way, as in any adventure worthy of the name.

After taking on two big stories—one by Pierre Mac Orlan, the other by Jack London—what mental gears persuaded you to bring this collection of stories to life?

Quite simply it's because I didn't find in my readings on this theme a complete story that could rival the first two. Thinking I couldn't do as well, I chose to do something different. So, since the idea of a trilogy was present at that moment, I found it pleasant to make a little overview out of the last volume of authors whom I admire and of different kinds of mankind's relationships with the sea.

**Men at Sea* is the third volume in a trilogy of adaptations of nautical literary stories. Though thematically similar, each is independent of the others. —ed.

Beyond the sea, don't these stories have another common denominator in being dark, even if lyrical and dreamlike? Is that what intrigued you?

The somber aspect was already largely present in the first two volumes, so that was a selection criterion as important as the maritime setting. That said, the stories each follow the style and preoccupations of the original writers. Because of this, one finds in them more poetry, more of the fantastic, more humor (black, of course) depending on the stories. And then, nothing amuses me more than drama.

What were your criteria for determining the sequential order of your stories?

As you realized, these weren't pages that were published here and there and collected here by happenstance. So I spent time organizing this puzzle in the hope that they'd all interlink in a coherent but varied fashion. What guided me first were rhythmic criteria about the length of the stories, then their kind of content. That being the case, each reader will make the trip in his or her own manner. They might read them out of order, as well. I have no expectations in this respect; I'm content with the role of orchestrator.

This book presents a different narrative mix than the two previous works since you also offer excerpts from great illustrated classic texts…

In *The Sea-Wolf,* on three occasions, you'll find purely illustrative double pages in black and white, even though they come across like breaths in a very dense story. The pleasure I had in creating them joined my preoccupation with wanting an "overview" for the third volume. It seemed to me it could be the way to complete and enrich this volume by illustrating texts by canonical authors whom I'll certainly never adapt for comics. And then, I've rarely come upon this association elsewhere, so it was exciting to escape the strict limits of narrative figuration.■

Published by Dead Reckoning
291 Wood Road
Annapolis, MD 21402

Originally published in French under the following title:
Hommes à la mer by Riff Reb's

Library of Congress Cataloging-in-Publication Data
Names: Riff Reb's, date, artist, adapter. | Johnson, E. Joe (Edward Joe)
    translator.
Title: Men at sea / [adapted by] Riff Reb's ; translated by Joe Johnson.
Other titles: Hommes à la mer. English
Description: Annapolis, MD : Dead Reckoning, [2019] | "Originally published
    in French under the following title: Hommes à la mer by Riff Reb's,
    ©Éditions Soleil, 2014"
Identifiers: LCCN 2018046315 (print) | LCCN 2018049528 (ebook) | ISBN
    9781682474419 (ePDF) | ISBN 9781682474419 (ePub) | ISBN 9781682473870
    (paperback) | ISBN 9781682474419 (ebook)
Subjects: LCSH: Sea stories—Adaptations—Comic books, strips, etc. | Graphic
    novels. | BISAC: COMICS & GRAPHIC NOVELS / Anthologies. | GSAFD: Sea
    stories.
Classification: LCC PN6747.R54 (ebook) | LCC PN6747.R54 H6613 2019 (print) |
    DDC 741.5/944—dc23
LC record available at https://lccn.loc.gov/2018046315

⊚Print editions meet the requirements of ANSI/NISO z39.48-1992
(Permanence of Paper).
Printed in the United States of America.

27 26 25 24 23 22 21 20 19   9 8 7 6 5 4 3 2 1
First printing